Media Rituals

'This is a very readable and important revision of the sociological study of the media. The author develops a concept of ritual that will be convincing to students raised in an age of a sometimes bewildering proliferation of reality-shaping media.'
(Professor George Marcus, Chair of the Department of Anthropology, Rice University)

Media are an inescapable part of our everyday life. But how can we understand those times of excess when the media has a significance completely beyond the routine? At times of crisis or triumph, how do media forge a public sense of community and shape people's private actions – or make us believe that they do?

Media Rituals rethinks our accepted concepts of ritual behaviour for a media-saturated age. It connects ritual directly with questions of power, government and surveillance, and explores the ritual space which the media constructs and where its power is legitimated.

Drawing on sociological and anthropological approaches to the study of ritual, Nick Couldry applies the work of theorists such as Durkheim, Bourdieu and Bloch to a number of important media arenas: the public media event; reality TV; Webcam sites; talk shows and docu-soaps; media pilgrimages; the construction of celebrity. In the final chapter, he imagines a different world where the media's ritual power is less, because the possibilities of participation in media production are more evenly shared.

Nick Couldry lectures in Media and Communications at the London School of Economics and Political Science. He is the author of *The Place of Media Power* and *Inside Culture*.

Media Rituals

A critical approach

■ **Nick Couldry**

LONDON AND NEW YORK

First published 2003
by Routledge
11 New Fetter Lane, London EC4P 4EE

Simultaneously published in the USA and Canada
by Routledge
29 West 35th Street, New York, NY 10001

Routledge is an imprint of the Taylor & Francis Group

Typeset in Goudy by Sparks Computer Solutions, Oxford
Printed and bound in Great Britain by
The Cromwell Press, Trowbridge, Wiltshire

British Library Cataloguing in Publication Data
A catalogue record for this book is available from the British Library

Library of Congress Cataloging in Publication Data
Couldry, Nick.
Media rituals : a critical approach / Nick Couldry.
p. cm.
Includes bibliographical references and index.
1. Mass media–Influence. 2. Mass media–Social aspects. I. Title.
P94 .C628 2003
302.23–dc21
2002012092

ISBN 0-415-27014-6 (hbk)
ISBN 0-415-27015-4 (pbk)

In memory of my father
Philip Couldry (1916–2000)

Contents

List of Illustrations

FIGURES

PLATES

[O]ur codes of conduct are as riddled with contradictions and as full of disproportions as are the forms of our social life, as is the structure of our society.

(Norbert Elias, *The Civilising Process,* 1994: 520)

[Contemporary societies] are required by their very dynamics to become increasingly mythical.

(Ernesto Laclau, *New Reflections on the Revolution of Our Time,* 1990: 67)

'Is this . . . is this for real?' I'm scanning the room, looking for signs of a camera, lights, some hidden evidence that a film crew was here earlier or is right now maybe in the apartment next door, shooting me through holes strategically cut into the crimson and black walls.

'What do you mean, Mr Ward?' Palakon asks. 'Real?'

'I mean, is this like a movie?' I'm asking, shifting around in my chair. 'Is this being filmed?'

'No, Mr Ward,' Palakon says politely. 'This is not *like* a movie and you are not being filmed.'

(Bret Easton Ellis, *Glamorama,* 2000: 425)

Preface

The title *Media Rituals* suggests a ready-made area of media research that is there to be explained and ordered. In fact, the position is more complex. There is a lot of talk about media in ritual terms, and there are a number of things that happen in relation to media that can properly be called 'ritual' which are the subject of this book. But we need to be critical of the assumptions about social 'order', and the media's supposed place within it, that underlie much talk of media rituals. I will be developing an anti-romantic approach both to media rituals and to the wider media process.

The topic of 'media rituals' cuts across the conventional organisation of media studies, and also across conventional assumptions that society has a 'centre', or that media are our route to such a 'centre', assumptions which saturate media studies and media sociology. These assumptions need to be challenged in many respects: not through philosophical elaboration (the post-structuralist subtlety of, say, Derrida provides few clues to interpreting a television talk show or a televised state funeral), but through the sociological study of how – from the smallest to the largest scale – the *idea* that the media 'stand in' for society's 'centre' is constructed and made to seem natural. From this different starting point, we can assess more clearly media institutions' own privileged position in the distribution of social power.

This book extends the argument of a previous book, *The Place of Media Power* (Couldry 2000a). Some aspects of the argument here are set out more fully in that book, but in many other respects, particularly the links I make to anthropology, this book is quite new, extending the range and clarifying the implications of my earlier argument.

Since January 2001, I have benefited greatly from the environment of the London School of Economics, particularly the support of a wonderful team of colleagues led by Roger Silverstone in Media@lse and the stimulation of many talented students. I particularly want to thank the students on my Media, Ritual and Public Life masters course for their inspiration and insight.

Many thanks also to Rebecca Barden and Christopher Cudmore at Routledge for supporting this book, and to Annette Hill and Routledge's other, anonymous, readers for their helpful comments.

Some of the material has been presented previously in different form. Parts of Chapter 5 were presented at the Crossroads in Cultural Studies conference at Birmingham University in June 2000 in a panel on 'Dialogues on Place, Scale and Power' and at the annual Society for Cinema Studies conference in Washington DC in May 2001 in a panel on 'Boundary-Work: Contemporary Film and Television Production' (thanks to Anna McCarthy and Vicki Mayer, respectively, for organising these panels). Parts of Chapter 6 were presented at the MeCCSA conference at University of Westminster in January 2002 in a panel on 'Reality TV' (thanks to Annette Hill for organising this). Related papers were presented in a seminar on Media Power at the Department of Culture and Communication, New York University (April 2000), at the LSE Media Research seminar (February 2001), and at a SOAS Media Research seminar (November 2001): thanks to Ted Magder, Roger Silverstone and Mark Hobart, the respective organisers. Thanks also to the audiences at each of these events for their helpful comments.

I am grateful to Roy Buergi and Wendy and Dave Laing for permission to reproduce two pages from the Website dedicated to pilgrimages to sites featured in *The Sandbaggers* (Granada TV, 1978–80).

There are many friends and colleagues with whom I have discussed ideas related to those developed here. Most helpful for this book's particular argument (and deserving of special thanks) have been Mark Andrejevic, Chris Atton, Karin Becker, John Caldwell, Henry Giroux, Todd Gitlin, Dave Hesmondhalgh, Matt Hills, Mark Hobart, Brian Kelly, Sonia Livingstone, Peter Lunt, Anna McCarthy, Kevin Robins, Clemencia Rodriguez, Roger Silverstone, Tiziana Terranova, and Jason Toynbee. Thanks very much to Garry Whannel for reading an earlier version of Chapter 6 and providing helpful comments. I am particularly grateful to Matt Hills for reading some chapters at a late stage and providing numerous insightful comments and criticisms. The remaining errors, of course, are my responsibility, not theirs.

Heartfelt thanks to my wife, Louise Edwards, for her support during a particularly busy and demanding time; without her, the book could, quite simply, not have been written.

This book is dedicated to the memory of my father, Philip Couldry, who knew all too well the personal cost of holding to one's own conscience, rather than accepting what passes for society's, and the media's, 'reality'.

Nick Couldry, London, July 2002

Chapter 1

Media rituals

The short and the long route

> ... the familiar is not necessarily the known ...
>
> (Lefebvre 1991a: 15)

There is something strange, even disorienting, about the media's impact on social life. We can recognise the reaction of Prime Minister Ramsay Macdonald to Britain's 'inventor' of television,[1] John Logie Baird. Macdonald thanked him for the television, this 'wonderful miracle' that had 'put something in his room which would never let him forget how strange the world was – and how unknown'.[2] But now we can only understand that early reaction against the grain of the enormous familiarity of television, and the familiarity of the worlds that television presents to us. The strangeness lies elsewhere, in our difficulty in grasping what difference it makes to the social world that the media is there. Understanding media means remembering that the familiar is not necessarily the known, and must therefore first be made strange.

This book uses theory – not abstract theory, but theory informed by empirical research – to understand the dimension of media we find most difficult to understand: the dimension left unexplained even when we have analysed all media texts and their source in the media industries. For we would still have to explain the media's role in ordering our lives, and organising social space. We would still have to explain those times when our attention to media seems more than casual, even necessary, and when the media appears to stand in for something essential about our lives together as social beings. To do so, we must look with a wider-angled lens than usual at how the social world is 'mediated'[3] through a media system that has very particular power-effects, and how the actions and beliefs of all of us are caught up in this process. I am introducing the term 'media rituals' to capture an aspect of this terrain.

By 'media' here, I will mean not any media, or process of mediation, but particularly those *central* media (primarily television, radio and the press, but sometimes film and music, and increasingly also computer-mediated communication via the Internet) through which we imagine ourselves to be connected to the social world. There is, as Todd Gitlin (2001: 10) recently argued, a dimension of our experience of media that differentiated studies of this or that medium miss: this is our sense of 'being with media' in their totality. This is the common sense notion of '*the* media', although in the age of media digitalisation its precise reference point is beginning to change. It is the media (in this sense) that underlies what I will call 'the myth of the mediated centre': the belief, or assumption, that there is a centre to the social world, and that, in some sense, the media speaks 'for' that centre. This myth underlies our orientation to television, radio and the press (and increasingly the Internet) as a social centre, and our acceptance of that centre's position in our lives as legitimate. If symbolic power is the socially sanctioned 'power of constructing reality' (Bourdieu 1991: 166), then the myth I am attacking can be expressed another way: as the belief that the concentration of symbolic power in media institutions is legitimate. My claim will be that media rituals are the key mechanism through which that assumed legitimacy is reproduced.

'Media ritual' is a term of art. There is a short and a long route to explaining it. The long route will be developed theoretically in Chapters 2 and 3 and then explored from various specific angles in Chapters 4, 5, 6 and 7. The need for a long route derives from the fact that, as the book's subtitle, 'A critical approach', indicates, I will work both with *and against* our instinctive sense of what this term means. I want to rethink common sense notions of 'ritual' in order to address the complexity of contemporary media's impact on social space. Understanding 'media rituals' is not simply a matter of isolating particular performances (rituals) and interpreting them; it is a matter of grasping the whole social space within which anything like 'ritual' in relation to media becomes possible. I call this wider space 'the ritual space of the media' (more on which later in the chapter).

Put more directly, 'media rituals' are any actions organised around key media-related categories and boundaries, whose performance reinforces, indeed helps legitimate, the underlying 'value' expressed in the idea that the media is our access point to our social centre. Through media rituals, we act out, indeed naturalise, the myth of the media's social centrality. The term 'media rituals' encompasses a vast number of things: from certain 'ritualised' forms of television viewing, to people's talk about appearing in the media, to our 'automatic' heightened attention if told that a media celebrity has just entered the room. Even this shorter route to understanding the term requires some background.

THE SHORT ROUTE TO UNDERSTANDING 'MEDIA RITUALS'

There are three broad approaches to the term 'ritual' in anthropology. These have understood 'ritual' respectively as:

1 habitual action (any habit or repeated pattern, whether or not it has a particular meaning);
2 formalised action (for example, the regular and meaningful pattern by which a table is laid for food in a particular culture);
3 action involving transcendent values (such as the Holy Communion, which in Christian contexts is understood as embodying a sense of direct contact with the ultimate value, God).

The first approach is uninteresting; sometimes in everyday language, I might talk about my 'ritual' of always having a drink and a snack when I get home after work, but in this case the word 'ritual' adds nothing to the idea of regular action or habit. The second and third approaches are more interesting and may overlap. Formalised action is much more than habit, since it implies that 'ritual' involves a recognisable pattern, form or shape which gives meaning to that action. To see 'ritual' from the third perspective – as action involving or embodying broad, even transcendent, values – is compatible with the second approach (indeed, ritual's formality is what enables it to be associated with something transcendent), but shifts the emphasis *away* from questions of pure form and *towards* the particular values that ritual action embodies.

Why should the term 'ritual' in these second and third senses (or a combination of them) help us understand contemporary media? Doesn't this fly in the face of many claims that we live in an age of 'de-traditionalisation' (Heelas *et al.* 1994)? Doesn't it ignore the progressive multiplication and diversification of media outputs and media technologies? Isn't it blind, finally, to the fact that in the 'information society' there is no possibility of anything as stable as ritual centres, only temporary regularities in a global 'space of flows' (Castells 1996; Lash 2002)?

To answer these questions fully is a task for the whole book, but there is a short answer for now. Just as ritualised action turns our attention to 'something else', a wider, transcendent pattern 'over and above' the details of actions,[4] thereby raising questions of form, so too it is the media's influence on the forms of contemporary social life – the wider *transcendent* patterns within which the details of social life make sense – that I intend to capture by the term 'media rituals'. It is not enough to make finer descriptions of media practice using our existing conceptual tools; only through a new concept, or so I will argue, can we *cut beneath* the apparently chaotic surface of everyday media practice. Once we do so, we will find more order than we expect and in the process add something to media and social theory, and also, I hope, to anthropological theory, where not only ritual but now mediation too are central concerns.[5]

The term 'media rituals' refers to the whole range of situations where media themselves 'stand in', or appear to 'stand in', for something wider, something linked to the fundamental organisational level on which we are, or imagine ourselves to be, *connected* as members of a society. I will explore the usefulness of this term in a number of specific examples: from media events (Chapter 4) to pilgrimages to media sites (Chapter 5) to the media's claims to represent reality (Chapter 6) to media sites for public self-disclosure (Chapter 7). What I do *not* want to do, however, by introducing the term 'media rituals' is to mystify what the media is, and its implications for questions of power. In speaking of 'media rituals', therefore, I intend to detach the term from its usual moorings.

'Ritual' has often been associated with claims that it produces, or maintains, social *integration*. This is a reading associated particularly with the tradition of social thought derived from the great French sociologist, Emile Durkheim. Durkheim was the leading French sociologist of the late nineteenth and early twentieth centuries, and contributed more than anyone else to our understanding of how modern, complex societies hold together, if they do. He explored these questions in two contrasting books: the early *The Division of Labour in Society* (1984) and the late *The Elementary Forms of Religious Life* (1995). One reading of the latter has emphasised the supposed unbreakable connection in Durkheim's thought between ritual and social integration. I will offer a different reading of why Durkheim matters. I will follow anthropological theorists such as Maurice Bloch and Pierre Bourdieu who have connected ritual not with the affirmation of what we share, but with the management of conflict and the masking of social inequality. Unfortunately, in media analysis, whenever 'ritual' has been introduced, it has been in the context of a rather traditional idea (derived from a particular reading of Durkheim's sociology of religion) that rituals 'function' to confirm an established social order that is somehow 'natural' and beyond question.

Instead we need to rethink 'ritual', including 'media ritual', and Durkheim's model of the social significance of ritual, to make room for new connections: between the power of contemporary media institutions and modern forms of government (Giddens 1985), between an understanding of ritual and the disciplinary practices of surveillance, between, that is, Durkheim and Foucault. For too long, media theorists have analysed the most dramatic examples of media power (the great media events of televised coronations and state funerals) in isolation from questions of government. As Armand Mattelart (1994) argues, the result is an impoverished account of the media's role in modernity. By contrast, a purely Foucauldian discourse analysis with its emphasis on flow, dispersal and discontinuity might well underestimate the real and consistent *pressures towards* order in contemporary mediated societies. (We can only guess, since Foucault did not, any more than Durkheim and with less excuse, analyse modern media!) That is why the theoretical framework of this book will draw on both Durkheim and Foucault, and many points in between, to grasp how media are entangled in the rhetoric of the contemporary 'social order'. It is worth saying something now about that difficult term, social order.

UNDERSTANDING THE 'ORDER' OF MEDIATED SOCIETIES

We cannot analyse the social impacts of contemporary media without taking a position on broader social theory. The underlying question, after all, is how are media involved in contemporary societies' holding together, *if* in fact they do. The approach I take to this question will be post-Durkheimian and anti-functionalist.

What do I mean by this? First, to be 'post-Durkheimian' is not to abandon Durkheim's social theory as a reference point, but to rethink our relation to Durkheim in a radical fashion; and, second, to be 'anti-functionalist' means opposing any form of essentialist thinking about society, not only functionalist accounts of society's workings (and media's role in them) but equally the idea that society is essentially *dis*ordered and chaotic. The two points are linked, since it is too weak a notion of social order that prevents some social theorists from seeing how much an anti-functionalist reading of Durkheim still has to offer in explaining contemporary media rhetorics. These points need some explanation.

Starting out from Durkheim

There are other roots than Durkheim for the study of 'ritual', of course, but it is Durkheim's sociology of religion (especially in *The Elementary Forms of Religious Life*) which is the unavoidable reference point for any account of ritual that is interested in wider questions of social order. It was Durkheim who insisted on the need to grasp the dimension of social life that transcends the everyday. He called this 'the serious life', *la vie sérieuse* (cf. Rothenbuhler 1998: 12–13, 25), and saw religion as its main, although not its only, manifestation. Durkheim, however, understood the term 'religion' in a rather special sense. For him religion:

> is first and foremost a system of ideas by means of which individuals imagine the society of which they are members and the obscure yet intimate relations they have with it.
>
> (Durkheim 1995: 227)

Religion, then, for Durkheim is not (whatever the claims it makes for itself) about cosmic order, but about the way social beings imagine the social bond that they share as members of a group. Instead of analysing contemporary religion, Durkheim offered a speculative account of the 'origins' of religious practice in aboriginal societies in perhaps the most brilliant product of 'armchair anthropology' (Pickering 1984: 348). Durkheim argued that our experiences of being connected as members of a social world are at the root of our most important categorisations of that world (such as, but not limited to, the sacred/profane distinction, which Durkheim argues underlies all religion in the usual sense of the term).

This argument can be broken down into three stages:[6]

1 At certain key times, we experience ourselves explicitly as social beings, as members of a shared social whole.
2 What we do in those moments, at least in Durkheim's imagined aboriginal case, is focused upon certain shared objects of attention, such as totems, and certain rituals which confirm the meaning of these 'sacred' objects or protect them from all other objects (the 'profane').
3 The distinctions around which those moments of shared experience are organised – above all, the distinction between 'sacred' and 'profane' – generate the most important categorisations through which social life is organised. This, in Durkheim's view, explains the social origin of religion and religious behaviour, and the centrality of the sacred/profane distinction in social life.

Durkheim's contemporary relevance

Why should Durkheim's account be of any interest to us today, either generally, or in a book on contemporary media? Surely Durkheim's method for developing his insights (if that is what they were) was neither plausible anthropology nor (even on its own terms) an analysis of modern religion.[7] So why have Durkheim's ideas fascinated a whole range of social analysts interested in contemporary forms of social order? The answer, paradoxically, is that Durkheim's insight, although projected back into the past, was in fact as much directed at an urgent question for *contemporary* sociology: how, if at all, do societies cohere, how is it that they are experienced by their members *as* societies? And more specifically: *are* there certain central categories through which we perceive the modern social world, and what is their origin?

This is the starting-point of certain influential accounts of the social power of media, that we can call 'neo-Durkheimian'. There are at least two variants, one explicitly and the other less emphatically Durkheimian. The first is based on the analysis of media events as special times when, it is argued, members of contemporary societies come together through media and become aware of each other as a social whole (Dayan and Katz 1992). Obvious examples would be the televising of major state events, such as state funerals, coronations and investitures. The second argument, by contrast, works outwards from everyday viewing (Silverstone 1981; 1988). If television (adopting the language of Durkheim (1995: 222) about the totem) is 'the abiding element of social life',[8] then through the various narrative and consumption patterns of television (and media in general) we are connected every day to the wider social world.

The second version of the neo-Durkheimian argument is, I would argue, more satisfactory than the first, because it insists on looking at the media's, particularly television's, role in the organisation of social life as a whole (cf. Silverstone 1994),[9] rather than just those exceptional media events whose rhetorical form is always, perhaps, resisted by some of the population (see Chapter 4). But the two versions are sides of the same coin: the exceptional sense of togetherness we may feel in media events is just a more explicit (ritualised) concentration of the togetherness, which, in a routine way, we act out when we switch on the television or radio, or check a news Website, to find out 'what's going on'.

These neo-Durkheimian arguments have a great asset: unlike many other approaches to the media, they take seriously our sense that *much more* is at stake in our relationship to the media than just distracted forms of image consumption. They share the underlying motivation of this book to address the 'excessive' dimension of the media's social impacts, but they also diverge from my argument in a crucial way. What is distinctive about the use of Durkheim that I propose (we can call it 'post-Durkheimian') is its emphasis on the process of social *construction* that underlies the *apparent* fit with modern societies of Durkheimian or neo-Durkheimian analyses of ritual and what we will bring under the term 'media rituals'.

I will be arguing throughout this book that we are *not* in fact gathered together by contemporary media in the way neo-Durkheimian arguments suggest. Even in the most dramatic cases of media events this is only an approximation; in most others it is purely a 'conventional expectation' (Saenz 1994: 576). To explain the ritual dimensions of media, we must read Durkheim against the grain, or at least against the grain of his most influential interpreters. At stake is not something archaic, as the term 'ritual' might suggest, or even a persistence of something very old into the modern era, but rather something intrinsic to modernity, indeed late modernity: the large-scale centralisation of power and social organisation.

Rereading Durkheim

I need, however, to get clear exactly how I will, and will not, use Durkheim's work on the 'origins' of religious life.

First, in adapting aspects of Durkheim's argument, we must offer something better than the speculative and generalised claims for which his account of the social basis of religion has been criticised (Gluckman 1971: 9–10; Pickering 1984: 345ff.). Difficult though it is, we must try to flesh out the sort of empirical link that Durkheim's account only dimly suggests: between our categorisations of the world and our shared experiences of ritual and simply being together as a group (Lundby 1997: 147–8; Pickering 1984: 401–2), and the involvement of media in both. That means complicating Durkheim's argument somewhat.

Second, since there are at least two ways of reading Durkheim, we have to be clear which one we choose. One reading stresses the foundational importance of collective emotions – the sensations of being together in one place, as members of a group – what Durkheim called 'collective effervescence' (Pickering 1984: 407). The other reading stresses not collective feeling but knowledge: that is, the cognitive processes and categorisations (inevitably more dispersed across space and not requiring us to congregate in one place) on which our knowledge of the social world is based. Both would seem to offer something important for thinking about the media's broader social impacts. My emphasis however will be primarily on the second, 'cognitive', reading of Durkheim (cf. Bourdieu 1991; Douglas 1984) rather than the 'emotive' reading (cf. Maffesoli 1996a; 1996b; Mestrovic 1997).[10] Only the cognitive reading – because of its reference to *everyday* practices of categorisation – captures the pervasiveness of the structural links between media rituals and social life. Simply put, the thought processes that underlie media rituals have resonances in our everyday thinking far beyond the local, sometimes emotional, context of media rituals themselves.[11]

Third, it is impossible to see Durkheim's image of 'primitive' social experience – a temporary gathering in the desert! – as anything more than a starting point for understanding the vast, dispersed complexity of contemporary societies, and how, if at all, they cohere. Indeed Durkheim himself had already argued in *The Division of Labour in Society* (1984) that modern societies are not principally held together by 'mechanical solidarity' (the thrill of mutual similarity expressed when people 'come together' that he later saw in the origins of ritual and religion). Modern societies, he argued, are linked primarily by 'organic solidarity', based in the divisions of labour and economic life: the systematic linking of people who are precisely different in their social roles.

This complexity in Durkheim's own writings has generally been ignored in neo-Durkheimian accounts of media, when they argue that television represents a 'return' to an earlier form of social convention, a new technologically enhanced form of 'mechanical solidarity'.[12] On the face of it, this reading of contemporary social forms is wildly implausible. Can we interpret a social gathering, such as an annual music festival, as the *source* of wider social categorisations, in the way that Durkheim imagined for gatherings in 'primitive' societies? Look around any such gathering, and you will quickly find in people's clothes, bodily style, language and so on, traces of countless *other* spaces and histories, all quite independent from that gathering and not specifically intended to be expressed there. Any simple 'representative' notion of place contradicts the insights of cultural geography that at every place many *incompatible* histories intersect (Massey 1994). So there is no contemporary parallel for the Durkheimian totemic ritual in the desert where all society's central meanings and values are at stake. But Durkheim's account can still help us grasp contemporary *rhetorics* of social togetherness, and the media's role in them, provided we adopt a more complex model of the way those rhetorics might work.

Beyond functionalism

This means avoiding the functionalism for which so many have criticised Durkheim and his followers.[13]

Neither too much order ...

By a *functionalist* account of the social – that is, our social values and their relationship to social order[14] – we mean an account which makes the following extra assumptions over and above a straightforward descriptive account of that relation:

1 that any such relationship is not just accidental, but a necessary result of the 'functioning' of the social whole and its parts;
2 that there is such a thing as 'the social whole', usually assumed to exist at the level of national territories;
3 that social integration is the principal sociological feature of societies, rather than just secondary or incidental.

In thinking about media rituals, I don't want to make any of those assumptions, as will become clear during the course of this book, nor do I want to overestimate the extent to which social cohesion actually exists. Instead, I want to use Durkheim's concerns with social order to help us analyse contemporary claims to social cohesion, and the contribution to them of media institutions and media practices. This means following Pierre Bourdieu's (1991: 166) radical reinterpretation of Durkheim as a thinker interested in social categories *not* simply because they embody something 'universal' about the human mind or social fabric, but because the claims to universality inherent in such categories are a fundamental, but also highly political, dimension of social 'order'.

This means foregrounding *the problem* of social order that motivated Durkheim's work: looking sceptically at whether contemporary mediated societies actually *do* hold together (with the help of media or otherwise) and (by extension) being cautious about projecting contemporary rhetorics of social integration outside the particular version of modernity that is dominant in 'the West'. Integrating history into the analysis[15] means allowing for other, quite different, paths towards complex social organisation, and opening out a less parochial analysis of conflict and power (Sahlins 1976: 120). The very idea of 'the social', which is assumed behind notions that rituals 'integrate' societies, is the result of a constant production (Hall 1977: 340); so too is our sense that in certain 'places' and times we 'come together' through media. The final chapter (Chapter 8) will use reference points outside the West to think beyond that very centralised notion of what media could be.

My argument still, perhaps, risks getting mistaken for a functionalist position, because it takes the media's *claims* to have a function very seriously, not for their truth, but for their effects. But, as the Israeli anthropologist Don Handelman has explained, taking seriously the representative claims of public events (a term he prefers to 'ritual') does not commit us to a functionalist position. It merely recognises that any social network will tend to have:

> media through which members communicate to themselves in concert about the characters of their collectivities, *as if* these do constitute entities that are temporarily coherent. Public events are convergences of this kind.
>
> (Handelman 1998: 15)

In contemporary societies dominated by highly concentrated media forms, the rhetorical pressures to believe in such 'convergences' are very great. To the extent that 'everything works *as if*'[16] there were a functioning social whole, media and media rituals are central to that construction – which is why we need to study them. Against the odds, then, Durkheim's 'primitivist' model can help us grasp the thoroughly modern claims of contemporary media to help states and societies hold together.

... nor too little order

My approach should also be distinguished from post-structuralist positions which argue that the very possibility of social order has been radically destabilised. Anti-essentialist positions, for example those influenced by Deleuze and Guattari (1988), risk obscuring quite how pervasive and consistent the social pressures *to believe* in the social order are, particularly in mediated societies. Ernesto Laclau (1990) in his short essay 'The Impossibility of Society', from his book *New Reflections on the Revolution of Our Time*, expresses the paradox very well when he points out that, even if philosophically we see 'difference' as radical and fundamental (luckily this is not an issue on which I have to commit myself here!), we still need a notion of ideology as the contingent, *but regular*, social process which encourages us to see meaningful 'order', even when it is absent. Deleuze and Guattari's work does, admittedly, emphasise that what they call forces of de-territorialisation (which evade ordering) confront forces of re-territorialisation (which reimpose order). There is a subtle difference between this position and that suggested here. In spite of the initial plausibility of the idea that globally accelerated flows of information, money and people result in 'the destruction of [social] reproduction by chronic production', thereby effacing 'the symbolic' (Lash 2002: 215), this ignores the extent to which principles of order remain, not just as compensatory devices for an underlying disorder, but embedded at the heart of our notions of who we are and where we belong. There is much more to be said, of course, on these complex issues. In a recent, radical rethinking of Deleuze and Guattari's work, Hardt and Negri's theory of 'empire', a similar problem is addressed and perhaps in some respects resolved (see Hardt and Negri 2000: especially chapter 1, section 2). There is no space, however, to pursue this further here.

A diagram may help to sum up where this book stands on these difficult general questions (Figure 1.1).

In addressing the role media play in sustaining our sense of social order, we need to keep our eyes fixed firmly on the two continuous lines, representing first, the actual levels of order (power concentrations) in contemporary societies and second, the relative degree of social disorder and chaos that coexists with them. At the same time we must reject (and see through) two opposing myths about the social process, represented by the dotted lines in the diagram: first, the myth of foundational order (functionalism) and, second, the myth of foundational disorder (some post-structuralist positions). Each myth blinds us to the real (if relative) order *and* disorder of contemporary social life. The media is involved in both those myths but particularly the first, and this is why, in thinking about media rituals, we need to stand outside media rituals rather than identify with them. We need to be sceptical bystanders, not celebrants, at contemporary media's ritual feast. The long-term aim

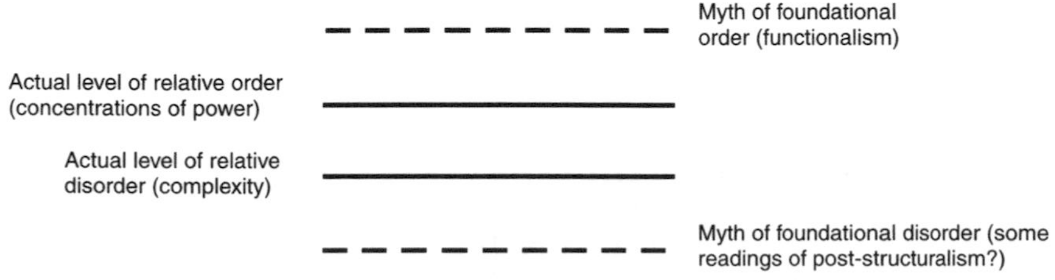

Figure 1.1 Myths/patterns of social order/disorder

of understanding media rituals, as we see in Chapter 8, is to help us imagine a world without them.

This book's perspective on media rituals is therefore not sympathetic, but critical. However, the version of media critique offered here differs from many previous versions in that it does *not* depend on claims that media reproduce particular ideologies (of the ruling class or whatever) whose origin lies outside the media system. The limitations (and indeed the implicit functionalism) of straightforward Marxist models for example, of how order is maintained in contemporary societies, have long been undermined (for example, Mann 1970), but in media sociology we have yet to discover a coherent alternative that sufficiently recognises the pervasive pressures towards order in mediated societies. I attempt to provide this through deconstructing one aspect of the 'ideology of media power' itself, that is the general ideology[17] condensed within our 'natural' assumption that media are our access point to contemporary social reality. This ideology of 'centrality' does not, of course, preclude, and indeed closely interacts in many places with, the successful reproduction of other specific ideologies (myths of the 'free market' or state populism), but it requires a distinct level of analysis: an analysis of the frame (the 'media frame': cf. Couldry 2000a) within which such specific ideologies are played out. This is the wider critical potential of deconstructing the often banal details of media rituals.[18]

TRACING MEDIA RITUALS ACROSS SOCIAL SPACE

I suggested earlier that in radicalising Durkheim's analysis of 'social order' we needed to go beyond the limited causal account he offers of how rituals work. How exactly?

A non-functionalist approach to rituals (including media rituals) is interested in them less for themselves as expressions of this or that idea – after all, what would that prove by itself? – than in the wider social processes of 'ritualisation' through which something like (media) ritual comes into being at all. The term 'ritualisation' connects with a shift in thinking about ritual in recent anthropology of religion, especially the work of Catherine Bell (1992; 1997), who draws not only on Durkheim but on Bourdieu and Foucault. 'Ritualisation', as explained more fully in Chapter 2, encourages us to look at the links between ritual actions and wider social space, and in particular at the practices and beliefs,[19] found right across social life, that make specific ritual actions possible.

The 'ritual space' of the media

The point here is to shift the emphasis in ritual analysis away from questions of meaning and towards questions of power.[20] Power is intertwined with the very possibility of contemporary ritual; similarly 'media power' (that is, the particular concentration of symbolic power in media institutions)[21] is intertwined with the very possibility of media rituals. There is a dimension of Durkheim's writings (neglected in neo-Durkheimian accounts) which was concerned with symbolic power (cf. Bell 1992: 218; Bourdieu 1991: 166), but to develop it fully we need a concept of the *space* in which ritual occurs that is not in Durkheim. How, and where, are key categories worked upon so that they can be drawn upon in the formalised distinctions of ritual performance? We cannot answer this without studying a wider space of ritualisation. Similarly, we can only grasp how some media-related actions make sense *as* ritual actions, if we analyse a wider space which I call *the ritual space of the media.*

I use the word 'space' here metaphorically,[22] as a convenient term to refer to the whole interlocking mass of practices that must be 'in place' for there to be ritual action oriented to the media. The term 'ritual space' is intended to help us think beyond the local context of what can be called 'media rituals' and through to a larger social scale, to the landscape whose contours constrain individual ritual practices at any particular time. In complex societies, the tightly defined contexts of formal ritual, such as religious ritual, are relatively rare. It is better to think of the ritual process as stretched across multiple sites, indeed across social space as a whole (cf. Silverstone 1981: 66–7). This wider landscape, which for convenience I call the ritual space of the media, is highly uneven. It is formed around one central inequality (the historic concentration of symbolic power in media institutions) but is shaped locally through many detailed patterns, particularly the categories (such as those of 'media' and 'ordinary' person, of 'liveness', and so on: cf. Couldry 2000a: 42–52) through which we understand our actions and orientations in relation to the media. Without this wider landscape, the patterned actions I call media rituals (the way we act in the presence of a media person or celebrity, the way a media event or a television studio is organised, and so on) would not make the sense, or have the resonance, that they do.

Studying media rituals in this non-functionalist way is the opposite of isolating particular moments and elevating them to special, even 'magical', significance. On the contrary, it means tracing the antecedents of media rituals in the patterns, categories and boundaries at work everywhere, from press and magazine comment to television newscasts, to our everyday talk about celebrities, to the way we act when we go on television. As illustrated by Figure 1.2, the 'ritual space of the media' is a metaphor for how media rituals condense media-focused patterns of thought and action that are latent everywhere (or almost everywhere).

Even in a post-Durkheimian version, however, media rituals direct our attention to a transcendental value associated with 'the media', that is, the media's *presumed* ability to represent the social whole. Behind this stand patterns of categorisation in everyday life whose net effect is to naturalise the hierarchy of things 'in' the media over things which are not 'in' the media (Couldry 2000a: chapter 3). My emphasis

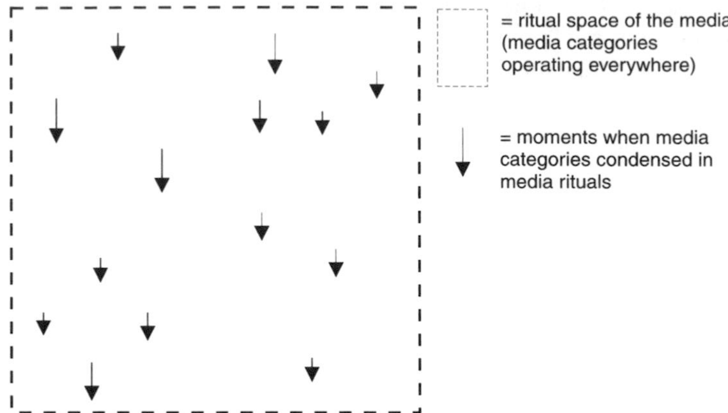

Figure 1.2 Relationship between 'ritual space of the media' and 'media rituals'

on 'categories', which is Durkheimian in spirit, might seem strange. In complex social worlds, with so many contradictory belief systems, can there really be any central categories that have a *privileged* relationship to social order, or what passes for it? Paradoxically there can, and a striking feature of media rituals is precisely the way they make natural (against all the odds) the idea that society is centred, and the related idea that some media-related categories ('reality', 'liveness', 'media person', and so on) are of overriding importance. This is the paradox of the media's social role in late modernity, but we cannot understand it by studying 'media rituals' in isolation.

We must, as the anthropologist Maurice Godelier put it, 'seek to use our theoretical imagination to penetrate the black box of those mechanisms which govern the distribution of the same representations among social groups with partially or profoundly opposed interests' (1986: 14). So too with the mechanisms that legitimate the uneven flow of media representations among a spatially dispersed and culturally diverse population.[23] But, as with any box, we cannot open it unless we have the right tools.

Ritual categories

Categories in the Durkheimian sense are the key to unlocking the black box of the late modern world's mediated rhetorics. What are 'categories' in Durkheim's sense? They are (quoting Marcel Mauss, Durkheim's main collaborator) the:

> principle[s] that elude examination [because they are the] principles without which ... judgements and arguments are not believed possible.
>
> (quoted in Bourdieu 1996: 8)

An interesting, but little asked, question is: what are these categories of thought in the contemporary mediated social world? I will offer some specific answers to this question later in the book, but the importance of the question has recently been reinforced by the political sociologist Charles Tilly's (1998) argument, outside a Durkheimian framework, that it is the apparently innocent work of 'bounded categories' that reproduces '*durable* inequality'. Durable inequality requires the persistent reproduction of categories, usually without our conscious monitoring, in countless micro-settings.

Social reproduction (on any level) is, however, never guaranteed – hence my qualification 'almost everywhere' four paragraphs back, when discussing the latent presence of media categories across social space. Here we *can* usefully draw on the insights of post-structuralist thought, particularly Deleuze and Guattari, in modelling the pervasive forces of de-territorialisation, which are at work across and within other processes of 're-territorialisation' (Deleuze and Guattari 1988). The difficult question is, however, how exactly to think that relation. Localised irony about a particular celebrity, for example, while not trivial, is unlikely to 'de-territorialise' the wider patterns of celebrity production across social space; indeed a certain amount of irony and laughter has always been a regular, even a necessary, part of the larger-space reproduction of social order (Bakhtin 1984). On the other hand, there are times when processes of de-territorialisation become crucial, even dominant, for example when localised patterns of disorder link up to produce a wider breakdown (the recent spread of protests against corporate brands might be an instance). I return to this issue in Chapter 4 when discussing 'media events'.

The term 'media rituals' is designed to imply neither a simple order nor a simple disorder, but a complex and never fully stable interaction between order and disorder. To retain the term 'ritual' at all, however, is to resist some scepticism about the vagueness of the term, both in anthropology (Goody 1977) and in media studies (Becker 1998; Corner 1999a). I will set out a more formal definition of media rituals in Chapter 2, but for now I hope to have shown that any apparent vagueness matters less than the type of work the 'media rituals' concept can do in helping us grasp the nature of contemporary 'social order' and media's place within it.

In developing the term, I will have to be selective. So, for example, I will not consider fan practices systematically, even though there is great scope for developing ritual analysis in relation to what fans do (see, however, Chapter 5). Nor will I discuss news production and consumption in detail. My primary examples will be pilgrimages to media sites, 'reality TV' and self-disclosure through media forms (not just television but also the Internet), since these seem to me the areas where ritual analysis can make the most immediate impact.

In the next chapter I explain in greater detail the key concepts we need for understanding media rituals, but first let me explain this book's context within the long-standing debates about how to evaluate the media's general effects on social life.

MEDIA RITUALS WITHIN THE WIDER FIELD OF MEDIA RESEARCH

If we look back over the past three to four decades, there has been a running, if often submerged, battle between two very different assessments of the media's consequences for social life. Some writers have seen them in a fundamentally negative light, while others have insisted on a positive evaluation. Such a general debate, we might argue, diverts us from more important questions about the details of this or that media text or production process, but it would be a mistake to dismiss it so easily. For at stake is the question of how we assess the impacts of media systems on social life and personal experience, which is much more than a question of technological development (cf. Robins 1995a: chapter 1). However difficult to resolve, this remains the fundamental question about media 'effects' (cf. Lazarsfeld and Merton 1969).

If it matters to analyse media rituals at all, it is because it allows us to get a better grasp on this fundamental question. Let me put my own answer in the context of others, negative or positive, in media studies and in media sociology.

Negative readings of the media's effects

There have been enough negative accounts of the media's social impacts to fill a book or two by themselves. A few highlights must suffice. Daniel Boorstin's early polemic *The Image: Whatever Happened to the American Dream* (1961) argued, across a number of areas, that media had effectively devalued social life, by reducing politics to 'pseudo-events', public personae to 'pseudo-people', and travel to an endless circulation among places already seen in the media. The broad similarity between Boorstin's and Jean Baudrillard's (1983) later, and better-known, analyses of media-induced social atrophy is clear. For Baudrillard, too, social space has been fundamentally transformed by the pervasiveness of media images and media models. Another French critic of the media, the Situationist Guy Debord (1983), had argued that 'the spectacle' (not only mass media, but the whole facade of consumerism) works by a claim to encompass the whole of social space:

> In the spectacle, one part of the world *represents itself* to the world and is superior to it. The spectacle is nothing more than the common language of this separation ... the spectacle is the map of this new world, a map which exactly covers the territory.
>
> (Debord 1983: paragraphs 29, 31)

For Baudrillard, Debord's analysis was, in a sense, too optimistic, because it still held onto the idea, first, of analysing media representations as if they could be isolated within the social flow and, second, of using that analysis to sustain a critical position on media outputs. Instead, Baudrillard argues, there can be no position outside media models in a society of 'simulation'; as he memorably put it, 'it is the map that precedes the territory' (1983: 2). Media form and social form, for Baudrillard, have merged absolutely. While, in his later writings, Baudrillard seems almost to celebrate this conclusion, the underlying analysis is hardly positive. Baudrillard's judgement on media's impacts on social life is that the question is undecidable, but only because (for good *or ill*, who can tell?)[24] those impacts are so pervasive and so complete.

Another negative assessment came later from Pierre Bourdieu (1998), in two lectures delivered, ironically enough, on a television channel, where he condemned the impact of television on the rest of the media (especially the serious press), on other arenas of cultural production (including the academic world), and on social life in general. Although this book has been widely criticised, both by media scholars and by the French media, it marks an advance on Baudrillard's broad philosophical speculations, because it connects the question of the media's social consequences with a sociological model of cultural production. I cannot go into its details here, but there is one point in Bourdieu's book which is valuable whatever the weaknesses of his detailed argument: his insistence on the simple, but profound, issue of television's symbolic power, its particular privilege of constructing social reality. We come back to this in Chapter 3. What is missing in Bourdieu's analysis, too, is any developed sense of media as a social process, involving not just producers but audiences.

Positive readings of the media's effects

What of writers who have evaluated the media process in positive terms? We will come in a later chapter to the specific debate on media events in the work of Dayan and Katz (1992), which represents one of the most important cruxes for assessing the media's social consequences, as well as the value of a neo-Durkheimian model of the media (Chapter 4). Here, I want to concentrate on other writers who have developed important arguments for a positive evaluation of the media process.

Paddy Scannell's work on television and radio is one of the broadest and richest bodies of work on contemporary media, covering history, phenomenology and the analysis of broadcast talk. Running through his work is a positive evaluation of the way media relate to another key term whose positive status he always assumes, 'ordinary life'. A central and positive dimension of contemporary media for Scannell is to speak convincingly from institutional settings to countless millions in the contexts of their everyday lives. For Scannell, this is a dimension of media that can never be grasped by political analysis. As he puts it: 'the only reality that media studies knows is a political reality. … It has great difficulty with any idea of ordinary unpolitical daily life, and its everyday concerns and enjoyments.' (Scannell 1996: 4) There is a questionable rhetorical move here, which becomes clearer if we talk in terms of 'power' rather than 'politics' (with its overtones of formal politics). Scannell assumes that we can simply bracket out not only the dimensions of power within ordinary life but, more importantly, the media's influence on the construction of what counts as 'ordinary life'.

This insulation from critical analysis of both 'ordinary life', and media's representations of it, is reinforced in Scannell's book *Radio, Television and Modern Life* (1996) where he draws on Martin Heidegger's philosophy of being (especially, Heidegger 1962). There is something interesting in Scannell's use of Heidegger (one of whose main themes was the necessary historicality of our existence) to analyse how everyday media connect us from hour to hour, day to day, and year to year to a broader historical process. But history gets bypassed in another sense – as a dimension which might influence our *evaluations* of the media process – when Scannell implies that Heidegger's profoundly general philosophical framework somehow supports his positive evaluation of the media process. Heidegger was concerned with 'being' in general, at a level unaffected by any conflicts of power at particular times and places.[25] As a result, real history (the material history of the media process and its consequences for social power) is excluded from Scannell's Heideggerian account of the media no less absolutely than from Baudrillard's philosophically framed analysis. If Baudrillard offers a negative 'theology' of the media (as Andreas Huyssen once put it, 1995: 188), Scannell offers a positive theology, and it is not 'theology' we need.

Less reverent, but no less impatient of questions of power, is John Hartley's (1999) engaging account of the 'uses of television'. Hartley is concerned to undermine broad arguments that contemporary media culture has a negative impact on education and public life by arguing that in its dispersed, often ironic form, media debates can educate, since they sustain a public space in which the terms of private and public discourse are open to negotiation beyond formal political control. This argument is no less theological in its way than Scannell's. While Hartley's rejection of automatic jeremiads against popular media is justified, he never addresses the implications of the massive concentration of symbolic power in media institutions. How does this affect our interpretation of the social 'uses of television'? Unless we rely on the jaded rhetoric of market liberalism, we can know nothing about the actual impacts, positive *or* negative, of contemporary media without considering, for example, the uneven symbolic landscape in which popular talk shows address their viewers and also their participants (see Chapter 7).

To summarise: positive evaluations of the media process address well how media penetrate the daily texture of private and public life, but fail to consider the social impacts of media power. Negative evaluations, by contrast, address media power, but lack engagement with media's place in our everyday lives. Yet the evaluation of media's overall impacts on society *remains* the central question for media studies and an important question increasingly for social theory, indeed philosophy too.[26] How can we move this debate forward?

Mediated 'reality' and power

The answer lies in a paradox. It was Henri Lefebvre who fixed on the *ambiguity* of everyday life in his writings in the early days of electronic media (Lefebvre 1991a: 18), the ambiguity that comes from the way the private space of everyday life is already crossed by countless trajectories of power (the economy, political order, media narratives). Maybe we can focus this paradox a little further for the media case. The central paradox we have to grasp in assessing the media's social consequences is that we cannot separate out *our* hopes, *our* myths, *our* moments of togetherness or conflict, from the mediated social forms which they now, almost always, take. Those forms in turn cannot be separated from the uneven landscape of power on which the media process is founded.

It is good to turn here to the American media theorist, James Carey (1989), whose work has an interesting relationship to Durkheim's theory of social order. Carey is well known for his call to media research to pay less attention to the 'transmission' mode of media (that is, to the transmission of media messages across space) and more attention to the 'ritual' mode (that is, media's role in the 'maintenance of societies in time'). Such an argument seems close to a Durkheimian concern with the maintenance of the social bond (Rothenbuhler 1993). Carey's reason for refusing to call himself a Durkheimian was that Durkheim pays insufficient attention to questions of power, and offers effectively a functionalist account of how societies work. These are precisely the reasons I have already offered for developing, not an anti-Durkheimian, but a *post*-Durkheimian (and anti-functionalist) account of media rituals.

It was Carey who, in spite of an occasional romanticism about 'communication' in a general sense,[27] put the paradox and challenge of the media's social impacts better than anyone else:

> Reality is a scarce resource … the fundamental form of power is the power to define, allocate, and display that resource.
>
> (Carey 1989: 87)

How can we doubt that the fundamental question about media is the question of power, the uneven distribution of the power to influence representations of social 'reality'? What, however, Carey's 'ritual' analysis of communication lacks is a detailed model of the *structured patterns* through which we live with, and even accept, the concentration in media institutions of the power to define reality. The point of the media rituals concept is to unlock these patterns. In media rituals, power and belonging are meshed together, for, as Philip Elliott put it in perhaps the first, but still most insightful, essay in this area, 'ritual ... is a structured performance in which not all participants are equal' (Elliott 1982: 145). Media rituals have provided a new setting for addressing Durkheim's fundamental question: what is social order? 'Society', Durkheim wrote, 'can only feel its influence in action, and [society] is not in action unless the individuals who compose it are assembled and act in common';[28] in contemporary mediated societies, almost *all* possibilities of 'acting in common' must pass through social forms (media forms) that are themselves inseparable from highly uneven effects of power. This paradox, as we shall see, is likely to stay with us even in the apparently more decentralised landscape of new media.

Chapter 2

Ritual and liminality

> The word 'ritual' like the word 'art' does not have one commonly agreed definition.
>
> (Lewis 1980: 19)

In this and the next chapter, I will introduce the key concepts we need to analyse the ritual space of the media, drawing selectively on anthropological theory. Ritual theory is not only one of the most contested areas of anthropology, but also a much larger area than we need to map for an understanding of media ritual, so it is important to keep to the central ideas with a minimum of technical detail. The main aim here, after all, is to understand media 'ritual' not for its own sake but as part of a broader understanding of the role of media power in the organisation of contemporary societies. As we move through this conceptual survey, the importance will become clear of certain critical anthropological theorists (such as Pierre Bourdieu and Maurice Bloch) who have tended to be ignored when media studies has addressed questions of ritual. This exploration will provide the basis for the detailed studies in later chapters of media events, media pilgrimages, reality television, and self-disclosure through the media.

RITUAL

The term 'ritual' in anthropology has a tangled history. In Chapter 1, I summarised the three basic senses of 'ritual' that can be distinguished: ritual as habitual action, ritual as formalised action, and ritual as action (often, but not necessarily, formalised) that is associated with transcendent values. In terms of how we *define* 'ritual', my overall preference is for the third, broadly Durkheimian, tradition, as developed in the early work of the American anthropologist Victor Turner (1974; 1977a). This stresses the wider social significance of the ritual process as a whole, in contrast with the analytical tradition that concentrates on defining ever more precisely the formal characteristics of specific ritual actions (Lewis 1980; Rappaport 1999; Tambiah 1985). But, as already indicated, I wish to bring to the Durkheimian approach, against its grain, a concern with rituals as instruments of power, and that will involve drawing on aspects of the second approach to ritual as well.

Ritual and the wider space of ritualisation

It is worth saying something about the first, banal, usage of the term 'ritual' – as 'habitual action' – because it is often confused with the other more substantive uses. The idea of 'ritual' – as the *merely* 'customary' or 'repetitive' – is often associated with ideas about the decline of 'real' ceremony in contemporary detraditionalised societies, and its replacement by observance for its own sake: an earlier substantive use of the term 'ritual' is seen to have degraded into a nominal usage. There are of course many serious arguments about the possible decline of ritual action in contemporary societies, and indeed about the media's role in this,[1] but they are not advanced by defining 'ritual action' loosely as *any* repetitive or habitual action. If we do that, then countless aspects of everyday life (from driving a car to checking our emails to, yes, watching television) are automatically included in the definition of 'ritual', but without any way of differentiating them! In media sociology, there have been some uses of the term 'ritual' to describe the habitual aspects of people's television viewing;[2] since, however, those uses make no serious use of anthropological theory and are themselves little more than habitual, rather than substantive, uses of the term, I will discuss them no further.

Nor will I be much interested in what we might call 'secondary' uses of the term 'ritual' in relation to media: that is, situations where media *portray already existing ritual action* (for example, the televising of religious ritual).[3] Clearly, if we use 'media rituals' in just this secondary sense, then we don't need to take any particular position on what the underlying term 'ritual' means. But I *do* want to give the term 'media rituals' a primary meaning, where 'media' adds something substantial (beyond the mere fact of broadcast coverage) to how we think about ritual. Nor (analogously) is this book simply about how the media represents 'liminal' social events (Martin 1981: 77); for this term, see the end of this chapter. Rather, and in line with most other substantive approaches,[4] I emphasise that the terms 'ritual' (and 'liminality') distinguish certain types of action and practice, with 'media rituals' being a special type of ritual action, distinguished by a particular type of relation to the media process, that we need to explain.

It is important, and not just pedantic, to be clear on such questions of definition, not least because of the difficulty in large, dispersed societies of accurately identifying patterns of ritual behaviour from the general mass of behaviour.[5] Recalling the term I introduced in Chapter 1, our aim is to study the wider *space of ritualisation* (Bell 1997), that is, the principles that have generated the media's 'ritual space' and which in turn therefore generate the possibilities of specific media rituals. But these are as difficult to see at first glance as the principles that generate a landscape over time. They are *latent* in the landscape of media power, with its glamorous highpoints and hidden depths. This landscape, while it provides the fundamental context for our orientations to the media, is, like any landscape, transformed by our actions, but very slowly and gradually: in the meantime, we have all to deal with the consequences of the media landscape we inherit, and the naturalising power of media rituals.[6] Our task is to denaturalise that landscape.

First, we need some building blocks for a substantive use of the term 'media ritual', drawing on concepts from anthropological theory: the patterning of action, the framing of attention, boundaries, and ritual categories. A full discussion of the media's 'ritual categories' is deferred until after the introduction of the concepts of 'symbolic power' and 'symbolic violence' in Chapter 3.

The patterning of action

As already explained, my main interest is in approaches to ritual that understand it in terms of the wider values and categories it embodies, but there are still important things to be learned from the anthropological tradition that analyses ritual purely in terms of the formal properties of special types of action. Primarily, this has focused on religious ritual – which means that the details of such analysis are often not our concern – but this is not a problem, since it is generally agreed that 'ritual' extends beyond religious ritual, as it must if the idea of media ritual is to get off the ground! This extended usage was already implicit in Durkheim's broad interpretation of religion and religious ritual, but it was made explicit in 1970s debates about secular ritual (Moore and Myerhoff 1977a; 1977b). Mary Douglas even went so far as to argue that 'very little of our ritual behaviour is enacted in the context of religion' (1984: 68).[7]

It is also almost universally agreed that ritual is a type or form of *action*, as distinct from a mere idea or thought or feeling (for example, Lewis 1980; Rappaport 1999: 38). To focus the discussion, it is worth looking briefly at some authoritative definitions of the term 'ritual'. The most systematic theorist of ritual, the late Roy Rappaport (and here I must leave aside his ambitious theory of why ritual action has wider cultural significance in the development of human civilisation) defined ritual as:

> the performance of more or less invariant sequences of formal acts and utterances not entirely encoded by the performers.
>
> (Rappaport 1999: 24)

Along with other definitions that are concerned above all to emphasise the formality of ritual action (cf. Tambiah 1985: 128), the underlying aim here is to capture the core of *religious* ritual, even if the definition is also drafted to encompass much more (Rappaport 1999: 24). In relation to formal religion, this emphasis on formality and exact (or almost exact) repetition is plausible and self-explanatory. That approach is less helpful, I suggest, if it excludes an interest in ritualisation in less formalised situations, including ritualisation focused around media. But, moving on, we should note two points about Rappaport's definition which are helpful. First, his insistence that ritual action is always more than it seems. Ritual action, he says, is performance of acts or utterances 'not entirely encoded by the performers'; in other words, in ritual, *wider* patterns of meaning are recognised as being enacted, although not necessarily intended or articulated, by the performers. Ritual action is action whose latent significance is much wider than its manifest form: this will be important later. Second, Rappaport, against the grain of much anthropological writing, emphasises ritual *behaviour* and not symbolism or ideas (1999: 26). While I too will use the concept of 'symbolic' power (as distinct from economic or political power: see Chapter 3), Rappaport's point is a different one. Clifford Geertz had erected symbolic activity to the centre of all anthropological analysis (1973: chapter 1) with the unhelpful implication that at the core of every ritual action were certain symbols or ideas which the action 'expressed'. Rappaport, by contrast, emphasises that ritual is always, fundamentally, action, not ideas; this is an important point for us in developing a theory of the actions we will call 'media rituals'.

Far from every ritual therefore expressing a hidden essence in which the performers explicitly believe, rituals by their repetitive form reproduce categories and patterns of thought in a way that bypasses explicit belief. On the contrary, if made explicit, many of the ideas apparently expressed by these rituals might be rejected or at least called into question; it is their *ritualised* form that enables them to be successfully reproduced without being exposed to questions about their 'content'. This will help us understand how ritual works in relation to media, where, quite clearly, there is no explicit credo of shared beliefs about media to which everyone signs up, but there are media-related patterns of action, thought and speech, which embody hierarchies that (silently, as it were) help legitimate media power.

Definitions of 'ritual' based solely on their expressive function are therefore unhelpful: for example, the definition offered by the American sociologist of religion Robert Wuthnow of ritual not as a type of action but simply as 'a symbolic expressive aspect of behavior that *communicates something about* social relations, often in a relatively dramatic or formal manner' (1987: 109, my emphasis). A media ritual, on this view, would be anything in the media that is expressive about social relations. But this loose definition neglects the primary dimension along which rituals are distinguished: the dimension of 'practice' (Asad 1993). Far from just being an expressive way of making media, media rituals are a particular type of formalised, media-related *action*, which (paradoxically, as we shall see) need not involve making media at all.

Even more helpful for us than Rappaport's definition is that offered by the American media sociologist Eric Rothenbuhler in an important review of the literature on ritual for media and communications theory:

> ritual is the voluntary performance of appropriately patterned behavior to symbolically effect or participate in the serious life.
>
> (Rothenbuhler 1998: 27)

Rothenbuhler, too, is clear that ritual action is a form of behaviour patterned in a way that relates it to 'the serious life' (Durkheim's term for the transcendent dimension of the social, which Rothenbuhler adopts: see Chapter 1), rather than an expressive form as such. *Media* rituals, then, we might suggest, are formalised actions organised around key *media*-related categories or patterns. We will later clarify what exactly these categories are, how media rituals work upon them, and why 'categories' matter so much in understanding rituals, including media rituals.

FRAMING

Already, in this very provisional definition of media rituals, there is an implicit link between the formal properties of ritual actions and a wider social space. We need a way of making this link more substantial. Here we can draw on another anthropological concept important in ritual analysis: the concept of 'framing'.

Ritual actions carry resonances of wider values or frameworks of understanding; in ritual action, we often have a sense that wider issues are somehow at stake. Indeed, because we are aware of that frequent connection, ritual form is one important way in which the legitimacy of assumed wider values can be confirmed and communicated. This is a crucial point in helping us understand, ultimately, how rituals are linked to power.

The idea that ritual is a means to direct, or 'frame', our attention to something wider that is 'at stake' in ritual performance has been emphasised by many writers, within both anthropology and media theory.[8] As Mary Douglas (1984: 64) put it, 'ritual focuses attention by framing; it enlivens the memory and links the present with the relevant past. In all this it aids perception'. 'Framing' is a useful term, derived from the sociology of Goffman (1975) and ultimately from Gregory Bateson (1973:

179–89). It captures how actions that can be described straightforwardly on one level – putting a ring on another person's finger – are recognised by all involved as signifying something else, whose exact nature depends on context (the act of marriage, the acting of a marriage ceremony in a scene from a play, a children's game?). As Goffman (1975: 79) put it, action in one register is 'rekeyed' in another.

The notion of 'framing' is important because it formulates precisely the connection with wider social values central to the Durkheimian view of religion and ritual. In ritual action, according to Durkheim, there is a sense (not necessarily explicit, as I've already emphasised) that wider values of sociality are at stake: rituals deal in some sense with what it is we have in common as members of a society. This connecting notion of framing (working through the way actions are understood) is common to many writers influenced by Durkheim: Turner (1977a: 96; 1974: 239), MacAloon (1984: 251, 274), Wuthnow (1987), and in media studies Real (1989). The same point is present in James Carey's famous analysis of the 'ritual mode of communication' (1989: 18, 21), although, as we saw in Chapter 1, Carey denies that his account is formally Durkheimian. The idea that ritual action is embedded in a wider frame of significance is central also to Victor Turner's account of the ritual process as associated with, or capable of expressing, social conflict and social drama. I return to Turner's concept of 'liminality' below.

What exactly do we mean by 'framing' in the context of 'rituals'? We can explain this by amplifying the provisional definition of media rituals offered above. Rituals are actions which, because of their patterning, stand in for wider values and frameworks of understanding. This connection (or 'framing') works as follows:

1 The actions comprising rituals are structured around certain *categories and/or boundaries.*
2 Those categories suggest, or stand in for, an underlying *value.*
3 This 'value' captures our sense that *the social* is at stake in the ritual.

By 'framing', then, in relation to rituals, we mean something more specific than the incidental associations of a ritual performance. We mean the way that a regular categorisation of the world *organises* particular ritual performances, and, in so doing, makes material a broader pattern, value, or hierarchy. The concept of 'framing', in turn, draws upon two other aspects of rituals: boundaries (to which I turn next) and media-related categories (dealt with more fully in Chapter 3). First, however, let me just clarify the way in which *media* rituals in particular might frame the social.

An example for the media field would be the organisation of ritualised meetings with celebrities around the distinction between the 'media person' (or celebrity) and the 'ordinary person'. The wider resonance, or framing, of such acts derives from the way that the media person/ordinary person distinction replicates a broader hierarchy

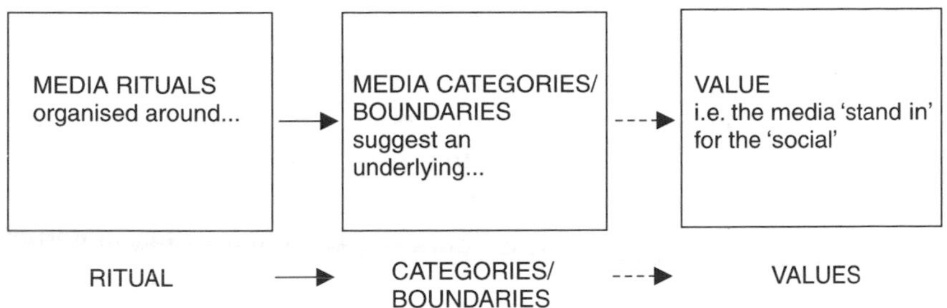

Figure 2.1 How media rituals 'frame' the social

between people/things/places 'in' the media over people/things/places not 'in' the media; this naturalised hierarchy, in turn, helps reinforce the special status of media themselves, and underlies, for example, the common reading of celebrities and their stories as if they stood for 'something more', something central about contemporary social life.[9] This boundary or category distinction suggests a broader, underlying value, which is that media somehow 'stand in' for, or represent, the social world as a whole. This link from ritual to categories to underlying value is represented in Figure 2.1.

Boundaries

Rituals do not so much express order, as *naturalise* it; they formalise categories, and the differences or boundaries between categories, in performances that help them seem natural, even legitimate. At first glance, this is merely a way of restating that ritual is formalised action, but, as Pierre Bourdieu argued, much more is at stake than that.

In an important brief article, 'Rites of Institution', reprinted in his book *Language and Symbolic Power* (1991), Pierre Bourdieu offered a radical revision of Durkheimian notions of ritual. Discussing rites of passage in van Gennep (1977) and transformative ritual in Victor Turner (1974), he argued that the conventional analysis of their impact should be overturned. Conventionally, the emphasis is on the transition that is ritually made (for example, from young boy to mature man; or from state of crisis to the restoration of social order). But Bourdieu argues that what matters is not the individual's passage from one state to another, but the social significance of the *line or boundary* that is crossed, the ritual boundary. This boundary, like all cultural boundaries, is an arbitrary one, based upon a particular construction of the world, but the fact that it is crossed in a ritual action reproduces it as significant and thereby helps in its continued legitimation; the crossing makes the boundary seem more real and less arbitrary (1991: 117–18). Yet at the same time, at least in the case of the rite of passage to manhood (the second case is more complex), there is a whole group of people (women!) for whom the boundary is not even, in principle, crossable. They cannot therefore take part in the rite of passage. So the underlying division – between man and woman – and its legitimacy in 'nature' is reproduced through the individual boy's ritual of transformation into a man. In this way, ritual reinforces not so much the 'content' of ritual – there need be no thing recognised as such – but the limits, or boundaries, within which we all (whether we take part in the ritual or not) have to act; it reinforces our individual sense of limits, making them seem natural (1991: 123). For Bourdieu, rituals are much more than formalisations of otherwise ordinary action; they are *rites of institution*, which institute as natural, and seemingly legitimate, certain key category differences and boundaries.

A further advantage of Bourdieu's approach is to reinforce the point, already suggested, that rituals may have power implications (broadly speaking, 'ideological effects') without necessarily having anything as explicit as ideological 'content'. Ritual performances may, even so, have specific resonances which are contradictory. Any term in a ritual may have condensed within it a range of references to both specific and general features of social experience: for Turner, the symbolic is inherently multi-valent and potentially contradictory (Turner 1977a). Ritual involves another, rather different, type of ambiguity, appearing to be both necessary and open to individual appropriation and reflection, since every ritual performance is always only a rough approximation to some imagined form. This potentially puzzling aspect of ritual is at the root of Maurice Bloch's analysis. Maurice Bloch (turning usual approaches to ritual on their head in a way that recalls Barthes' (1972) notion of myth as a 'turnstile' that alternates continually between 'reality' and 'myth') claims this very ambiguity of ritual is central to its effectiveness (Bloch 1989: 130); it is rituals' oscillation between timeless history and contingent adaptation that allows us to believe in their overriding 'truth'. While none of the media rituals I discuss make claims to be exactly 'timeless', Bloch's notion of ambiguity captures something important to which I return in Chapter 6, when we discuss reality game-shows such as *Big Brother.*

In ritual, then, things seem open, just when they operate to secure a wider closure: this is a question of form, more than explicit belief, and this may help to capture part of what is most puzzling about media (and particularly media rituals). This helps, more generally, explain why the Cambridge anthropologist Jack Goody's (1977: 32) famous attempt to debunk the notion of ritual could be right in suggesting that ritual tells us less about people's explicit beliefs than we normally suppose, but wrong in suggesting it must be abandoned. In describing certain forms of action from the perspective of power, people's beliefs – which may, or may not, be expressed through ritual – matter less than the organisational principles embodied in ritualised action.

MEDIA RITUALS AND THE 'SOCIAL ORDER'

We are ready now to formalise our definition of media rituals: *media rituals are formalised actions organised around key media-related categories and boundaries, whose performance frames, or suggests a connection with, wider media-related values.* This definition combines the second and third conceptions of ritual discussed earlier (as formalised action, and as action associated with broader, shared values), while ignoring the first (ritual as mere 'habit'). But there are further points to be noted as well. What makes a ritual action distinctively a media ritual is *not* whether it is performed in the media, or involves an act of media production or consumption, but the media-related categories around which it is structured and the media-related values to which it directs our attention. In understanding media rituals, then, our primary concern is not with the 'ideas' that might be 'expressed' through, say, a media text, but with the formal relations at work in a particular type of action.

It was Baudrillard who in an early essay suggested that the power implications of contemporary media were always, in part, questions of 'form' (1981: 169), that is, of the 'social division' which the media constitutes between producers and consumers of representations. Quite separately, Bourdieu argued that 'in the symbolic domain, takeovers of force appear as takeovers of form' (1991: 213), while Maurice Bloch transvalued Durkheim's theory of religion as social form into an analysis of ritual as 'the use of form for power' (1989: 45). What are the implications of this argument about form in the case of media rituals? To anticipate Chapter 3, media rituals are practices through which the arbitrariness of the limits around participation in the media sphere – that is, media institutions' heavy concentration of symbolic power – is naturalised. Every media claim to speak 'for us all' naturalises the fact that generally we do not speak for ourselves.

No more than rituals in general, however, can media rituals be analysed in isolation from the larger hinterland of ritual*isation*: that is to say, separated from the wider analysis of the whole gamut of patterns of action, thought and speech, more or less routine, which generate the categories and boundaries on which media rituals are based and constitute the ritual space of the media. It is this hinterland of everyday action, thought and belief that make the special cases of media rituals possible.

As Catherine Bell puts it (in relation to religious ritual, but the point applies to media rituals equally well), the most central quality of ritualisation is how it organises our movements around space, helps us to experience constructed features of the environment as real, and thereby reproduces the symbolic authority at stake in the categorisations on which ritual draws. The background ritualisations of practice underlying media rituals work in a similar way: through the organisation of all sorts of social actions around key media-related categories ('media person/thing/place/world', 'liveness', 'reality'; for more detail, see Chapter 3). These categories are reproduced right across social space: I have called this hinterland 'the ritual space of the media'. It is this wider patterning that the theoretical term 'the ritual space of the media' allows us to grasp as connected.

All social life lies behind the condensed actions of ritual, including media rituals. This is why the arguments of this book range widely: across television shows, press comment, Websites, actions at tourist sites, behaviour in studios, and so on. Ritualisation is a dimension of all social space and, in relation to media rituals, incorporates the categorising logic of societies that, increasingly, are organised around media 'centres'. As Catherine Bell puts it:

> The orchestrated construction of power and authority in ritual ... engage[s] the social body in the objectification of oppositions and the deployment of schemes *that effectively reproduce the divisions of the social order.* In this objectification lie the resonance of ritual and the consequences of compliance.
>
> (Bell 1992: 215, my emphasis)

Note, however, that 'social order' is used here (cf. Chapter 1) to mean, not a 'foundational' social order whose status is uncontestable, but a relatively ordered social world, one of whose dimensions is precisely the continual construction of its own relative order as something 'more' than that, as something necessary, *as value* (see Figure 1.1 in Chapter 1). This construction is a real (not constructed!) process and has real effects on how we act, think and speak (cf. Peters and Rothenbuhler 1989).

From this perspective, we can rethink the anthropological legacy of ritual analysis in a radical way, breaking in the process from most earlier thinking about ritual in media studies. As John Corner has suggested (1999a), this is no bad thing, since media studies has until now lacked a clear primary sense for the term 'ritual'. Ritual, on the Durkheimian model, matters because of its special relationship to the integration of society, but, as is well-known, such questions of 'effects' have always been difficult to establish in relation to media. This is why the term 'media rituals' until now has had little substance, because we have lacked the means to explain how media rituals are grounded in everyday practice, relying instead on the vague assumptions about 'effects' implied in the Durkheimian model.

Our focus, by contrast, (following Catherine Bell's reorientation of work on ritual in the anthropology of religion) shifts attention to the smallest details of categorising practice through which the media's authority as a social 'centre' is reinforced. The existing approach to media rituals closest to mine is that of the Swedish-American anthropologist Karin Becker. Another interesting parallel with my approach, which there is no space to pursue here, is Paul Little's essay on the Rio Earth Summit (Little 1995), although media are less central to it than to Becker's piece. In a very clear and illuminating article, Karin Becker (1995) analyses an event in the Swedish calendar

– the submission of the annual Swedish tax return – which is now a televised event. She describes, for example, how people hesitate for a second with the form in their hand above the collection box, so that the camera can register the moment of delivery. Becker's argument is developed quite deliberately on a micro-level and outside the grand claims of a Durkheimian argument, but it is very suggestive in showing how in the case of the media ritualisation works through the body (cf. Chapter 3). Becker's wider claim is that the presence of television cameras gives rise to a new formalisation of action that we might call ritualised.

What is common to our arguments is the insistence on looking closely at the patterning of action in media ritual and the categories of thought such patterning implies. I would, however, draw a somewhat different conclusion from her argument. In certain cases, the presence of cameras encourages formalisation and the playing with, and working upon, media categories such as celebrity, reality and liveness (cf. Becker 1995: 639–44). But the presence of cameras is not essential for this process, which may be prompted in other ways. We could easily imagine a parallel media ritual to Becker's, not televised but simply hosted by a television 'personality'. Equally, the presence of cameras does not *itself* transform every aspect of an event into a media ritual; many football matches are televised, but this does not result in the whole game becoming a media ritual, even if ritualisation remains a potential dimension of details in the match. The presence of television cameras, then, which Becker highlights, is but *one of many* ways in which action oriented towards media may become formalised and ritualised.

Chapter 3 pursues this in more detail, but first we must introduce another key term of ritual analysis, 'liminality'.

LIMINALITY

'Liminality' is a term which, like ritual, still has its uses within a non-functionalist perspective, even if its usage has been particularly associated with the neo-Durkheimian theory of ritual found in the early work of Victor Turner.

Underlying 'liminality' is the idea of separation, and through that 'framing'. 'Framing' clearly implies some separation of ritual action and everyday action (see above). The idea that ritual action is distinct from, even sealed off from, the everyday (da Matta 1984: 236–7; Tambiah 1985: 132) may be expressed literally. So some ritual performances happen in physically separate sites, away from the flow of everyday action (da Matta 1984: 221 on carnival; and see Chapter 6 on media pilgrimages). More generally, in various ways ritual action is 'extraordinary' action, set apart from the actions of 'ordinary' life (Bell 1992: 74; Durkheim 1995: 222; Smith 1987: 109). The concept of 'liminality', however, takes this notion of separation much further.

Liminality and the temporary suspension of social order

'Liminality' attempts to capture the way that, unlike everyday action whose significance is purely local, ritual actions take on wider resonances, that encompass the whole of society. Here is a passage where Victor Turner describes one such moment:

> Following the breach of regular, norm-governed social relations, a phase of mounting *crisis* supervenes, during which, unless the breach can be sealed off quickly within a limited area of social interaction, there is a tendency for the breach to widen and extend until it becomes coextensive with some dominant cleavage in the widest set of relevant social relations to which the conflicting or antagonistic parties belong.
>
> (Turner 1974: 38, original emphasis)

The term 'liminal' was used first in anthropology by Arnold van Gennep (1977) in his classic analysis of 'rites of passage' in traditional societies. The *limen* (Latin for threshold) was van Gennep's term for the boundary crossed in such rites, whether the boundary between boyhood and manhood or (in van Gennep's own extension of the term) the boundary between the person who has not yet made their pilgrimage and the person who has. The term entered wider usage in anthropology through Victor Turner who adapted it to cover a range of circumstances not confined to ritual in the strict sense, such as situations of major social conflict (Turner 1974; 1977a). Turner's insight (cf. Gluckman 1971) was to see that van Gennep's model of ritual passage could explain the form which transitional social crises, even in more complex societies, regularly take.

The quotation above comes from a description of the second of what Turner identified as the three stages of a 'social drama':

1. the initial social breach;
2. its widening to become a general crisis, enveloping social relations as a whole;
3. the resolution of the crisis, at which point the wider sense of social order is also restored, indeed reaffirmed (Turner 1977a: 91).

By extending the relevance of Durkheim's analysis of ritual as social form to the more chaotic and complex flow of public events, Turner overcomes one implausibility in Durkheim's theory of the social bond: its over-reliance on situations of consensual experience, and lack of attention to moments of conflict (cf. Ettema 1990; Rothenbuhler 1989). In addition, Turner suggested how conflict and social order were structurally related in a broader alternation between two types of social organisation: *societas*, which is equivalent to formal social organisation and prevails in normal conditions, and *communitas*, which is the type of loose, unstructured sociality or 'togetherness' that prevails in times of crisis (1977a: 96–7). Liminality (and the *communitas* it involves) is for Turner a process by which the social bond is not just reflected upon, but actually constituted and reconstituted: 'major liminal situations are occasions in which a society takes cognizance of itself' (1974: 239). Turner captures here the ambiguity of 'play' in its most serious sense: the forms through which alternative forms of social order are imagined, even if they can not be enacted (cf. Silverstone 1999: 59–67). This explains how Turner's later work came to be concentrated increasingly on performance (including theatrical performance) and left behind the Durkheimian concerns with social order of his earlier work.

Turner's concept of liminality is a powerful idea that attempts to bring conceptual order to a range of public events that by their nature almost defy analysis. Its usefulness for understanding heavily mediated public events (so-called 'media events') is obvious and will be discussed further in Chapter 4. Perhaps less plausibly, 'liminality' has been used by various theorists to capture more ordinary and less conflictual events or practices connected with the media: from the televised Olympic ceremonies (MacAloon 1984: 252) to the Rio Carnival (da Matta 1984: 224) to Disney World (Moore 1980) to the general functioning of television as a mythical medium that we tap into every day (Silverstone 1988: 22, on television as a 'liminal space'). There are traces also of this sense of everyday liminality, although without the term, in Henry Jenkins' work on fandom, particularly fans' attempt to escape the constraints of their normal working lives in 'a weekend-only world' (Jenkins 1992: 282–3).

'Liminal' and 'liminoid'

The term 'liminality' is therefore highly adaptable, but it risks being used loosely without attention to the caveats which Turner himself applied. As Turner pointed out, what was crucial about the liminality of ritual in less complex societies was that participation in them was *compulsory*, whereas participation as a viewer in the Olympics, or as a member of the Rio carnival, let alone everyday television viewing, is voluntary (Turner 1982: 42–3). For that reason, 'when used of processes, phenomena and persons in large-scale complex societies, [the] use [of the term liminal] must in the main be metaphorical' (Turner 1982: 29; cf. Turner 1977b). Like Durkheim, Turner saw a fundamental historical break with the institutionalisation of the division of labour and the resulting separation of play, or 'leisure', from work (1982: 36–7). Yet a sense of the 'liminal' lives on in complex societies in various events and pastimes (the F.A. Cup Final, the Super Bowl, and so on) and for this Turner reserves the word *liminoid*, that is, 'liminal'-*like*.

The liminoid is a dispersed form of the liminal, not strictly segregated from the rest of social life and often heavily integrated into commercial organisation, as with sport. When claims are made in sporting contests, especially great sporting climaxes, that wider social values are at stake, these are largely rhetorical, but that does not mean that they are trivial, and it is this playing with wider claims for social connection – the 'as if' of great sporting events and spectacles – that Victor Turner's term 'liminoid' captures. Turner extends 'liminoid' to aspects of contemporary religious experience, including pilgrimage (Turner 1974; Turner and Turner 1978). Turner saw pilgrimages as an adaptation in large-scale societies of the idea of the rite of passage. We return to this in Chapter 5 on media 'pilgrimages'.

Does it matter that contemporary societies are characterised more by 'liminal'-like (liminoid) experiences, than by the truly liminal? It matters much less once we drop the claim that at certain moments the social is *truly* expressed through ritual: from a post-Durkheimian perspective what matters is only the *claims* to totality that are made in association with rituals or ritualisations, and these can be found as much in liminoid leisure activities as in the most serious and compulsory ritual – indeed in contemporary societies, the boundaries between the two are often blurred. Within a neo-Durkheimian perspective, however, the difference between liminal and liminoid remains crucial and therefore problematic: it represents precisely the difference between fake rituals and the ritual process proper (which really does, it is claimed, connect us to a social centre).

In fact, Turner's distinction between liminal and liminoid articulates a wider difficulty with the neo-Durkheimian account, which Turner perhaps was the first to see clearly. By making a sharp distinction between truly liminal and merely liminoid, Turner raises the issue of whether true liminality, true ritual, is still possible in contemporary, highly dispersed societies. There is a genuine difficulty here:[10] how can we distinguish the 'ritual' (or 'liminal') from the 'non-ritual' (or merely 'liminoid') elements in everyday life? Traces of liminality, wherever they occur, are not *genuine* liminality in Turner's sense; we must avoid arguing, simplistically, that sport and popular culture have simply taken over the 'liminal' role previously performed by religious ritual (Goethals 1997). There is no evidence for that, and indeed it is not even clear what this claim means. There is a difficult balance to be struck between, on the one hand, appreciating that many forms of ritual activity *have* declined – and perhaps the general preconditions for developing new forms of ritual have declined (Douglas 1984: 69; cf. Durkheim 1984: 106) – and, on the other hand, not ignoring the media's possible contribution to *new forms* of ritual experience with a different, but not trivial, relationship to the flow of everyday life. The latter possibility is crucial to the argument of this book.

CONCLUSION: THE REINVENTION OF RITUAL IN LATE MODERNITY?

The concept of liminality, and Turner's caution about its overuse, lead then to a broader issue about the value of ritual analysis in contemporary societies.

Various writers have spoken of how media fictions infiltrate the very textures of daily life, creating what Alejo Carpentier (1990), one of the founders of Latin American 'magic realism', once called 'the marvellous in the real'.[11] It can even be argued, plausibly, that, as the formal settings for ritual (including the formal social differentiations around which ritual action can be structured) decline, so the need for other forms of 'ritual' to compensate increases: these may be a different type of ritual, rituals of just 'being-together' or, as Mary Douglas called them, 'rituals of enthusiasm' (1970: 154). This argument has been extended more recently by the French sociologist Michel Maffesoli (1996a; 1996b) to suggest that 'liminality' of a particular sort may be increasing, not decreasing; the media, he argues, are central to what he calls neo-'tribal' experiences of 'sociality'.[12] In a sense, as the Durkheimian scholar Pickering (1984: 410–11) pointed out in relation to Douglas' early version of this argument, this is at odds with Durkheim's original argument that *formal* ritual was essential to the maintenance of the social order, but it may nonetheless capture in an interesting way the context in which certain rhetorics (and rituals) of togetherness are intensifying, just as the material basis of shared experience is becoming more, not less, precarious.

We will return to this difficult issue in Chapter 6, when discussing *Big Brother*, but for the time being let me highlight the direction where my argument is heading, which is very different from Maffesoli's. I am not concerned to argue that contemporary societies actually do hold together, even in very complex ways, around a shared world-view and shared values. My interest is in how in large societies the pressures *to claim* that society 'comes together' increase, especially, perhaps, as their basic plausibility decreases. Such claims are inextricably bound up with various dimensions of power, including the operation of the economy and the sustaining of consumer demand, the demands of governments for attention and compliance, but also (most relevant to us) the need of media institutions for audiences and social status (in media, the pressures of government and economy intersect). In question, in other words, are the real concentrations of power that lie behind the myth of a valorised social 'centre'. If so, it makes less sense than ever to analyse rituals, including media rituals, in isolation from a broader analysis of power.

Chapter 3

Ritual space

Unravelling the myth of the centre

> Although the generations change, the image remains the same. It is the abiding element of social life.
>
> (Durkheim 1995: 222)

> One of the characteristic constitutive elements of ideology is the power to remain unchanged when other things are changing.
>
> (Bloch 1989: 134)

These contrasting quotes capture the choice to be made between seeing rituals as the expression of something permanent and universal and seeing them as the articulation of contingent and historically specific (even if persistent) patterns of power. In this chapter I argue in greater depth for the second, less comforting interpretation. This chapter completes our exploration of the theoretical terms we need to understand 'media rituals'; these are then put to use in the specific analyses of later chapters. Chapter 1 introduced the basic moves of a post-Durkheimian approach to media rituals, and put it in a wider context; Chapter 2 discussed some key concepts for a media analysis that draws on anthropological theory, particularly ritual and liminality. The result is to rework radically many of those concepts for a media age. In this chapter, I want to explain more fully why the study of media rituals must be grounded in a critical analysis of media power. That will enable us to be more specific about the types of action covered by the term 'media rituals', and also to suggest more concretely how a critical analysis of media rituals can intersect with other critical readings of media production, for example in terms of class, gender, or ethnicity.

SYMBOLIC POWER AND SYMBOLIC VIOLENCE

How are ritual performance and ritual practice connected to differences of power, and the unequal distribution of resources? Economic or political (coercive) power has often used ritual, but the closest link is between ritual and the form of power engaged in ritual performance itself: that is, *symbolic power* (Thompson 1995: 15–17) or, as another social theorist has it, 'ideological domination' (Scott 2001: 25). (I prefer the term 'symbolic power' because it emphasises that such domination always requires, as its medium, symbolic forms (speech, writing, performance, images, and so on), and its exercise may or may not involve explicit ideological content (see Chapter 2).[1] Second, it suggests there are power implications involved in such symbolic forms themselves, given that the ability to produce symbolic forms is not evenly shared.)

The connection of 'ritual' to symbolic *power* – that is, to the differentiation of people from each other in terms of the differential symbolic resources they possess – is in one way obvious; ritual forms have always involved priests or functionaries, with special power and authority. But many writers have proceeded to analyse ritual communication without analysing the uneven distribution of symbolic resources on which ritual practice relies. In contemporary mediated societies, where there is such an enormous concentration of symbolic resources in particular institutions (the media), it is not tenable to ignore ritual's connections with symbolic power. This much, perhaps, is uncontroversial. More controversial is the argument I develop in this chapter that the particular inequality of symbolic power represented by the *existence* of media institutions lies at the very heart, first, of media rituals' organisation and, second, of their social consequences. If this is correct, we cannot analyse media rituals without a developed concept of symbolic power and the related term, symbolic violence.

Symbolic power

Neo-Durkheimian accounts of ritual do not pay much attention to 'symbolic power', for the simple reason that they are not concerned with the conflicts that arise over its possession. Yet they assume that rituals have 'powerful' effects. Indeed they attribute enormous power to rituals – to externalise social reality, even to make certain experiences possible (Douglas 1984: 64; cf. Rappaport 1999: 119–21, 138) – but without dwelling on the potentially divisive notion of symbolic power. Similarly when Mary Douglas (1984: 114) states that 'the idea of society is a powerful image … it has external boundaries, margins, internal structure. Its outlines contain power to reward conformity and repulse attack', she does not unpack the nature of this 'power' – who possesses it, who does not, and under what conditions. Clearly Douglas would accept that the organisation of ritual practice raises issues of power, but this is of secondary interest in her account.

The concept of 'symbolic power' is in fact surprisingly underdeveloped. A weak notion of 'symbolic power' can be found outside the Durkheimian tradition, for example in John Thompson's generally helpful analysis in *The Media and Modernity* (1995). Drawing on Bourdieu but also Michael Mann's work, Thompson valuably insists on the symbolic as a dimension of power alongside the political and the economic. But his precise definition of 'symbolic power' is less satisfactory. He defines it as 'the capacity to intervene in the course of events, to influence the actions of others and indeed to create events, by means of the production and transmission of symbolic forms' (1995: 17). This definition captures what a number of social institutions (the media, the church, educational institutions) do, but it does not capture the wider impact that certain *concentrations* of symbolic power may have. A *strong* concept of symbolic power, by contrast, would insist that some concentrations of symbolic power (for example, the concentration from which contemporary media institutions benefit) are so great that they dominate the whole social landscape; as a result, they seem so natural, that they are misrecognised (to borrow a term from Pierre Bourdieu),[2] and their underlying arbitrariness becomes difficult to see.

Here we are simply following through the consequences of the fact that symbolic power has rather different effects from other forms of power. All forms of power have countless ramifications across social space: economic power, for example, is not confined to one sector of life (economic production) but affects all sectors of life, through the commodification of leisure and so on. But symbolic power impacts upon wider society in an even more pervasive way, because the concentration of society's symbolic resources affects not just what we do, but our ability to *describe* the social itself; it affects the perception of the inequalities in the social world, including the unequal distribution of those very symbolic resources themselves. A concentration of symbolic power is both a fact in its own right and a factor affecting the representation of *all* social facts (this one included). Effects of 'misrecognition' are then inherent in the uneven distribution of symbolic power, in the way that they are not with other forms of power (economic or political). That is why we need a strong concept of symbolic power which recognises the impacts of its uneven distribution on social space as a whole.

Symbolic violence

This notion of misrecognition – which as we will see is particularly important for thinking about the power implications of media rituals – has been developed more precisely by Bourdieu through his concept of 'symbolic violence'. As originally introduced, this term had quite a limited scope: 'symbolic violence, the gentle, invisible form of violence, which is never recognised as such, and is not so much undergone as chosen, the violence of credit, confidence, obligation, personal loyalty, hospitality, gifts, gratitude, piety' (1977: 192; cf. 1990: 127). 'Symbolic violence', then, began as a term for indirect forms of domination which operate without formal compulsion or violence. From this perspective, symbolic violence is less necessary in complex societies where a wider range of institutionalised or contractual forms of control are available, although Bourdieu does note (1977: 196–7) that, as the operation of economic domination itself becomes exposed, new forms of disguise or symbolic violence become necessary. An example of the latter might be the corporate strategies of charitable giving, environmental protection or 'putting people first' in which so many global corporations have invested heavily over recent decades.

For complex societies with an advanced division of labour, however, Bourdieu's original usage hardly captures the 'symbolic violence' associated with the specialised sectors of society directly concerned with *symbolic production*, including the media. Yet what better example could there be than the media of symbolic violence – violence (Bourdieu 2000: 170) which 'is set up only through the consents that the dominated cannot fail to give to the dominator ... when their understanding of the situation and relation can only use instruments of knowledge that they have in common with the dominator, which ... make this relation appear as natural'? If we could see media representations differently, as the production of just one limited sector of society merely claiming to be the voice of us all, the media's status in society would be very different (and in authoritarian states where media are explicitly subordinated to easily recognised forms of state power, it is).[3] But it is because in most cases we cannot simply see this that media rituals work.

From this perspective, the weakness of most Durkheimian and neo-Durkheimian accounts of ritual becomes clearer. It is not that they lack a notion of symbolic power; what they lack is an understanding of that power's inseparability from symbolic violence. Dayan and Katz's analysis of media events, for example, depends on a notion of symbolic power; without it, their idea that television makes possible new forms of social togetherness would make no sense (Dayan and Katz 1992: 17). But they do not challenge the unequal distribution of symbolic power without which these effects would be impossible (see Chapter 4). Such questions of power get lost behind the comforting sense that 'we' are all somehow involved in the process of constructing 'our' reality through media rituals and media events. Take, for example, the following from another neo-Durkheimian writer:

> Media serve as the central nervous system of modern society. The search to understand these media draws us into a search for the centre of all that is life in the 20th century. Our media, ourselves.
>
> (Real 1989: 13)

The functionalism of this approach could hardly be clearer. Once again, it was James Carey who put the point most directly in this passage which might almost have been written by Bourdieu:

> In our time reality is scarce because of access: so few command the machinery for its determination. Some get to speak and some to listen, some to write and some to read, some to film and some to view … there is not only class conflict in communication but status conflict as well.
>
> (Carey 1989: 87–8)

To say that 'reality' is scarce is a vivid, if general, way of saying that the social world is continually misrecognised, because of the uneven distribution of symbolic resources that characterises it. Symbolic violence is therefore *inherent* to the media's operations but it can only be unpacked through a theory of the specific rituals and ritualisations that sustain it on a day-to-day basis.

BEYOND THE MYTH(S) OF THE CENTRE

First, we need to isolate and name one form of misrecognition that helps frame all the other specific misrecognitions involved in media rituals. I shall call this the 'myth of the centre', and explain its relationship to another myth which I will call 'the myth of the mediated centre'.

Disrupting classic myth-making

Edward Said wrote of the image of 'centrality' in American society (Said 1988: 159). There have been countless other diagnoses of US society apparently more relevant to media culture, from Baudrillard's travelogue in 'hyperreal' America to Neal Gabler's recent account of American reality 'conquered' by entertainment (Baudrillard 1988; Gabler 2000), but it is Said's image which is the most penetrating, and the most useful for our analysis. The US is a society saturated by media to an extraordinary degree; and the image of 'centrality', if real, must have some connection with that. But the idea of society's 'centre' is also at the root of all Durkheimian and neo-Durkheimian accounts of how society holds together through ritual, so there is much more at stake here than an argument about one nation's television consumption.

A classic statement of the myth of the centre was Edward Shils' *Center and Periphery* (1975). Shils was the eminent sociologist working in the Parsonian tradition who, with Michael Young, wrote one of the earliest analyses of television's role in contemporary ritual (Shils and Young 1956) (see Chapter 4). It is precisely such an idea of society's 'sacred centre' on which the plausibility of classic Durkheimian and neo-Durkheimian arguments depends. When Shils wrote it, he was still cautious because he had not yet made the neo-Durkheimian move of arguing, against the direction of Durkheim's own historical analysis, that modern media, especially television, can 'reconstruct' this sense of the centre. This, however, is what Dayan and Katz (1992: viii, 23) explicitly argue, quoting Shils approvingly, and insisting that media recreate 'mechanical solidarity' through an entirely modern technology of social coordination (the broadcast schedule, satellite distribution, and so on).

In Chapter 2, I suggested that this idea is both true and false: true, because it registers the enormous pressures in late modernity (in which the media are involved) to construct a sense of society's centre, but false in that it ignores that these are precisely processes *of construction*. The analysis cannot, however, stop there. If society's 'centre' is indeed a myth – or if (put another way, adopting Habermas' famous distinction between 'system' and 'lifeworld') contemporary media fail to speak the 'lifeworld's' truth to the 'system', because they are in crucial respects *part of* that 'system' – then we need to explain why this myth stays in place and how it connects with the wider legitimation of media power. For this, we need to link the concepts of 'symbolic power' and 'symbolic violence' to the construction of a ritual body: how are the media's ritual categories incorporated in specific ritual actions and ritual mastery?

Note that this begins to shift media analysis away from media texts and into broader questions of governmentality (Rose 1996: 42) and the regulation of social practice in late modern states. Once we drop the assumption that society has a core of 'true' social values waiting to be 'expressed', then we are free to reread contemporary processes of social and cultural definition for the open-ended conflicts that they really are. Perhaps the most fundamental term of conflict is the definition of 'reality' itself, although 'reality', of course, is registered in different ways in a range of contexts: the 'reality' addressed by government policies of social control, economic 'reality', the 'reality' of national mood, the 'reality' of the fashion and entertainment worlds. Because society's symbolic resources are very unequally distributed (with media institutions being the main beneficiaries of that inequality), these ongoing conflicts of definition are marked by symbolic violence: certain definitions have enough weight and authority to *close off* most other alternatives from view, although such closure can never be total and is always, in principle, open to challenge. It is here that the deconstruction of media rituals connects to other more specific ideological deconstructions of media outputs, because it challenges our belief in the media as *the* space where we should look for expression, let alone resolution, of specific conflicts about how to understand the social world.

Counter-codes and strategies of surveillance

If we want to grasp such conflicts around symbolic power, and the play of symbolic violence, but *without* relying on any 'myth of the centre' or other functionalist assumptions, then we need a further concept which captures those local definitional battles beneath the surface of apparent social 'consensus'. This is the concept of *naming*, introduced by the late Italian political sociologist Alberto Melucci. Operating outside the Durkheimian tradition, and indeed outside the study of ritual entirely, Melucci emphasises the importance in late modernity of ongoing contests to 'name' reality. He argues that, while we live in societies where there is no sacred at all (1989: 62, 109), our lives *are* organised towards other, more problematic forms of consensus, through the standardisation of consumption and market forces (1989: 55), and the strategies of governments. In such societies there are conflicts over 'the production of information and symbolic resources' (1989: 55) and 'access to knowledge becomes a new kind of power' (1989: 84). Individuals have a stake in these battles through their own local attempts to define themselves, by appropriating common symbolic resources. In his 1996 book *Challenging Codes*, Melucci turns more specifically to the media. Contemporary societies' domination by media, he argues, requires 'a new way of thinking about power and inequality' (1996: 179), which recognises the importance of control or influence over what he calls the 'master codes'. 'The real domination' he argues, 'is today the exclusion from the power of naming' (Melucci 1996: 182).

Melucci's main interest is the role of social movements as contesters, against the odds, of the normal concentration of the power of 'naming' in governments, corporations and media institutions. Social movements operate, he argues, both inside and outside the system of representation (1996: 309). Naming, and contests over naming, open up a very different perspective on the attempts to monopolise the 'reality' of historical events which we see in 'media events' (see Chapter 4). These contests operate not just in local and national media, but also the intrinsically global, dispersed new medium of the Internet. Recent years have seen a number of symbolic conflicts where the 'naming' of central social realities has been at stake, for example the Seattle and Genoa anti-globalisation protests in 1999 and 2001, and the protests against corporate power analysed and championed by Naomi Klein (2000).

The concept of 'naming' is productive for a post-Durkheimian account of media ritual in other ways too. If we see ritualisation as involving a particular way of naming the social world, this links it to other everyday practices of apparently little relevance to 'ritual'. I mean the everyday categorising practices of governments. The Israeli anthropologist Don Handelman (1998) has offered an interesting recent commentary on these issues. Instead of 'rituals' he prefers to talk of 'public events', because he wants to reject entirely the implication that such events consensually represent 'the wider social order' (1998: xii). Handelman's interest lies elsewhere, in how public events come to be constructed as such, 'the logics of their organisational design' (1998: xi). Handelman's wider aim is to analyse the coordinating patterns which make up public events and their connection with 'bureaucratic logics'. Quite plausibly, Handelman argues that, rather than being dazzled by the mediated show of 'social togetherness' in, say, sporting events or carnivals, we should think more closely about how those events' organisation depends precisely on the implementation of bureaucratic categories (1998: xxxviii, xxxix).

Here, and elsewhere, I want to invoke a counter-reading of the Durkheimian legacy that foregrounds not the consensual nature of 'the symbolic' but the inherently contested nature of symbolic power. As Pierre Bourdieu suggested in 'On Symbolic Power', reprinted in *Language and Symbolic Power*:[4]

> Durkheim has the merit of designating the *social function* ... of symbolism in an explicit way: it is an authentic political function which cannot be reduced to the structuralists' function of communication. Symbols are the instruments of knowledge and communication ... they make it possible for there to be a *consensus* on the meaning of the social world, a consensus which contributes fundamentally to the reproduction of the social order.
>
> (Bourdieu 1991: 166, original emphasis)

Don Handelman echoes this point: 'the control over processes of classification is a most powerful means through which to shape and control social order' (Handelman 1998: xxxi). This means that, as analysts of ritual and especially media rituals, we should be particularly *suspicious* of public spectacle. Contemporary public spectacle, far from being a revelation of underlying timeless 'truths' about social life, can be seen instead as:

> The representation of social order under surveillance, under control, manipulated by its compositors and auditors ... magnified through the exact, clinical, optic gaze of televised and videotaped events.
>
> (Handelman 1998: xxxix)

The connection between ritualisation and surveillance is an important one which I apply in Chapter 6 to thinking about the ritual dimensions of 'reality TV'.

Mythical deconstruction or ideological analysis?

For the sake of clarity, it is important to acknowledge one possible misreading of the argument I've developed so far. This would see the argument as a latter-day Marxist debunking of media rituals as ideological processes that mystify an underlying level of domination. The media, and media rituals, would be the vehicle for power interests that lie outside the media, above all economic interests; this could take support, for example, from Maurice Bloch's ideological reading of ritual as the misrepresentation of power relations (Bloch 1989). Philip Elliott's fascinating 1982 essay on 'press rituals', which sadly he did not live to develop, offered a definition of 'ritual' for media contexts along similar lines, although he emphasised political, not economic, domination in the first instance:

> Ritual is rule-governed activity of a symbolic character involving mystical notions which draws the attention of its participants to objects of thought or feeling which the leadership of a society or group hold to be of special significance.
> (Elliott 1982: 147)

The danger of this type of argument is that, in vigorously rejecting the classic Durkheimian view of rituals as socially integrative, it repeats functionalist assumptions in a different form: it claims that media rituals work to implement an underlying functional necessity, deriving from society's economic base as reflected through government structures. Elliott himself at the end of his essay (1982: 168–73) seems to have been uneasy about such a reductive approach.

As suggested in the introductory chapter, the approach to media rituals developed in this book is different from an ideological reading in Marxist vein. I am not saying that media rituals work *necessarily* as vehicles for any particular ideology as that term is normally understood (messages that support the interests of particular states, corporations, or other entities such as religious institutions). My analysis focuses not on the specific messages communicated through media rituals, but on the more basic mystification inherent in the *form* of media rituals, *whatever* their content and indeed whether or not they have any content. This is the idea that society has a 'centre'. Of course, in contemporary social life, there are many parallel and linked processes of central*isation*, some operating on a national scale, some increasingly on a global scale (regulatory pressures, market pressures, and so on); we have governments, after all! But this idea goes much further than that, by claiming that *beneath* these real pressures of centralisation is a core of 'truth', a 'natural' centre (different 'centres', of course, depending on where we live) that we should value, as the centre of 'our' way of life, 'our' values. This is *the myth of the centre*, and it is connected with a second myth that 'the media' has a privileged relationship to that 'centre', as a highly centralised system of symbolic production whose 'natural' role is to represent or frame that 'centre'. Call this *the myth of the mediated centre.*

In reality, and whatever the competing pressures of social centralisation and (we should not forget) the rival pressures of decentralisation, there is no such social centre that acts as a moral or cognitive foundation for society and its values, and therefore no natural role for the media as that 'centre's' interpreter, but there are enormous pressures to believe in each. So great are those pressures that it even seems scandalous to name these myths as such. Yet it is essential to do so. The idea that society has a centre helps naturalise the idea that we have, or need, media that 'represent' that centre; media's claims for themselves that they are society's 'frame' help naturalise the idea, underlying countless media texts, that there is a social 'centre' to *be* re-presented to us. (The reality is different and more complex. An intense (but not total) concentration of coercive power in modern states works alongside, although not always in step with, the intense (but not total) concentration of symbolic power in modern media institutions: again, recall Figure 1.1 in Chapter 1.)

These two connected myths underlie a number of categorical distinctions, boundaries and hierarchies that help organise media discourse and are played upon in the practice of media rituals. The central principle underlying all these distinctions is the hierarchy of what is 'in' the media over what is not 'in' the media (cf. Couldry 2000a: 17). I will come shortly to the details of these categories, but it is important first to see both how this differs from a standard ideological analysis of the media and how it might support, not undermine, that separate ideological analysis. Media rituals operate to naturalise the notion of a 'mediated social order' within which all specific ideologies must compete, as well as legitimising the particular representational privilege of the media (as a centralised system for producing and distributing images, information and opinions).

Media rituals remain, in this respect, 'ideological', but in a transformed sense of the word, suggested by Ernesto Laclau's reworking of contemporary Marxism in 'The Impossibility of Society', from *New Reflections on the Revolution of Our Time*: 'the ideological would consist of those discursive forms *through which a society tries to institute itself as such* on the basis of closure, of the fixation of meaning, of the non-recognition of the infinite play of differences' (1990: 92, my emphasis). The claims of media – familiar from every news bulletin and marketing campaign – to represent society as a whole are almost always ideological in this general sense, and are intrinsic to media institutions' self-image. That, of course, is not all media do: in particular places and for particular purposes (whether on narrowcast cable channels, or in the women's or men's magazine markets), another discourse of fragmentation and segmentation is important. But this rarely, if ever, operates against an underlying sense that there is a centre of attention represented by media ('what's going on') to which the audience or readership in question should pay attention. Modern societies exhibit very intense concentrations of all forms of resources – economic, political, symbolic – and these generally need to be legitimated if people are to live comfortably with them. One of the main things media institutions do, as the principal beneficiaries of society's concentration of its *symbolic* resources, is to legitimate that very concentration. They do so by circulating discourses which make media seem like the natural representatives of society's 'centre'. Media rituals are the actions where such discourses take their most condensed and naturalised form; as such, they are a principal means through which the misrecognition of media power is reproduced.

The point, then, is not to replace other deconstructions of specific ideologies played out in media productions, locally and globally. On the contrary, the myth of the mediated centre is one of the most powerful tools of such specific ideologies (whether the continued legitimation of gender, class, ethnic or racial inequality, or inequalities based on differences in sexuality). The very idea that 'the media's' supposed resolution at particular times and places of a particular ideological conflict is *definitive* for the audience addressed can be deployed for their own ends by all those involved in that conflict. Deconstructing the myth of the mediated centre is therefore a tool in analysing those other debates, which is not to deny either that, for particular purposes in particular struggles, both within and beyond media institutions, the myth has a strategic use. None of this, however, should blind us to the importance of a level of analysis beyond specific ideologies.

My position is, of course, not without its own paradoxes: to identify the language of the mediated social centre and its power, you have to speak it and thereby, in a sense, continue its life. But speaking the language of 'the centre' is compatible with learning to speak another language too, when we reflect on media. This will be explored in Chapter 8.

THE MEDIA'S RITUAL CATEGORIES

The 'myth of the mediated centre' is a label for something more complex and more messy: the mass of practices through which media power is legitimated. Media power seems legitimate because, through all sorts of arrangements of speech, thought and action, it is made to seem natural. There are many dimensions to this process, as I argued in *The Place of Media Power* (Couldry 2000a) and only some are connected to media rituals. Those that I called 'banal practices of ordering' (Couldry 2000a: 48) involve the ways in which social practice is, increasingly, organised around media sources and media access. Media have become 'obligatory passing points'[3] in many areas of public and private life, and this is an everyday fact of social organisation. None of this, however, requires anything so formalised as media rituals.

'Media rituals', by contrast, are condensed forms of action where category distinctions and boundaries related to the myth of the mediated centre are worked upon with particular intensity. In media rituals, no actual networks are directly created or strengthened, but instead categories of thought that naturalise media power are acted out. For convenience, let's call these *the media's ritual categories*. What are they? First, and most important, the basic category difference between anything 'in' or 'on' or associated with 'the media', and anything which is not. There is no type of thing in principle to which this difference cannot apply; that is what it means to say that it is a *category* difference. Like Durkheim's distinction between 'sacred' and 'profane', it cuts across everything in the social world; anything can be 'in' the media. The 'difference' between what is 'in' and not 'in' the media is therefore not natural, but a difference which, through continual usage, is constructed as natural (cf. Couldry 2000a: 41).

We can observe ourselves and others constructing, as different, things, events, people, places or worlds 'in' the media. In Chapter 4, we see this in the construction of particular events as 'media events'. In Chapter 5, we will look closely at the specialness of media places, as places of 'pilgrimage'. And at various points in the rest of the book, we will come across the category difference between media people and non-media people, in the construction of celebrities, stars and 'personalities'.

So far we have looked at the category difference, and hierarchy, between what is in the media and what is not. This is the primary distinction through which the myth of the mediated centre is naturalised. But there are important *secondary* differences as well; these derive from the assumption that what is in the media must have higher status than what is not, but are distinct in their reference point. For example, the term 'liveness' (discussed in detail in Chapter 6) derives from the status of what is presented in the media, but suggests a little more explicitly that the reason media things matter more is because they are part of society's *current* 'reality'. That 'reality' is changing from moment to moment, as media coverage changes, which means that whatever is being shown *now* must, relatively, have a higher status than what is no longer being shown: hence the status of live transmission. Even more explicit, but still naturalised, are the distinctions drawn between the 'reality' of the different things media present: the debates, for example, about 'reality television' that we also discuss in Chapter 6, or the pursuit of the 'really real' moment of 'true' emotion in the televised talk show (Chapter 7).

The media's ritual categories, like all important organising categories, are reproduced in countless different circumstances. They become automatic, unthinking: so you might say to a colleague or partner, 'Call her, she was once in that show, she might make a difference to our profile ...', and think no further of the category distinction you are reproducing. In media rituals, we see these category differences internalised in particular action forms which both test out their workings and naturalise their significance. I turn next to how the media's ritual categories are internalised through bodily performance.

RITUAL ACTIONS AND RITUAL BODIES

If the conventional notion of ideology involves specific contents believed as such, ritual's relation to belief is more indirect. Category differences may be worked upon in actions and embedded in the organisation of, and the body's orientation in, space, but that does not mean that these categories are necessarily articulated in the beliefs of those who enact them. On the contrary, once reflected upon, they become open to contestation in a way that, when naturalised in bodily action, they are not. Ritual action lies somewhere between pure internalisation and explicit articulation; the emphasis and exposure, as it were, that ritual action brings can encourage certain types of dispute and debate, but they tend to stay within the ritual framework, whose organisation has already naturalised the most important category differences.

The internalisation of categories

What connects the everyday space of ritualisation and ritual action is the body that passes between them: the ritual body which has internalised the organising significance of ritual's category differences. To grasp how this connection works, we can draw on some more terms of Pierre Bourdieu. For example, when discussing how official language comes to have legitimacy, Bourdieu writes that this recognition is 'inscribed in a *practical* state', in 'dispositions' as are all forms of symbolic domination (1991: 50–1, my emphasis): for 'symbolic violence ... can only be exerted on a person predisposed (in his habitus) to feel it' (1991: 51). We do not need to go here in any great detail into Bourdieu's difficult concept of 'habitus' that underlies this passage; we can simply adopt a working definition of the term as capturing how people's individual actions are shaped, at two removes, by:

1 the forces which structure the principles that, in turn,
2 constrain the range of practices in which they can engage.

These constraints (the 'habitus') work through the body; they are a dimension of the organisation of our actions and practices that is *already* in place before we perform, reflect on, or articulate them. This operates 'below the level of consciousness, expression and the reflexive distance they presuppose' (Bourdieu 1990: 73). Bourdieu does not just refer to the organisation of the individual body in isolation, but to the organisation of the spaces such as the home, where bodily experience is orchestrated among its world of objects (1990: 76), and the 'practical mastery' that every agent has to acquire as she moves through space (Bourdieu 1977: 87–95, discussed by Bell 1992: 107–8).

Catherine Bell has usefully developed these ideas to argue that it is such practical mastery that is the end-point of religious ritualisation, 'the body invested with a "sense" of ritual' (1992: 98).The sense of ritual – of certain forms of action as heightened – is a way in which a broad hierarchy is reinforced through performance. As Bell puts it: 'ritualization is a way of acting that is designed and orchestrated to distinguish and privilege what is being done to other, usually more quotidian, activities' (1992: 74). In this way ritual performance is able to suggest a 'higher' order of things:

> Fundamental to all strategies of ritualization ... is the appeal to a more embracing authoritative order that lies beyond the immediate situation. Ritualization is generally a way of engaging some wide consensus that those acting [in ritual] are doing so as a type of natural response to a world conceived and interpreted as affected by forces that transcend it.
>
> (Bell 1997: 169)

You might object that *media* rituals cannot invoke a transcendent order equivalent to that invoked by religious ritual (which is Bell's subject). Recall, though, that, insofar as media rituals invoke media as a representative of the social centre, it is exactly such transcendental claims that follow from a neo-Durkheimian account of the media. My argument, while opposing that claim, takes very seriously the idea that, embedded into certain types of formalised practice we perform in relation to media, are category differences that naturalise the *idea* that media are socially central.

What seems difficult, however, is to see how something very large (a claim about the whole social world and media's place in it) can be reinforced, in miniature as it were, through something so small. But this is what is most radical about Bourdieu's concept of 'practical mastery': his insight that the most minute details of bodily deportment and language can reproduce larger patterns of social ordering (or at least, images of social order). This principle is as relevant to 'complex' societies as to 'simple' ones. Bourdieu discusses this link in the following passage:

> If all societies ... set such store on the seemingly most insignificant details of *dress, bearing,* physical and verbal *manners,* the reason is that, treating the body as a memory, they entrust to it in abbreviated and practical, i.e. mnemonic, form the fundamental principles of the arbitrary content of culture. The principles embodied in this way are placed beyond the grasp of consciousness, and hence cannot be touched by voluntary, deliberate transformation, cannot even be made explicit; nothing seems more ineffable, more incommunicable, more inimitable, and, therefore, more precious, than the values given body, *made* body by the transsubstantiation achieved by the hidden persuasion of an implicit pedagogy, capable of instilling a whole cosmology, an ethic, a metaphysic, a political philosophy, through injunctions as insignificant as 'stand up straight' or 'don't hold your knife in your left hand'.
>
> (Bourdieu 1977: 94, original emphasis)

But, you might say again, can contemporary *media* – surely, in its details, the most *contested* of institutional sectors – be the focus of injunctions so ideologically saturated as the bodily instructions Bourdieu mentions?

To allay your doubts, here's a thought experiment. As you read this page, imagine that you are told that a well-known television personality has just entered the building: would you go on reading, and in the same way? If you agree with me that almost certainly you would *not*, then we have identified one dimension of contemporary social life to which the term 'media rituals' alludes. Media rituals (and ritualisation) capture that 'extra', largely naturalised, dimension of social life, that acknowledges in condensed form the framing power of 'the media'. We all know this instinctively, but what is hard is to find ways of isolating this dimension with greater precision.

Where are media rituals?

Certainly, unlike with religious rituals, we cannot look for media rituals in a single confined space, such as the church or the mosque. Media processes are too dispersed across space for that. Indeed your action of turning round, and staying turned around, when a media person enters the room, is not yet a media ritual, but it *is* an action organised on a principle (media people are special, therefore worthy of special attention) that can be played out in formalised action, for example in the highly organised spaces of the television studio. Small-scale media rituals can occur even within wider spaces that are not, as such, ritual spaces. So, while much of what goes on at the media theme parks, such as Granada Studios Tour in Manchester, that I researched for *The Place of Media Power* (Couldry 2000a) is not ritual (queuing for food, chatting, looking at exhibits), some things that go on there are media rituals: the occasional meetings with celebrities, the chance to appear 'on camera' (or pretend to do so), and so on.

What we are looking for is not just categories at work, but ritualised action. We need to identify those actions where latent media-related categories are put to work in ways that are formalised enough for us to call them media rituals. There are a number of places, still little researched or studied, where we should look for such ritualised actions:

- sites where people cross from the non-media 'world' into the media 'world', such as studios, or any place where filming or media production goes on;
- sites where non-media people expect to encounter people (or things) in the media (for example, celebrities);
- moments where non-media people perform for the media, for example posing for a camera, even if this takes place in the course of action that is otherwise not formalised.

In all these situations, people act out in formalised ways category differences that reproduce in condensed form the idea, or derivatives of the idea, that media are our access point to society's 'centre'. Here are some examples of the type of thing I have in mind:

- people calling out as their presence 'on air' is acknowledged (the studio chat show host turns to them and asks them to clap, 'show what they feel');
- people either holding back, or rushing forward, at the sight of a celebrity;
- people holding back before they enter a place connected with the media, so as to emphasise the boundary they cross by entering it (cf. Couldry 2000a: 111);
- performances by media people that acknowledge their own specialness before a crowd of non-media people;
- performances by non-media people in certain types of formalised media context, such as a talk show (Chapter 7).

Note, finally, that calling something a media ritual (for example, a talk show performance) does not prevent it from also having intense *personal* significance. The ritual of televised confession is one contemporary media setting where Bourdieu's theory of practical mastery meets Foucault's theory of power as productive of new regimes of the self. Foucault (1981a) analysed how the ritual of confession (before the priest, the doctor, the psychoanalyst) is structured by the power differential between confessor and interlocutor. In spite of the greater complexity of its audience, the television confession too is a ritual form, structured around certain category differences (host versus confessor, ordinary space versus studio space, ordinary stories versus stories that have passed through television) that only make sense because of the power differential which they both disguise and naturalise. Given this, it is a form open to any number of individual and temporary negotiations, as part of the contests over any socially marked difference (whether gender, class, ethnicity, or sexuality). My main emphasis will be on the questions of form, rather than such individual contestations, but my argument is quite consistent with the importance of the latter as well. More on these points in Chapter 7.

Media ritualisation spans, then, intense personal performance (a person revealing private truths before unknown millions) and the seeming banality of everyone turning round because a media celebrity has entered the room. Both – and everything that lies between them – are part of how we live out as 'truth' the myth of the mediated centre.

SOME POSSIBLE COUNTER-ARGUMENTS?

Before we turn in later chapters to more detailed cases, let me address two objections to the argument so far.

First, it is important to emphasise that in developing the concept of media rituals, I do not deny the possibility of resistance to, or continual negotiation of, the media's ritual categories. Throughout, I have been arguing that categories and myths get reproduced through action, thought and belief right across social space, but this implies that it is always possible for such reproduction *not* to take place. I will not in this book be considering in great detail practices that directly contest the centralisation of symbolic power, but they are important and perhaps they are increasingly gaining prominence (see Chapter 8).

Quite apart from strategies of resistance, there are much more common ways in which ritual categories are appropriated, turned to ends other than a simple reproduction of power. The whole practice of media-based fandom, for example, can be read in terms of such appropriations. But this again does not generally undermine the concept of media rituals, notwithstanding the critical potential of some notions of fan practice; on the contrary, it is an essential feature of rituals that (unlike formal ideology) they *are* available to personal appropriation:

> Ritualization, as any form of social control ... will be effective only when this control can afford to be rather loose. Ritualization will not work as social control if it is perceived as not amenable to some degree of individual appropriation.
>
> (Bell 1992: 222)

Understanding media rituals means acknowledging both the details of individual appropriations and the pervasive forms that get reproduced through those appropriations. While fan practice is not a primary focus of this book, this position is broadly compatible with the most recent and sophisticated work in this area (for example, Hills 2002: conclusion).

Second, it might seem that my attack on the myth of 'the centre' simply reproduces it in a new form by insisting on its importance at a time when, arguably, new *decentralised* media forms are becoming dominant: the Web, the mobile phone and text messaging system, and so on. But these new media, whatever their centrifugal potential, are quite ready to be co-opted within the myth of the centre. New media, whatever their differences from older media forms, are not disconnected from the material processes by which society's symbolic resources are centralised, and this is why many are concerned, for example, at the impacts of corporate pressures on the 'ethics of cyberspace' (Hamelink 1999). This indeed is why we need to grasp the *ritual* dimensions of new media too (Jones 1998: 30). The very idea of new media as automatically 'transformative' in their social impacts is perhaps just the latest and most fashionable version of the myth that through media we access both our central realities and our future.[6]

Chapter 4

Rethinking media events

> In ritual one lives through events …
>
> (Turner 1982: 86)

> … the lesson [history] teaches is … [is] to be on our guard against the event … not to think that those actors who make the most noise are the most authentic; there are other silent ones.
>
> (Braudel 1972: 25)

Media events are a good place to start applying our theory of media rituals, for a number of reasons. First, they are the subject of Dayan and Katz's classic book *Media Events: The Live Broadcasting of History* (1992), which poses more clearly than anywhere else the advantages and the difficulties of a study of media rituals. It does so not through general cultural commentary or textual analysis, but through one of the most systematic attempts to date to bring anthropological theory to bear on media.[1] Second, it is in evaluating media events that differences between neo-Durkheimian and post-Durkheimian approaches to media ritual emerge most starkly. This is partly because of the rhetorical power of Dayan and Katz's argument, but also because of the intrinsic connection between media events and the ritual space of the media. If James Carey (1989: 18) is right that 'the ritual view of communication' addresses the media's role in maintaining society through time, then media events are the times, often as short as a week, when the media does this most actively. *Or so it seems*. For, if 'in ritual one lives through events' (Turner 1982), then it is around media events that the debate over how to theorise media ritual comes most fiercely to life. Following the argument of the first three chapters, this chapter will show that media events are in crucial respects *constructions*, not expressions, of 'the social order', processes which construct not only our sense of a social 'centre', but also the media's privileged relation to that 'centre'. Media events, then, are privileged moments, not because they reveal society's underlying solidarity, but because they reveal the mythical construction of the mediated centre at its most intense.[2]

I side with those who are suspicious of 'events' as the source of deeper truths. The great French historian Fernand Braudel's suspicion of events was based partly on a structuralist's natural antipathy to short-term patterns when compared with the *longue durée* ('events' he once wrote, 'are dust'),[3] but in the quotation above the motivation is more directly relevant to media rituals and their complexity. Braudel asks whom we should listen to in interpreting events: the voices on the surface, or the voices who appear nowhere on the surface, the 'silent ones'? Braudel was thinking about the erasures in historical records, but contemporary stories of media events are subject to a censorship no less ruthless. How are the structures of the media's ritual space (its permanent inequalities) worked out through media events? The idea that social truths are 'expressed' through those structures is surely too simple. We must beware as well of loose usage of the term 'ritual' (cf. Becker 1998; Corner 1999a) in the emotive atmosphere of media events. Even so, 'ritual', as we shall see, captures something crucial about the pressures that construct media events, and our (apparent) sense of their social centrality.

MEDIA EXTENSIONS OF PUBLIC EVENTS AND RITUALS

First, we must review the prehistory of the term 'media events', which is important for understanding its current usage.

Alternative histories of the media event

Dayan and Katz's analysis of media events did not emerge out of the blue, but followed in a line of work on television's role in mediating British royal ceremonial. The starting point was Shils and Young's article (1956) on Queen Elizabeth's coronation in 1953. This influential article interpreted the meaning of the coronation in post-war Britain. Shils and Young read it in classic Durkheimian terms as a 'rededication of the nation' (Shils 1975: 137), 'the ceremonial occasion for the affirmation of the moral values by which the society lives … an act of national communion' (Shils 1975: 139). The article described the details of the coronation ritual itself, and the way it was amplified to a wider audience through a crucial departure from previous royal ritual: the fact that the ceremony could be experienced in a family setting in front of the television or radio set. In a theme echoed in all subsequent accounts of media events, Shils and Young emphasise the way people watched television in groups (Shils 1975: 145), creating a sense of a wider 'national family' watching in parallel in homes across Britain.

Shils and Young do not emphasise the term 'ritual' but in effect they run together a number of possible senses in which we could think about what media do to ritual. David Chaney distinguishes between three such senses which cut across, but do not contradict, the rival definitions of ritual discussed in Chapters 1 and 2:

- ritual that the media reports;
- ways of reporting the rituals that are themselves ritualised;
- the situation where 'the medium may itself be a ritual or collective ceremony' (Chaney 1986: 117).

What was striking about media coverage of the 1953 coronation was that through television an already established ritual could be simultaneously enacted for an audience stretched across multiple locations.

This point was developed in historical work by Chaney (1983) and by David Cardiff and Paddy Scannell in their history of the BBC's acquisition of a privileged role in covering British national rituals (Cardiff and Scannell 1987; Scannell and Cardiff 1991). With occasional caveats,[4] this work operated broadly within a Durkheimian framework. 'The essence of a ritual' Chaney (1983: 120) argued, 'is that a collectivity is postulated or affirmed which might otherwise only have an ambiguous social existence'. While the phrase 'postulated or affirmed' is cautious, the caution is relatively undeveloped in Chaney's work; and for Cardiff and Scannell 'ritual *always* works to transform [society]' and the transformation in British rituals in the twentieth century lay in the way television 'provide[d] a fragmented audience with a common culture, an image of the nation as a *knowable community*' (1987: 168–9, my emphasis). The strength of this research was its revelation of the historical struggles underlying the televising of royal ritual; the BBC needed to establish itself in relation to the British state, and obtaining the right for television cameras to be present at royal ceremonies was an important way of doing this. Chaney quotes from the correspondence before consent was granted, with the BBC's Head of Religious Broadcasting writing to the Dean of Westminster that 'there are strong religious and national reasons for letting as many people *share in the service through television*' (Chaney 1983: 131, my emphasis). It was through such negotiations that the right of the camera to be present 'at the most intimate moments of symbolic ritual' was established (Chaney 1983: 134). Note how effectively Durkheimian arguments were used by those negotiating this historic shift.

Generalising their analysis, Cardiff and Scannell argue that, although television in general is no longer 'about' exceptional events but fully integrated into the routines of everyday life,[5] television retains the role of representing national ritual (1987: 171–2). Whether this remains the case in an era of multiple television channels and the Internet is uncertain (see below). But this early work at least established that through television the nature of public ritual itself had fundamentally changed,[6] with the informed participation by huge populations absent from the ceremonial site itself (cf. Scannell 1996).

The most detailed study of the implications of this shift is Dayan and Katz's *Media Events* (1992). By 'media event' they mean an event that is broadcast 'live' and is 'remote' from its audiences, which is a real event occurring at society's 'centre', not set up by the media itself. Its broadcast must also be preplanned, but constitute an interruption to the normal flow of broadcasting (1992: 3–7). We will return shortly to the details of this definition. The televisation of public ritual, for Dayan and Katz, is more than the transmission of an otherwise unchanged public ritual. Television transforms events on the ground into a multi-local narrative that has no parallel in previous ritual practice and which is available for viewing in the home (1992: 94–5). Without losing a sense of the specialness of ritual as local action (viewers' distance from the ceremonial events being reinforced in other ways), Dayan and Katz argue that television 'offer[s] unexpected ways of participating in the ritual experience … [and] maximise[s] the power of spectacle' (1992: 101). Television builds the 'liturgical context' of the events (1992: 103) through its highly selective reading of both the ritual event itself and the preparations for it, people's reactions to it, and so on. The mediation process is certainly not a simple ideological imposition, and Dayan and Katz analyse the complex negotiations involved in making the media event succeed (many fail miserably; 1992: chapter 3). But, if successful, they argue, media events work to integrate society.

Before turning to the details of Dayan and Katz's argument, let us notice that we could have chosen a very different precedent for studying media events, giving a rather different direction to our argument. I refer to the early US work on the impact of mediation on public events: Lang and Lang (1969) and Merton (1946). It is Robert Merton's study, *Mass Persuasion*, that yields perhaps the most interesting alternative context for a study of media events, because he operates without any assumption that such events have a wider, transformative significance. On the contrary, he is critical of such claims. For now let me just sketch the main features of Merton's work.

Merton studied how people were persuaded to contribute money to a US government warbond drive in 1943 through broadcasts by a well-known radio celebrity, Kate Smith. Smith conducted on live national radio a marathon series of short appeals (each lasting only a few minutes but occurring regularly over a period of eighteen hours). At first sight, this is a purer form of media event than Dayan and Katz's, because it was a formalised action constructed *only* through the media, yet carrying the resonances of a public event that engaged public emotions (combining the second and third senses of media 'ritual' that Chaney distinguished).

Kate Smith was already well-known as a professional performer; indeed she had hitherto led several shorter warbond drives (for this one she said she would give her services free). People identified with Smith's performance and her struggle to overcome exhaustion. Merton identifies various features of the event that we might call 'ritualised': its formalisation and the developing sense that a wider collectivity was involved in the interaction between the national audience and Smith the performer. What is most interesting is how Merton makes no grand claims that something deeper was expressed by this process. His analysis is more caustic:

> The very same society that produces [a] sense of alienation and estrangement generates in many a craving for reassurance, an acute need to believe, a 'flight into faith'.
>
> (Merton 1946: 143)

> A society subjected ceaselessly to a flow of 'effective' half-truths and the exploitation of mass anxieties may all the sooner lose that mutuality of confidence and reciprocal trust so essential to a stable social structure.
>
> (Merton 1946: 189)

Merton's research was conducted within the now unfashionable tradition of 'mass society' media critiques, but that does not undermine the *empirical* evidence he offers (to which we return later in the chapter). If only as a counterweight to Dayan and Katz's highly rhetorical analysis of media events' social significance, Merton's comments are worth keeping in mind.

Media events or media rituals?

One final point needs to be clarified before we move on to a detailed analysis of Dayan and Katz's position: what is the connection between 'media events' and 'media rituals'? In Chapter 2, we defined 'media rituals' as 'formalised actions organised around key media-related categories and boundaries, whose performance frames, or suggests a connection with, wider media-related values'. In Chapter 3, we explained that the media-related values to which media rituals direct our attention are based in the myth of the mediated centre: the construction of a social centre, and the construction of media as our privileged access point, or 'frame', to that 'centre'. The 'media rituals' discussed in Chapters 2 and 3 were specific, local actions structured around categories and boundaries connected with that underlying myth. But 'media events', as we have already seen, are large collections of actions across multiple locations (the broadcast event, millions of viewing situations, the circulation of discourses around the broadcast event). In what sense then do 'media events' comprise, or encompass, media rituals?

The exact definition of media events is something that we will debate throughout the chapter, and against the grain of Dayan and Katz's assumptions. However that debate is resolved, the basic connection between media events and media rituals is clear. Media events are large-scale public events which connect actions across multiple locations within an overall action-frame that is focused on a central, broadcast 'event' (which need not itself be a ritual). The link to 'media rituals' comes in the organisation of that overall action-frame: what makes a mass of actions in many places come together *as* a 'media event' is the fact, or the construction of the fact (for now, I leave this point open), that through the narrative frame of that media event a social collectivity is affirmed, reinforced or maintained. Media events, in other words, are large-scale media-focused social processes whose overall organising frame is precisely the values, or at least the *assumed* values, that underlie a Durkheimian reading of media rituals: the affirmation of the social bond through the media process. Within the frame of media events, therefore, many local actions can occur which deserve the title 'media rituals', because that action-frame connects them with media-related values. In fact, this remains true, whether or not we pursue a Durkheimian, or a post-Durkheimian, reading of those actions and the wider 'media event'.

The key question of this chapter, however, is precisely whether a Durkheimian reading of media events, and the media rituals that take place within them, needs to be replaced by a post-Durkheimian, anti-functionalist reading.

From this perspective, there is no need to dispute two important points which Dayan and Katz's study established: first, that television (and modern media generally) changed the conditions of contemporary ritual (cf. Bell 1997: 242–6), and second that, in the context of media events, a special mode of viewing often occurs – usually with others, accompanied by formalised behaviour (perhaps the laying out of a meal, certainly the exclusion of interruptions to the broadcast) – which in itself deserves the name 'media ritual'. Dayan and Katz call this 'festive viewing' (1992: chapter 5). 'Festive viewing' has been studied for other media spectacles: the Super Bowl (Real 1975), the Olympics (Real 1989; Rothenbuhler 1988). Note that 'festive' in Dayan and Katz's sense does not mean happy or celebratory, since it encompasses times of shared sadness. On the day of Princess Diana's funeral in September 1997, I observed an extension of this when hundreds of thousands of people (myself included) watched the funeral coverage live on large television screens in public parks a mile or so from the ritual centre of Westminster Abbey. Here, no less than for the millions of families watching the event in their living rooms, 'the "social" was experienced directly as a *shared* viewing situation' (Couldry 1999: 84, changed emphasis), or at least that is how the viewing experience was constructed. These forms of social watching are definitely media rituals: they are formalised actions, organised around their difference from 'ordinary' viewing, with the difference demarcating situations when the media's role as access point to the social centre is particularly affirmed.

DEFINING MEDIA EVENTS

Having introduced Dayan and Katz's term 'media events' and its historical trajectory (or trajectories), I want to review it in detail before, in a later section, developing an alternative way of thinking about media events.

Dayan and Katz's neo-Durkheimian reading

For Dayan and Katz, media events are defined as preplanned, but non-routine, live transmissions of real events. They are also much more than that. So far I have concentrated on the uncontroversial part of their thesis, that media, particularly television, rework older forms of public event and public ritual. 'Media events' do not just relay what would have gone on without them, but rearticulate the elements and sites of an existing ritual process into a fully *mediated* event whose form was unimaginable before electronic media (Dayan and Katz 1992: 17). Quite rightly, they reject the dismissive view of Daniel Boorstin (1961) that television leaves us with only an unending procession of 'pseudo-events'. On the contrary, as Dayan and Katz argue with great conviction, media events produce complex multi-author, multi-sited event-texts, sometimes of great power, that Boorstin's reductive analysis simply fails to grasp. So far, so good.

This, however, is only the beginning of Dayan and Katz's argument for the wider significance of media events. There are some wider claims embedded in the basic definition already given. The insistence on 'liveness' is not, on the face of it, necessary, although as an historical accident mediated public events had to be 'live' for the first decades of television's history (I discuss 'liveness' in more detail in Chapter 6). Nor, on the face of it, is Dayan and Katz's insistence on the 'reality' of the broadcast necessary. Why isn't the live broadcast of a *telenovela*'s climactic episode before huge national audiences a media event, as it would be but for these restrictions?

There is, however, a substantial, not purely formal, reason for these limitations built into Dayan and Katz's definition of media events, which relates to their explicit neo-Durkheimian purpose. Media events, as they see them, are occasions where television makes possible an extraordinary shared experience of watching events at society's 'centre'. That is why media events must be 'live' *and* 'real', and it is because they are live and real that the act of viewing them simultaneously with others is itself extraordinary. Dayan and Katz draw here on Shils' notion of society's 'sacred centre' (cf. Chapter 3). Media events:

> are events narrated ... by television ... [yet] their origin is not in the secular routines of the media but in the 'sacred center' (Shils 1975) that endows them with the authority to preempt our time and attention.
>
> (Dayan and Katz 1992: 32)

Through media events, viewers themselves 'actively celebrate' (1992: 13). Indeed, in these events, we see 'the rare realisation of the full potential of electronic media technology' as a force for social integration (1992: 15). Television in Dayan and Katz's account answers Durkheim's concern a century earlier at the decline of experiences of social solidarity. They are writing, as they put in the preface to the book, 'in a neo-Durkheimian spirit that holds that the "mechanical solidarity" [enabled by television] ... is at the foundation of the "organic solidarity" of differentiated ... politics' (1992: viii). This is a classic neo-Durkheimian analysis of why ritual matters, but for Durkheim, of course, ritual was under threat in modernity (Durkheim 1984). This, then, is the destiny of television, at least for Dayan and Katz: to reunite the broken parts of Durkheim's wider argument.

This purpose gives a real rhetorical power to Dayan and Katz's book, and requires some additional restrictions to be built into their definition of the 'media event'. Thus media events are not only times when large societies are 'together', but when this togetherness is experienced as something *positive* (clearly 'togetherness' need not be positive, as in civil war). Media events 'celebrate reconciliation, not conflict'; they are hegemonic, not destructive of social bonds; 'these broadcasts integrate societies in a collective heartbeat and evoke a renewal of loyalty to the society and its legitimate authority' (Dayan and Katz 1992: 9). As a definitional restriction, if nothing else, this is rather arbitrary, as we shall see in a moment. Media events are more than mere repetitive, commemorative acts, in which people take part out of habit. They are actually 'persuasive', at least in democracies (1992: 21–2), where the complex negotiations between media institutions, political institutions and audiences that underlie any successful media event are, they argue, very different from attempts to impose consent through broadcast media in twentieth-century fascist states (1992: x). Once again, Dayan and Katz's concentration on media events in democracies suggests special pleading. Finally, they argue, media events turn the home into a public space (1992: 22), actually *connecting* centre and periphery (1992: 191). Dayan and Katz must make this assumption, otherwise their Durkheimian ideal of revived public ceremonies risks fracturing into a mass of separate, not necessarily connected, viewing situations.

Dayan and Katz's model is not, however, entirely Durkheimian. They add a refinement from Weber's tripartite distinction between rational, charismatic and traditional authority. Each of these types of authority corresponds to, and is confirmed by, three types of core narrative enacted by media events: contests, conquests and coronations (1992: 24, 43–5). This, however, is not my concern here and in any case it is the larger Durkheimian claim (about how society is bound together by certain core experiences of togetherness) that drives their argument. From this Durkheimian base, it is only a small step to add the Turnerian conclusion that media events are 'liminal' (1992: 117–18; cf. 201–21, 104–5, 107) and socially transformative (1992: 160, 167). Dayan and Katz are, of course, aware of Turner's own doubts (see Chapter 2) about the use of the term 'liminality' in complex dispersed societies, but (as with Durkheim) they argue such doubts are transcended by the possibilities of television to unite scattered populations (1992: 118, 145–6), even to create a new form of sociality (1992: 197). For Dayan and Katz, television, at least in media events, changes what can be thought of *as* social experience; here, in effect, they extend to mediated societies Mary Douglas' view that 'ritual can come first in formulating experience' (Douglas 1984: 64).

This bold argument was developed for at least a decade, before being published in final form in *Media Events* (Dayan and Katz 1992), and it has been influential. Michael Real (1989), for example, gives it a postmodern twist: in societies of media saturation and very high levels of shared media literacy (societies of 'super media' as he puts it) the boundaries between media producers and audience are less important, making moments of social togetherness through the media increasingly easy to construct. (Dayan and Katz would perhaps be less sanguine about that.) And the same broad Durkheimian argument had already been presented in a more subtle form in John MacAloon's analysis of the 'neoliminal' dimension of televised Olympic ceremonies (1984).[7] Indeed the term 'media event' has been widely adopted in later analyses of Olympic events, on which there is a large literature.[8] Provided we mean by media rituals no more than television's role in extending the scope of contemporary (non-mediated) ritual and the socialised viewing associated with media events in that limited sense, then there is no difficulty. The problems begin when we examine the wider assumptions underlying Dayan and Katz's argument.

Problems with the neo-Durkheimian reading

In spite of its rhetorical power and many local insights, there are a number of difficulties with Dayan and Katz's account of media events. Since it represents the strongest formulation of a neo-Durkheimian position in current media research, it is important to go through these carefully if we are to show the usefulness of a different approach.

The first difficulty is in a sense merely descriptive, but hardly trivial. I have already suggested that the extra limitations in Dayan and Katz's definition help to ensure that media events for them always have positive, hegemonic effects. But, given that they are hardly naive about the ideological conflicts involved in constructing media events (see, for example, 1992: chapter 6), this limitation is rather arbitrary. To call a media event hegemonic depends on a certain reading of the event; even Dayan and Katz do not claim that the media events they analyse attracted *no* dissenters or apathetic bystanders, and their choice of what counts as a media event – requiring in it a *positive* 'hegemonic' effect – itself involves a value judgement.

If we take one obvious recent candidate for Dayan and Katz's definition – the televised funeral of Princess Diana in September 1997 – the question of whether it was 'hegemonic' is hardly straightforward. As Robert Turnock's study (2000) shows, in relation to the British television audience at least, there were still many who did not watch, and of those who did a surprisingly large number do not appear to have conformed to the expectation of grief or shared emotion. To this, Dayan and Katz could object that in any mass ceremony (especially a multi-local televised ceremony) there will always be variations in individual reactions. Of course, but this variability only becomes an issue if you assume, as they do, that media events are hegemonic in their effects. The problem, if it lies anywhere, lies with Dayan and Katz's Durkheimian assumptions.

Once we bracket out those assumptions, there are a great many potential media events which do not necessarily help integrate society. One example, following Tamar Liebes (1998), are the 'disaster marathons' on Israeli television, for example the 72-hour non-stop coverage following the suicide bomb attacks in Israel in March 1996. It is true that these are not 'preplanned' media events, and therefore fall outside an explicit restriction that Dayan and Katz impose on the definition of the media event, however high the audiences and however intense the viewing involved. Arguably, however, this only shows how artificial that restriction is. Once you remove it, you must surely include within media events this type of disaster coverage (familiar of course in many other countries) which does *anything but* integrate society. Instead it heightens a sense of crisis, broadening the scope for conflict, and without any prospect of narrative closure (Liebes 1998: 74). Such events are 'liminal' in Turner's sense, but usually lack any affirmative outcome.

Other examples increase these doubts. There are plenty of events which (but for Dayan and Katz's restricted definition) we would want to call 'media events', but which are not socially integrative or, if they appear to be, are so only from one, highly contested, perspective. Daniel Hallin (1994) has discussed the example of the Reagan–Gorbachev summits in the 1980s; Eoin Devereaux's analysis of television charity fundraisers such as Band Aid and Live Aid (1996) is another interesting case. In each case, 'media events' begin to merge with the wider, more obviously contested, terrain of mediated politics, once again suggesting how artificial Dayan and Katz's restricted definition of the media event is. In their defence, Dayan and Katz might develop a counter-example from the events after Diana's death. These, it could be argued, involved a clear contrast between the uncertainty of the conflict surrounding the media coverage in the days up to the funeral, and the affirmative televised media event of the funeral itself. If so, it is arguable that the shared viewing experience of Diana's funeral brought the conflicts of the previous week 'under control' as far as possible, thereby fulfilling the integrative social function by which Dayan and Katz seek to distinguish the *media event proper.* But we lack any evidence to substantiate this and such evidence as there is (as already noted) is ambiguous, to say the least. In addition, by automatically excluding from the definition of media events highly mediated situations which are *contested*, such as those in the week leading up to Diana's funeral, Dayan and Katz exclude some of the most interesting cases, where the media's narrative authority is tested and worked upon.

So the descriptive force of Dayan and Katz's theory of media events is distorted by their desire to make it work for neo-Durkheimian ends. Perhaps a less restrictive definition, combined with a clearer separation between general analysis and the special cases which fit best with the Durkheimian position, would be a way forward. But this is only the start of the difficulties.

There is a problem with the assumptions underlying Dayan and Katz's argument as a whole. In a classic essay which predates their theory but reviews Durkheimian arguments (such as Shils and Young's on the 1953 coronation) for the socially integrative role of political ritual, Steven Lukes (1975) brought out two fundamental weaknesses in those arguments. One weakness is a generalisation of the descriptive problem I have just been considering: that, by focusing exclusively on the supposed *integrative* effects of political ritual, those arguments ignore most of the terrain to be studied. What about rituals which work to *oppose* society's value system, or which exacerbate social conflict, or which do not achieve a stable hegemonic interpretation, against the intentions of their producers (1975: 300–1)? Even if it *is* unusual for media events to oppose society's value system, this only brings to the surface just how *ideological*, and implicitly conservative, the theory of media events is! It treats as natural, even ideal, the fact that the media's ritual resources are generally focused in support of one set of values, those that happen to be dominant ones.

The other weakness identified by Lukes in neo-Durkheimian accounts of political ritual is even more fundamental. Durkheimians argue that such rituals are significant because they 'hold society together' and do so by affirming a common set of values. But this begs a number of questions: 'whether, to what extent, and in what ways society *does* hold together' (Lukes 1975: 297). The fact that societies are stable (in the sense that they are not in the throes of civil war) does *not* necessarily mean that they have a shared set of values (Mann 1970; Parkin 1972), or (even if they do) that it is these values, rather than something else entirely (inertia, coercion in its various forms, despair – the list of possible causes is endless!) that 'holds them together'. And what of societies which are in conflict and lack obvious consensus? Lukes mentions

Eastern Europe (he was writing before 1989); today one might mention, among many possible examples, Israel, recalling Liebes' argument.

The problem, then, with neo-Durkheimian views of political ritual (into which Dayan and Katz's theory of media events clearly falls) is that they obscure all the interesting questions about whether and, above all, how societies do hold together, *if* they do; in other words, they reproduce what we have called 'the myth of the centre'. The only way forward in Lukes' view is to resituate the analysis of political ritual 'within a class-structured, conflictual and pluralistic model of society' (1975: 301). This is a broader task for political sociology, but for media sociology we can concentrate, more modestly, on how media events work to *construct* a sense of the 'centre', and the entanglement of the media's ritual power in these constructions. Entangled here too are the strategies of contemporary states to use media events as vehicles to shore up their own authority – but again this is primarily an issue for political sociology.

The need for this rethinking of media events is reinforced by two further concerns; the first relates to channel and medium multiplication, the second to the global applicability of Dayan and Katz's model.

Dayan and Katz's argument brackets out the growing complexity of the contemporary media audience. How, for example, should we understand the effect of more than two decades of cable television in the US, one decade of cable and satellite television in the UK, and almost five years of broad Internet availability in both countries upon the possibilities for the *simultaneous* mass audience that Dayan and Katz assume? We need, certainly, to be suspicious of hasty marketing rhetoric which claims the days of the mass audience are over; things are not so simple (Couldry 2000a: chapter 9; Curran 1998). One important factor, even if media distribution channels multiply, is that, at times of intense crisis or shared interest in a common event, those multiple outputs can easily be connected up intertextually to *recreate* a sense of a compulsory mediated 'centre', albeit with countless tributaries reaching out from that centre. This, I would argue, is the best way to interpret the sense of 'compulsory' viewing that, in Britain but elsewhere too, sustained a live television audience for Princess Diana's funeral in 1997 claimed to be in excess of two billion people (at a time when cable and satellite television were widespread in many countries).

A related issue arises when we rethink Dayan and Katz's model of media events on a global scale. In principle, their model ought to be extendable; there is nothing in their book to say it shouldn't apply globally, many of the events they discuss had a transnational significance (for example, President Sadat's visit to Jerusalem), and some important global events have occurred since their book was published which would seem to be natural candidates for 'media event'. These include the televised inauguration of Nelson Mandela as President of South Africa in 1994 and the funeral of Princess Diana in 1997. But, while the scope of Dayan and Katz's argument is potentially global, the implausibility of some of their underlying assumptions only increases on the global stage. Can we really claim that *any* public event, broadcast across more than a hundred nations, could have a socially integrative impact in every such location? Surely not. If so, the choice seems to be: *either* drop that requirement from the definition of media events (but at the cost of endangering the neo-Durkheimian conclusion of the argument) *or* maintain this condition, but only include global media events on the stringent condition that they have positive social impacts across the globe. Both approaches leave the neo-Durkheimian position weakened in the end, especially when it relies on an implicitly *national* model of 'societies', and indeed sociology (Urry 2000), which is now coming under challenge.

In the face of all these difficulties, we should, I suggest, redefine the term 'media events' more cautiously just to cover *those large-scale event-based media-focused narratives where the claims associated with the myth of the mediated centre are particularly intense.* This allows us to retain many of the descriptive insights of Dayan and Katz's argument, but detach them from the increasingly unwieldy apparatus of the neo-Durkheimian position. I explore this possibility further in the next section.

A NEW PERSPECTIVE ON MEDIA EVENTS

What would it be like to think about media events, but without relying on the myth of the mediated centre?

Constructing the media's authority

The first, and most obvious, difference would be to foreground how, in the course of a media event (as just redefined), the myth of the mediated centre is in fact reproduced.

Here it is helpful to return to Merton's classic (1946) account of the US warbond drive, our alternative starting point. What was interesting about that media event is that, although obviously connected with the state's war aims at the time and therefore easily readable as merely constructed, it did acquire a wider social significance. How exactly? First of all, the uniqueness of the event was constantly asserted by Kate Smith and by the radio station:

> I don't think anything even remotely like this has ever been done before.
> (quoted in Merton 1946: 22)

> [It is] the most wonderful ... the proudest ... day of my whole life.
> (quoted in Merton 1946: 23)

> All regular business at this station has been suspended.
> (quoted in Merton 1946: 23)

Second, many claims were made that the performance aspects of the event (Kate Smith's struggle with her vocal chords) somehow represented something wider, 'a totality of a particular type', as Merton puts it, 'a race or an endurance contest' (1946: 29). (Remember that 'contest' was one of Dayan and Katz's categories of media event narrative.) It was asserted that the audience, too, were participating in this event: as we would now put it, the event was 'interactive'. Merton notes how the rhetoric of the performer was picked up in the language of audience members:

> [W]e can do it together ... we can put this greatest of all warbond drives across.
>
> (quoted in Merton 1946: 55)

> [W]e did something, I was part of the show ... we felt that others had been impressed and bought a bond. And the fact that so many people felt the same made me feel right – that I was in the right channel.
>
> (quoted in Merton 1946: 56)

In addition, the sincerity of Kate Smith was asserted when she recalled personal experiences and was believed by most listeners, even though this was, for her, very much a professional role (1946: 82). It is true that Dayan and Katz, too, stress rhetoric in their account of media events; but the difference is that in a neo-Durkheimian account the rhetorical constructions of a media event get transformed magically into something 'higher' and more representative. As we have seen, Merton refuses such a move.

A similar scepticism enables us to see such rhetorical forms in the events after the death of Princess Diana: the assertion that the event was unique, that the whole nation was involved, and that the media was the event's privileged interpreter. Here are passages taken from newspaper coverage in the week after Princess Diana's death:

> Crowds on a scale never witnessed before began to gather in London today as the nation prepared to say farewell to Diana, Princess of Wales.
>
> (*Evening Standard*, 5 September 1997: 8)

> Mr Blair could not disguise his own feelings that Diana's death was 'something more profound than anything I can remember in the totality of my life.' He went on, 'We must commend a sense of national grief at the moment. It's not just grief as a nation. It is personal to each and every one of us.'
>
> (*Daily Mail*, 5 September 1997: 2)

> The word was shock and it spilled from people's lips and gripped their hearts yesterday. Millions woke in disbelief at the early morning news bulletins on

> radio and TV and at the hastily reassembled front pages of the Sunday newspapers.
>
> (*Daily Mail*, 1 September 1997: 10)

In media events, such claims spill over from one agent to another: we find them in the mouths of media and of government, and attributed by each to individual citizens. There is a feedback loop, which is only partly the result of anyone's strategy, since it is inherent in the process of mediation itself (cf. Lang and Lang 1969): media, governments and audiences pick up signals from each other, and the overwhelming sense of an 'event' develops. Regardless of its detailed origins, the event becomes a 'frame' within which people know they can participate with others, as reflected in the comment of this woman shortly after Diana's death:

> I am not a royalist. I admired [Diana], but I never realised that I loved her. I wanted to be part of it all. It's the most moving thing that's happened in my lifetime.
>
> (quoted in *The Times*, 6 September 1997: 10)

In structural terms, we have here for complex societies an effect analogous to the 'contagion' of the 'effervescent assembly' in Durkheim's model. Such feedback loops, however, are inseparable from a distinctive and unequal structure of power. Just as in the 'ritual space of the media' generally, so too underlying the media event there is a gulf between the media's privileged status as interpreter of the social world and non-media people's secondary authority to speak. Indeed we can argue that it is precisely within the exceptional context of media events that media work hardest to ground the representational authority on which they rely for their everyday practice.[9]

This idea might seem cynical, but in one sense it is common ground between all analysts of media events, whether neo-Durkheimian or not. Paddy Scannell acknowledges in passing that 'the coronation of 1953 is widely regarded, in retrospect, as having "made" the BBC's television service' (1996: 80). Barbie Zelizer, in a more critical account of the construction of journalistic authority following President Kennedy's assassination, argues that US journalists used that time to 'strengthen … their position as actual authorities concerning events of the "real world"' (1993: 2–3) and as shapers of the American public's memories of the event. So media may continue to construct their position as privileged interpreters of the social 'centre' long after the media event itself is over, by recalling that event and how they told the story.

Related to this is the media's claimed authority to speak *for* the 'ordinary person'. Here is an example, once again from the press coverage of the events after Diana's death:

> Valerie Adams froze in front of the book. New Malden is where she is from. She rehearsed on the early train and remembered. 'I said it to myself for the whole hour I waited in line,' she said. She wrote with ease. 'Dear Diana, Rest in Peace. You were a lovely lady and you always will be.' ... The flowers led you to the People's Princess in London yesterday. They were in the hands of children and the ordinary people [Diana] said she loved.
>
> (*Daily Mail*, 2 September 1997: 2)

In the formalised language of this report (aimed no doubt at solemnity and the affirmation of a wider community), notice the patronising division between the 'ordinary person' (observed) and the 'media person' (observing and narrating). The effect was no doubt not deliberate, but neither is it accidental; the inequality of symbolic resources reworked here is the very same inequality without which the writer's authority would not exist.

We have, in effect, reversed Dayan and Katz's argument that media events, through their exceptional nature, reveal 'truths' about contemporary mediated societies which in normal circumstances are invisible. On the contrary, claims for the uniqueness of the media events and the media's special role in interpreting them are merely intensified versions of the media's ordinary claim to be the representative of 'the centre'. Like the 1970s British nightly current affairs programme *Nationwide*, in Brunsdon and Morley's classic analysis, the media's discourse reproduces the 'myth of "the nation, now"' (1978: 87), both within the exceptional context of media events and on a daily basis. To adapt Dayan and Katz (1992: 1), media events show us not the media on holiday (they are never on holiday!) but media *power* 'on holiday'. For it is in the special emotive setting of the media event that the media's everyday claims to authority have their best chance of being mistaken as necessary.

Media events and liminality

In the contemporary world there are few, if any, moments of 'togetherness' which are not already crossed by the mediated power structures that influence all spaces of expression.[10] This, however, does not mean that media events are readable only as reproductions of those structures. On the contrary, within the frame of media events, there is always the possibility of social interaction that is truly 'liminal' and disruptive, and I want to explore how we can describe this without relying on the myth of the mediated centre.

Such liminality may take the form of explicit conflict, as illustrated by Larson and Park's (1993) careful study of the production of the Seoul Olympics in 1988, planned under an authoritarian regime. Their book is primarily a study in political economy, but they analyse a number of controversies which arose in spite of the elaborate media planning. There was, for example, a controversy over an allegedly biased US commentary on an incident involving a South Korean boxer; the undiplomatic comments of the US commentator were relayed to Korea via broadcasts made to the US troops stationed in Korea, from where they were picked up more widely. Larson and Park, while keeping Dayan and Katz's definition of media events in mind, conclude that the Seoul Games were 'an event-centered communication process, rather than simply a media event', since in addition to their planned elements, they were 'also … a source of unplanned and, at least in the short term, disruptive news events' (1993: 238). A parallel might be the 1953 British coronation incident (Scannell 1996: 86), where a US reporter's 'disrespectful' comments on the ceremony were picked up by the UK press, creating a short-term scandal. These two examples show how unstable are the hegemonic processes of a media event, especially when, as is now common, they spill out beyond national borders to other countries where the appearance of consensus is less assured.

Media events may also, by their scale, provide opportunities for underlying conflicts to be expressed or negotiated, including conflict over the underlying inequality of symbolic power on which the media's authority to narrate those same events is based. As John Fiske puts it:

> a media event … is a point of maximum discursive visibility … also a point of maximum turbulence … It also invites intervention and motivates people to struggle to redirect some of the currents flowing through it to serve their interests; it is therefore a site of popular engagement and involvement, not just a scenic view to be photographed and then left behind.
>
> (Fiske 1996: 8)

In media events, the structure of the media's ritual space may itself be contested, or at least renegotiated, in the temporary opportunities media events provide for *acting* (not merely spectating) in public events. As I have argued elsewhere (Couldry 1999), one of the most striking things about popular symbolic production in the mourning period for Princess Diana was the way people took up opportunities to speak (or write) and to be heard (or read) before a guaranteed, if temporary, audience (in the walls of tributes at central places in London, and elsewhere). In these situations, both difference and unity were expressed in a way that, on the face of it, fits a Durkheimian framework, but whose long-term consequences are much more uncertain. Were power structures and boundaries permanently challenged, let alone the media's representational authority? Almost certainly not. In such cases, even within a post-Durkheimian perspective, Turner's point – that the liminal is a period *out of* the ordinary that precedes the restoration of social order – remains a useful reminder of the pressures towards order.[11]

The sheer complexity of a media event – a space of discursive production by thousands, even millions, of people, even if media institutions have the privileged position within that space – often exceeds the rhetorical claims made for that event's integrative power. We have already seen this in relation to the audiences for the televised funeral of Princess Diana. There are other examples of how the vastness of a media event makes possible ideas and images that accept no part (on the face of it) of the rhetoric of social inclusion: the most obvious would be the jokes that swarm around cyberspace in the wake of large-scale mediated disasters,[12] but this is only one example of a broader process whereby the strategic frame of a media event can be used tactically to pursue other agendas. The result is 'liminality', not in Turner's sense, but in a sense closer to Michel de Certeau's (1984) well-known discussion of 'tactics': that is, productions that operate on (not across) the margins or boundaries of the media event. Clearly, then, social integration is not the only use to which the frame of media events can be put: hence (once more) the need to analyse them outside the constraints of classic Durkheimian assumptions.

It is here that the work of Deleuze and Guattari (1988) offers a useful, because diametrically opposed, perspective to Dayan and Katz's. As mentioned in Chapter 1, Deleuze and Guattari, whose philosophical work has had a major impact on social theory, were interested (like Durkheim) in the question of 'order', but in understanding order not as natural, but as the interaction between two opposed forces, of 'de-territorialisation' and 're-territorialisation' (cf. Chapter 1). This provides us with a fresh perspective on the chaotic surface of media events. Deleuze and Guattari proposed a new word for the non-unitary coming-together of properties and things right here and now in an event: the 'haecceity', for example (their example) 'a cloud of locusts carried in by the wind at five in the evening' (1988: 263)! The haecceity (the artificiality of the term, while bizarre, is not really the issue!) is the very opposite of the media event in Dayan and Katz's conception; it is a coming-together which speaks of, or expresses, *nothing deeper*. It is this possibility of banality that the rhetoric of media events consistently resists. This is not to say that we can just ignore that rhetoric, since its effects are all too real, but simply that we need never think that alternative formulations are impossible. I will return to the question of alternatives to the myth of the mediated centre at the end of the book.

Media events and the reality of symbolic conflict

Does my argument show that media events are *only* constructions, or that there are never occurrences that have a shared significance for everyone in a particular territory? Certainly not: there are natural disasters which are significant for everyone, and there are non-natural events (for example, catastrophic challenges to a political or social order) which are similarly universal in their basic significance, if not their interpretation. These are not media events, first and foremost, although they may quickly become media events in their aftermath, including for audiences far beyond the territory where they have automatic significance (cf. Wark 1994, on the fall of the Berlin Wall). As a form of rhetorical construction, the media event can only grow in relevance in a globalised media system. There is a connection here to the terrible attacks on New York and Washington DC on 11 September 2001, which I want to explore, however tentatively.

In one way, the blanket coverage of those attacks (and people's intense pursuit of the breaking news) fitted perfectly into the exceptional forms of media engagement Dayan and Katz describe, even if the attacks themselves were not media events in their definition since the coverage was not preplanned. The initial coverage of the attacks (but not just when live: also when repeated through that and the following days)[13] had an immediacy that was unarguable; in the face of such appalling images, and the vivid memory almost all of us retain of them, can we still argue that the 'mediated centre', as I have put it, is a myth? Yes – and it is all the more important to do so in reflecting upon the implications of those terrible events, not least because it was one highly developed dimension of that myth which was at stake in those attacks.

The September 11 attacks had, of course, many dimensions and motivations, but surely one was as an attack on a symbolic centre, whose significance as an object of attack was linked to its involving real sites associated with the concentration of the world's material and symbolic resources: the Twin Towers in New York City, at the heart of Manhattan's financial, governmental and media centre. The attacks, of course, were not themselves rituals, but an attempt to destroy part of the ground on which today's media rituals are produced. The implied targets were far more numerous than those who tragically lost their lives, since countless millions of the world's population are bound up in various ways with sustaining the idea of America as 'the insurmountable [symbolic] horizon of our time' (Mattelart, Delcourt and Mattelart 1984: 100–1). That horizon was contested by a physical attack on one of the most obvious symbols of its natural legitimacy. Inseparable from that horizon is a wider landscape of symbolic inequality (Couldry, forthcoming) that, while on a different and global scale, is analogous to the inequalities we have analysed beneath the rhetoric of media events: I mean the uneven landscape of global production and distribution that theorists of media and cultural imperialism attacked in various forms for decades.

It would, of course, be crass to claim that the implications of September 11 can be reduced to an ultimately academic debate about the social rhetorics of media production in the early twenty-first century (the media event). But there is something, I would claim, in the separation insisted upon throughout this chapter – between media representations and the claims made for media representations – that it is useful to carry over to the longer-term analysis of the implications of September 11, a task which itself lies well beyond this book. That is why, paradoxically, I have not in this chapter foregrounded the September 11 attacks, even though in many respects their media dimensions conformed to what we can retain from Dayan and Katz's notion of a 'media event'. For at the same time those events showed us that, for any understanding of contemporary forms of power, we must *look beyond* the claims of order on which such forms of power rely, and concentrate instead on the conflictual reality with which they are entangled.

CONCLUSION

This chapter has dealt with complex events where for a time the ritual space of the media is closely involved with the historical unpredictability of non-media events. In the next chapter I want to look more closely at the entanglement of media rituals with the organisation of social space, as reflected in pilgrimages to media sites. We will see some overlaps with rhetorical patterns discussed in this chapter.

Chapter 5

Media 'pilgrimages' and everyday media boundaries

> The space of a (social) order is hidden in the order of space.
>
> (Lefebvre 1991b: 289)

In the last chapter we deconstructed the idea that the media's 'special times' reveal anything special or universal. Rather they are times when the construction of the media's authority is most intense; since it is this authority that underlies media rituals, we can say that in media events the symbolic work of ritualisation is also at its most intense. In this chapter, I will similarly attempt to deconstruct the media's 'special places' and uncover the hierarchical spatial order that underlies them. In studying this uneven landscape, we encounter the most directly spatial aspects of what metaphorically I have called the 'ritual space of the media', that is, the hinterland of categorisation and ordering that lies behind the practice of media rituals.

We are already familiar with aspects of this landscape from work on celebrity and fandom, particularly fan journeys to places featured in programmes or films (Gamson 1994; Harrington and Bielby 1995; Hills 2002: chapter 7; Jenkins 1992; cf. Couldry 2000a: part 2). From another perspective, this landscape represents the 'myth of the mediated centre' mapped onto actual space, and the privilege of particular places within it. My interest here is, however, quite specifically in the ritual practices which are focused in such places, and their relationship to wider patterns of 'ritualisation'. In particular, we will explore the usefulness of the concept of media 'pilgrimage' to describe such journeys. Note these journeys are made by a much wider group than just fans,[1] which is why they are part of the study of media rituals, not just the study of fandom.

The metaphor of 'pilgrimage' may have become so routine, so laden with irony and parody, that it has lost analytic value – if, that is, we regard clichés as empty. I prefer to follow the social psychologist Michael Billig's argument that it is precisely the patterns of *banal* language which, by attrition, reinforce large-scale patterns of thought that are anything but banal in their consequences (Billig 1995; 1997). This is especially so for the term 'pilgrimage' if, as its religious metaphor seems to require, it refers not just to ideas, but to a form acted out in journeys across space. The metaphor of 'pilgrimage' links banal language to (perhaps) banal action, potentially a double reinforcement, but of *what*?

The general significance of the 'pilgrimage' cliché beloved of journalists and also academics (Reader and Walter 1993) – a chosen journey to a significant place – derives from the way that contemporary societies are overlain, unevenly, with shared narratives of significance. We make 'pilgrimages' to distant places which have not only personal significance, but a guaranteed social importance too; they in principle matter to an imaginable group of others, even if, when I set off on a pilgrimage, I do not know who in particular I will meet on that journey. 'Pilgrimage' points are potential gathering points where the highly abstract nature of contemporary social connection can be redeemed through an encounter with a specific place. In general sociological terms, therefore, pilgrimage points are places where the 'disembedded' nature of late modern communities can be 're-embedded' (Giddens 1990) in the specific form of a journey to a chosen, but distant, site.

'Pilgrimage' in this broad sociological sense, far from being a trivial aspect of modern states, is endemic within them. The phenomenon was noted, for example, during Hitler's rise to power in 1930s Germany. Let me quote from Ian Kershaw's pioneering study of the 'Hitler myth':

> 'The Obersalzberg [the area of Hitler's residence in Bavaria] has become a sort of pilgrimage place,' noted one report. 'The area around Wachenfeld House is constantly occupied by men and women admirers. Even in walks in isolated spots the Reich Chancellor is pursued by a throng of intrusive admirers and inquisitive persons.'
>
> (Kershaw 1987: 60)

Kershaw's footnote to this passage even refers to people taking pieces of Hitler's garden fence 'as relics'.

Media pilgrimages (cf. Couldry 2000a: part 2) are specifically journeys to points with significance in media narratives. Through media pilgrimages, not only is the abstract nature of the media production system 're-embedded' in an encounter, for example, with a site of filming or a celebrity, but the significance of places 'in' the media is more generally confirmed. The media pilgrimage is both a real journey across space, and an acting out *in space* of the constructed 'distance' between 'ordinary world' and 'media world'. Media pilgrimages therefore enact a key structuring principle of the ritual space of the media, and not surprisingly are the focus of many detailed media rituals.

To use the word 'pilgrimage' is emphatically *not* to claim any religious significance for such media-related journeys (although, as we will see, research on religious pilgrimage does yield useful insights, by way of a structural analogy). It *is*, however, to take seriously the sociological implications of the ordering of space around certain privileged points, whose privilege naturalises underlying boundaries and hierarchies. As the geographer Henri Lefebvre put it, the only way to analyse forms of power that for their effect rely partly on their own abstraction in space is to analyse the actual spatial operations which they involve (1991b: 7, 289). To grasp these, it is no use 'reading' media spaces as if they were 'texts'; instead we must study the actual spatial operations (and particularly the boundary work)[2] which underlie the media's symbolic authority.

In doing so, we must beware of two dangers: first, of inflating the significance of such journeys in neo-Durkheimian fashion into expressions of the social bond; and second, of collapsing their significance in line with some postmodern arguments. We also need to think carefully about what changes the Internet has, and has not, brought to the ritual space of the media and the journeys with which it is associated.

GETTING MEDIA PILGRIMAGES INTO FOCUS

I have explained what media pilgrimages are in abstract terms, but what specifically do we mean by this term? Examples are all around us, in the form of journeys to media theme parks and other tourist sites which market their status as current or past filming locations (Couldry 2000a: 31–4, 65–6). Increasingly, as we see later, individual fans are creating their own pilgrimage sites on the World Wide Web. Indeed any journey to a distant location or person 'in' the media can potentially be a 'media pilgrimage'. Before turning in detail to my own approach to media pilgrimages, I want to review some other possible interpretations that leave them still, partly, out of focus: first, a Turnerian account of media pilgrimages as journeys to places associated with society's central values; and second, a postmodern debunking of media pilgrimages as deluded travels in 'hyperreality'.

Durkheimian readings?

Media pilgrimages are still very little studied (except from the limited perspective of fandom), so it is hardly surprising that no full-blown Turnerian analysis of them exists, although there are traces of it in the literature. However, such an account can be constructed straightforwardly by combining a neo-Durkheimian view of contemporary media's operations as an expression of society's 'centre' (Real 1989) with Victor Turner's influential theory of modern pilgrimage as a special journey to a place associated with central values (Turner 1974; Turner and Turner 1978). For Turner, even religious pilgrimages are strictly limin*oid* (merely 'liminal-like'), not liminal, experiences; they are from the beginning manufactured and commercialised. In addition, in line with Durkheim's general rethinking of religious experience in terms of experiences of sociality, Turner's concept of pilgrimage encompasses journeys without any link to religion:

> Both for individuals and for groups, some form of deliberate travel to a far place intimately associated with the deepest, most cherished axiomatic values of the traveler seems to be a sort of 'cultural universal'. If it is not religiously sanctioned, counseled or encouraged, it will take other forms.
>
> (Turner and Turner 1978: 241)

So there is no 'sacrilege' in extending the term pilgrimage to secular forms that involve the sense of a compulsory journey (Reader 1993: 233–5). Indeed, once (following Turner) we ground 'pilgrimage' in the need to discover in the flesh some of the abstract multitudes with whom we share membership of a society (Turner and Turner 1978: 192), then pilgrimage of any sort can be traced back to Durkheim's basic insight about the need to affirm the social bond.[3] There is nothing strange about a neo-Durkheimian notion of media pilgrimages: it is a journey to a special place valued in the media and therefore the spatial correlate of Dayan and Katz's media event (a time whose media coverage takes on a special, valued status).

The problem with a straightforward Turnerian theory of media pilgrimage is that it ends up naturalising the idea of a mediated 'centre', which is precisely what we must deconstruct. At this point, and without any implication that media pilgrimages are religious in nature, it is worth noting the critiques made of Turner's theory by anthropologists of religion. First, it has been argued that at actual pilgrimage sites, far from a unified set of values being affirmed, there is considerable conflict, including *differences* of interpretation over religious values and the meaning of the pilgrimage site; indeed the pilgrimage site is 'almost a religious void, a ritual space capable of accommodating *diverse* meanings and practices' (Eade and Sallnow 1991: 15, my emphasis).[4] This point could perhaps be accommodated within a revised version of Turner's thesis, which argued that pilgrimage sites involve not so much the affirmation of shared values, as a forum where important value-*differences* are worked out. Second, however, it has been doubted whether pilgrimage typically *does* involve the special moments of community and togetherness that the neo-Durkheimian argument requires. According to another scholar of pilgrimage, Morinis, such moments are rare (1992: 28, note2); more prevalent is the search for 'predictable experiences', and the *retrospective* sense of having done something special when you return to the 'everyday' routine: 'while the sacred is the source of power ... it is at home once again that the effects of power are incorporated into life' (1992: 21, 27). Third, it has been argued that Turner's model treats pilgrimage sites in isolation from their wider context. As Glenn Bowman puts it, 'to comprehend pilgrimages in the particularities of their practices, anthropologists must explore the many disparate sites [i.e. other than pilgrimage sites] at which the concepts of the sacred, and desires to engage it, are forged' (1991: 120). Morinis (1992: 22) makes the same point more formally when he argues that, to understand pilgrimage sites, we must grasp 'the [general] code of pilgrimage which underlies the concept and practice of pilgrimage within a culture'.

These debates within the anthropology of religion raise important issues for any attempt to read media pilgrimages in neo-Durkheimian fashion, suggesting that we should be sceptical about any claim that journeys to special media sites are simply affirmative; we cannot fully make sense of journeys to such sites unless we consider their relationship to the domestic space from which the media 'pilgrim' sets out. This fits with what we know from the sociology of tourism, that it operates within the general polarity of 'ordinary' versus 'extraordinary' experience (Urry 1990: 101–2). Any account of media pilgrimages needs, as with religious pilgrimage, to analyse the wider cultural and ritual space within which the act of pilgrimage makes sense: this fits with my argument earlier that media rituals can only be understood as part of a wider ritual space.

None of these doubts, however, requires us to abandon the notion of media pilgrimage altogether, since it points to a significant pattern of action which we need to understand, albeit outside a functionalist framework. This is important, given other arguments that reject media pilgrimages as of only illusory significance in a postmodern age.

Postmodern dismissal?

A postmodern argument, following Baudrillard (1983) on the annihilation of place and Boorstin (1961) on the death of travel through media saturation, would deride as an illusion the idea that a pilgrimage takes us to a 'special' place. From this perspective, no place is special anymore, since every place has already been saturated by media narratives. Indeed, on the face of it, *media* pilgrimages are the most obvious candidates for this reductive approach, since by definition they contain things already encountered on television! This was exactly why I first became interested in them: why spend time and money visiting a place you've already seen, maybe thousands of times? I was convinced that there was more to say on these journeys than postmodern theory allowed for.

There are, however, more sophisticated variants on this reductive postmodern line of argument. Mestrovic (1997) has acknowledged that there is real emotion expressed at sites such as media theme parks, rather than just boredom or deflation, but he argues it is a sort of preprogrammed emotion; people 'emote', because that is what they know they are expected to do (we return to this issue from another perspective in Chapter 7 in relation to talk shows). As a general comment, this is suggestive, but it gives us few tools for interpreting the detail of what people do at such sites, and why people go there in particular.

Critical geography has undermined these postmodern arguments by analysing the long-term spatial impacts of the industrialised production of fantasy. Far from this reducing all space to 'hyperreality', the result is to reinforce still further the significance of *particular* places as having a privileged status in networks of symbolic production. As Sharon Zukin's work has shown, sites such as Disneyland are profitable constructions of the *illusion* of a symbolic centre, and that illusion has a power which is not reducible to an excuse for showing emotion: 'Disney World suggests that [its] architecture is important, not because it is a symbolic of capitalism, but because it is the capital of symbolism' (1991: 232). This not only fits well with general sociological arguments about the close interlocking of the organisation of leisure with the organisation of work (Rojek 1993: 213),[5] but also reinforces our concern with analysing media pilgrimages as journeys within a highly structured and uneven symbolic landscape, the ritual space of the media.

Media 'pilgrimages' and the ritual space of the media

How are media pilgrimage sites related to the ritual space of the media? On the face of it, the answer seems simple. Media pilgrimages are journeys to media-related places. As such, they reinforce those places' special significance and thereby the key structuring hierarchy of the media's ritual space: the hierarchy of places 'in' the media over those which aren't. Before getting into greater detail, we have to acknowledge that such connections between media and spatial organisation, indeed the spatial aspects of the media landscape as a whole,[6] have been almost completely ignored in general media sociology. Almost unique are Stewart Hoover's reflections on the visits by fans of Pat Buchanan's religious programme in the 1980s, *The Seven Hundred Club*, to its studios. Working at that time within a Durkheimian framework, but drawing on his own extensive empirical research, Hoover argues that television's 'cultural significance' cannot '[lie] only in its manifest "messages" or "symbol systems". Television, religious or not, must necessarily entail consciousness of space and distance on the part of its viewers' (1988a: 174). Yet, as he notes, this spatiality of television has been almost entirely neglected.

On the face of it, this is unsurprising. The whole point of television, as a broadcast medium, you might argue, is to create a '*despatial*ised commonality' (Thompson 1995: 231, my emphasis). But here we need to return to Lefebvre. We cannot deny that television operates in some places, not others: its distribution and production operates to a certain spatial grid, and its consumption is equally patterned in place (McCarthy 2001). In other words, the media process has a *spatial order*, which we usually forget. Indeed, it is precisely part of the workings of the myth of television to collapse that very real spatial order into the myth of 'the mediated centre'.

EVERYDAY MEDIA BOUNDARIES

Analysing media pilgrimages within a post-Durkheimian framework, we need, first, to think carefully about the everyday spatial boundaries that the wider media process involves.

The organisation of media space

Our starting point is the fact that media production happens in particular places, here and not there. It is associated with metropolitan centres, although filming (rather than, say, editing) may in principle take place anywhere. The media do not simply reinforce existing metropolitan bias, because marginal areas (whether geographically, politically, economically, culturally) can have attractions for media production, for example as the sites on which nostalgic narratives of the past can be projected. So I was wrong to be surprised when, on holiday last year in the remote Outer Hebrides off the Scottish coast, I found Ben Fogle, the star of BBC's 'reality TV' series *Castaway*, opening the local Highland Games and a television crew filming a period drama on a beach. Rather than a simple centralisation of media production, there is instead a grid in which key *nodes* (for media inputs and outputs) are associated with central locations, although under certain conditions the network may reach out to the 'margins' as well. The issue in any case is not only what spaces get represented, but where the resources of media production are concentrated. Above all – and this is a point so obvious that it is easily forgotten – those resources are concentrated in media institutions, which are largely situated in a few metropolitan centres.

Real boundaries are placed around media institutions. These are not natural boundaries, although they are so regular that one might easily mistake them for natural. To remind ourselves that the significance of these boundaries is socially constructed, not natural, it is worth recalling the early days of British radio in Manchester (the station '2ZY' which operated from 1924 to 1926), when members of the audience frequently *went down to* the studios to take part in, or interrupt, programmes, treating the studios as a public space which they were entitled to enter![7] This historical detail seems curious to us now, because it implies a completely different understanding of media space from our own: the idea that the media are a public communication *space*, which, as members of the public, the audience is entitled to enter. The history of British broadcasting (and broadcasting almost everywhere) can be understood in terms of an increasing concentration of scarce production resources into particular controlled spaces (such as the BBC's Broadcasting House). This history was not fundamentally changed by the availability of more mobile production facilities from the 1960s onwards (portable sound recording, video, camcorders, and so on), because submerged in that history is another broader theme. This is the process by which populations became accustomed to the idea that the physical space of broadcasting was *not* a space to which, as members of the public, they had a right of entry, so that boundaries around media production emerged as natural and legitimate.

Non-mainstream media practice may still involve a strikingly different concept of the media process's spatial dimensions, as in this account by one of the organisers of Black Liberation Radio (Springfield, Illinois), Napoleon Williams:

> Now Black Liberation Radio has actually become the voice of the community of Decatur. We have drawn people who two years ago would never have listened to me on the radio as daily listeners. *They will call in* ... If you are depressed you might just call in for a simple conversation which is what you need at just that moment. No other station in Decatur is that accessible. The people feel that it is their station, which it is. They built it. They bought the transmitters and everything ... It's my house, but it's the radio station too, so I guess you could say it's a community center. You will have people *knock on my door* four or five o'clock in the morning wanting to get on the radio right then and there. So whatever I'm doing, I get up and let them get on the air.
>
> (interviewed in Sakolsky and Dunifer 1998: 109–13, my emphasis)

Far more typical of broadcasting history, however, is the strict spatial order experienced by audiences every day of the week in major studios. Here is an account of being in the audience for the BBC's *Saturday Night Live* National Lottery programme in the mid-1990s by John, a clerical worker from the South of England. I interviewed him in November 1996 to discuss his visit to the set of the British soap *Coronation Street*, but he told this story without prompting:[8]

> [I] enjoyed the studio thing [i.e. the programme] [but] did not enjoy the BBC itself, it was dreadful the way you were treated. You were told to get there, 6 o'clock I think it was, but the programme doesn't go live until 7.50, so you think, 'Oh well, I'm going to be in the studios, it'll be nice and warm.' And you get there and you stand outside on the main road, at the BBC studios, it was freezing cold, it was

> November, and it started to rain, so after about half an hour, they then let you in and you go to a Portakabin and you're searched, frisked ... and you go through a barrier like you do at an airport ... and then you get out of there and you queue up again for about another 20 minutes and they take you round where it says 'BBC' ... and then you stand in another queue outside and then they take you in, and you think, 'Oh, I'm going into the studios, wonderful.' And then they take you into this enormous room which is geared to very expensive ... tea, coffee, BBC videos, BBC books ... it's like an airport lounge, and you sit there for an hour, and you think, 'Oh, the studios must be just there, just off this room,' ... no such luck ... you go through a set of double doors and the ushers open the doors, I was expecting to go onto the studio and I ended up outside again ...
>
> (interview, November 1996)

The boundary around the media production process here is, like most territoriality (Sack 1986), connected with the protection of material resources: maintaining scarcity of access to media production skills and equipment, and thereby the symbolic capital of those who have that access. But this separation (cf. Couldry 2000a: chapter 3) is also part of what legitimates the enormous concentration of symbolic power in media institutions. This separation is always, potentially, at odds with the idea that the media is a public space, which you and I as members of the public are entitled to enter. There are particular advantages, then, in such boundaries being reproduced in ritual form.

Ritualised boundaries around the media world

There are boundaries placed around most types of workplace. But there is something odd about the idea of boundaries around the (in principle) public space which things or people 'in' the media inhabit. Let us start with a purely symbolic version of such a boundary, that is, one whose material basis was almost entirely illusory.

On holiday in 1997 on the North-West coast of Skye in Scotland's Inner Hebrides I revisited a lighthouse at Neist Point, a remote windswept spot which I'd enjoyed walking to before. You reach the lighthouse by descending a long series of steps cut in the cliff edge and, as I climbed down, I was surprised to see a graveyard in front of the lighthouse quarters. Coastal graveyards are a feature of the Hebrides, but from my previous visit I couldn't remember one at this spot. It seemed appropriate and moving, until I got closer, when I read the painted sign on the fence around the gravestones (see Plate 5.1):

> Neist Point was the location during 1995 for the making of a film called 'BREAKING THE WAVES'. This Grave yard was built for a scene in that film. There are no real graves here and the ground is not CONSECRATED. No offence is

Plate 5.1 'Graveyard' film set from *Breaking The Waves* in 1997

> intended to the Church or Church Goers. The film Won The Silver Medal In The 1996 Cannes Film Festival.

Like those with me (none of us churchgoers), I felt angry at the tastelessness of leaving fake gravestones near where many real people had, quite possibly, lost their lives at sea. In any case, why had a film set been thought worth preserving? Why was there a fence around the 'graves' with a large 'No Entry' notice, when no real graveyard (with much more to protect) would have such a restriction? There was something curious about this territorial claim on open land, and the boundary it implied: could a media space – a space of representation – be legitimately protected in a way that the real space (of which it was a simulacrum) could not? Here was the reproduction of an original physical boundary (around the space of filming) claiming a ritual force, and quite effectively: I saw no one break it, nor, in spite of our misgivings, did we.[9]

The significance of this case, in itself quite bizarre, is the background expectation it sought to draw upon that it was *natural* to restrict access to what had once been a site of media production (even if the notice was merely ironic – which I doubt – the *thought pattern* reproduced is the same).[10] The same logic is at work in countless tourist sites across the world which assert that they were *once* locations for filming, whether for television or cinema, and therefore automatically more significant; but the category difference is not always enforced in ritualised form.

Such ritualised boundaries should, generally, make sense to visitors. If we look closely at what visitors to such sites do, it is common to find them marking a formal boundary in their action between everyday space and media space. So visitors, talking about going to the outdoor set of the soap opera *Coronation Street* at Granada Studios Tour, Manchester, implied a physical boundary that in fact wasn't there when they wrote or spoke of 'stepping *onto* the Street'. At one time, the entry point *was* marked, physically and symbolically, by a pretend military border post named 'Checkpoint Charlie'. As the 1991–2 brochure for Granada Studios Tour put it: 'watch out for border guards … keep those passports to Weatherfield handy, or you may not make it to the Rovers' (cf. Couldry 2000a: 108–9).[11]

The idea of an invisible, but symbolically significant, barrier between ordinary world and media world is something we know, more dramatically, from fans' accounts of their meetings with celebrities, for example the accounts in Fred Vermorel and Julie Vermorel's book *Starlust* based on interviews with pop music fans in Britain in the 1980s. Bear in mind that such fans were likely to have encountered the objects of their fandom principally through television, so the relevance of their comments extends beyond music:

> *Barry Manilow fan*: Our seats were in the fifth row and I couldn't believe how close to the stage our seats were. I remember walking down to my seat and my legs were shaking so much, I felt a tremendous relief when I sat down. Then the concert started, and after all those months of waiting he was here. I knew Barry was standing there, but my mind wouldn't accept it. It was like a mirror image of the TV screen.
>
> *Hollies fan*: As we walked through the door I saw Allan Clarke … I couldn't believe it, I nearly shouted out loud – here was this great star sitting drinking tea in an ordinary café, and being ignored by everyone. We sat down nearby. I felt ill, I thought I was going to be sick, my stomach churned so much. I wanted desperately to talk to him but didn't know how to. In the end my wife could stand it no longer and we got up together and went over. I said: 'Mr Clarke, sorry to bother you but may I have your autograph?' He looked up and said: 'Of course' … He wrote: 'Thanks, Allan Clarke' … then we thanked him and sat down, and he carried on as if nothing had happened!
>
> (Vermorel and Vermorel 1985: 122–3)

In these accounts, the barrier between ordinary world and media world is quite palpable. No doubt many individual emotions were triggered by these meetings, but we also see reproduced the regular boundary between ordinary and media worlds that underlies the media's ritual space as whole.

Not that boundary reproduction is all that goes on at such sites of media pilgrimage. A wide range of experiences may be triggered by such visits (cf. Couldry 2000a: part 2) and the *meaning* of that boundary will be different if the media site has been discovered (and in a sense therefore recreated as a narrative object) by the fans themselves, as when fans track down unmarked places that were once a filming location (see Hills 2002: 147–9, on the pursuit of *X-Files* sites in Vancouver).

It is time now to look at behaviour at media pilgrimage sites in more detail.

MEDIA PILGRIMAGES AND RITUAL PRACTICE

Any particular media pilgrimage site will contain multiple conflicting discourses, just like religious pilgrimage sites (Eade and Sallnow 1991). That in itself does not tell us much, since, as noted earlier, it is not enough to read sites as texts; we must get beneath their surface to the processes through which they are produced as meaningful sites. We have already begun to do this across the media landscape as a whole, but an actual media pilgrimage site should tell us something particular; not 'truths' about the social 'centre' (we have already deconstructed that idea), but certainly evidence of how certain types of ritualisation are enacted there. We can analyse this internalisation of ritual norms as a type of embodied practical mastery (in Bourdieu's sense; cf. Chapter 3). Potentially, this is a very large subject, so we can hardly be exhaustive, but let us at least examine what clues media pilgrimage sites provide about this process.

Parcelling out

There is what Lévi-Strauss called 'parcelling out':[12] the marking out, as significant, of differences in ritual space. The differences may themselves be minor, but the process of differentiation helps to confirm the category differences in which the ritual itself is based. Media locations are rife with the marking of such minor differences. Going to see a place 'in the media' is, after all, from the outset an act of comparison (comparing the actual location with what you saw on the media) and much that I observed at Granada Studios Tour, Manchester, involved confirming the significance of such seemingly minor differences. Together these small acts of comparison confirmed the special significance of the media world, as opposed to the 'ordinary world'. Here is the comment of Julie, one visitor to the outdoor set of the soap *Coronation Street* whom I interviewed in her home:

> I tell you one thing that I have never noticed, that I did notice, that there's an alleyway. You've got the Rover's Return and then there's the alleyway and *then* there's the houses. Now I never noticed that before until I went to the Street ... that was another thing that amazed me.
>
> (quoted in Couldry 2000a: 86)

Julie was not the only visitor to remark on this difference between the set as seen on television and the actual set.

I found a similar process at work when I visited NBC Studios Tour in New York in April 2000. Much of the tour was quite mundane (videos of old programmes, long corridors, explanations of special effects); indeed, everyone seemed to be taking it as routine. So I was not ready for the gasps which my touring party let out when they entered the studio for the *Rosie O'Donnell Show* (a popular talk show with a celebrity host and frequent celebrity guests). People talked quickly: they wanted to know *exactly* where 'Rosie' sits, where her band sits, and how the impression of a larger space is created for television.

We can give this (and similar actions) a very bland explanation, of course: people just like the show and therefore find the set interesting. But 'gasps' signal a little more than interest. Studio sites are, after all, the place where the latent hierarchy of media space (latent, because it is despatialised in the process of broadcasting) becomes manifest. True, there is always a fascination to witnessing how 'presence' is manufactured, but television studios represent not just any illusion of presence; they show us the mechanisms through which *society imagines it sees itself.* They are one site where the myth of the mediated centre is produced. And, of course, they are real places, so that visiting them seems to confirm as natural the symbolic hierarchy whose terms they embody.

The meaning of such precise differentiations (or 'parcelling out' as Lévi-Strauss called it) is clear: it confirms in the form of a practical mastery the significance of the difference between media and ordinary locations. The skill lies in monitoring the precise configuration of the 'extraordinary' (media) location, when seen in its 'ordinary' state without cameras (Couldry 2000a: 84–5; cf. Smith 1987: 109–10).

Not all forms of ritual mastery are equal

At this point, however, we must emphasise a major difference from religious ritual. Unlike religious ritual, which is usually enacted against a complex background of explicit and shared beliefs, media rituals are not played out in an even, consensual space. The ritual space of the media is crossed by other forces, which, although they originate in the very same inequalities of symbolic power, distort the apparent significance of the ritual actions of particular actors. We know those forces well from the recent literature on fans, and particularly the discrimination (reported by many researchers) that television fans experience, because of their low status in social hierarchies of taste.[13] Usually this discrimination is read purely as a contest over taste, but it is tied also to the organisation of the media's ritual space and its hierarchical division of people and things 'in' the media over those which are not. This helps to make sense of why ritual acts of 'pilgrimage'carried out by a *media* person are treated with respect by the media, but carried out by a non-media person are mocked.

Here, first, is an account (from a British tabloid newspaper) by Mark Pearson, a fan of the 1960s and 1970s BBC situation comedy *Steptoe and Son*. His hobby is tracking down the locations used for filming the programme:

> So far, I've found almost 90 per cent of the locations. The rest don't exist any more. When I find one I tend to go back about 15 times just to reassure myself that it's the right place. I like to look at it from all angles and try to work out where Harry [the lead character] stood as the scene was shot. Then I take photographs and write an article about it for the [Steptoe and Son Appreciation] Society's quarterly newsletter, The Totting Times – 'totting' means salvaging items from refuse, which is what the Steptoes did. I get letters of congratulation and that makes me feel close to a little band of about 300 people who share my interest.
>
> (quoted in *The Daily Mirror* (The Look supplement), 18 April 1998: 5)[14]

Mark Pearson's account is framed by the newspaper with three others under the headline 'ADDICTED', with the byline: 'Mary Keenan meets four fanatics who admit they put their quest for telly trivia before friends and even their family'.

Contrast that with an account from the celebrity magazine *OK* of television presenter Gail Porter's visit to Tunisia to the locations for *The Phantom Menace* (Lucasfilms 1999). The film had its UK release around that time and Porter had been flown out by the magazine for a photo-shoot with her mother, with a tie-in competition for readers to win a holiday seeing the locations. Porter's desire to stand on the film location – which, as with the *Steptoe* sets, had no traces left of the actual filming process – was treated reverentially, and in colour:

> Gail flew out to Tunisia to visit the fantastic settings of the movie. 'It was certainly the experience of a lifetime,' she says. 'There I was, standing on the steps of the fortified granaries in Medenine, which feature in the film, with my arms wide open pretending I was Darth Vader and saying, "I am your father."'
>
> Gail spent four days travelling by jeep from the Mediterranean coastal resort of Hammanet through the desert and back to the capital, Tunis, for a short flight home. What may sound like a gruelling journey – a lot of the driving was off-road – was all part of the excitement for the intrepid Gail ... she will always remember

> the hotel that was on the site of Luke's house from the original [*Star Wars*] movie. 'I was just blown away to see that. I could just picture the crew there.'
>
> (*OK* magazine (vol. 170), 16 July 1999: 31, 36)

Here the headline was: 'ON THE SET OF THE NEW "STAR WARS" FILM GAIL PORTER THE TV STAR GOES ON SAFARI IN TUNISIA TO TRACK DOWN THE LOCATIONS WHICH WERE USED IN "THE PHANTOM MENACE"'. So the closeness of 'ordinary people' to media sites seems strange, even 'mad', whereas the closeness of media people to media sites seems right, indeed 'natural'. This precisely duplicates the category difference between media people/locations and non-media people/locations that underlies the ritual space of the media.

There may also be cases where, having recognised the specialness of the pilgrimage site and the meaning of visiting it, visitors affirm its boundaries (and categorical distinctions) more explicitly. The media pilgrimage works, in other words, as 'a rite of institution' (in Bourdieu's sense; see Chapter 3) that confirms the legitimacy of the divisions that underlie the ritual. So, to pick one of many examples, one visitor to Granada Studios Tour, John (whom we last saw queuing outside a BBC studio), hesitated at the door of one house on the set of *Coronation Street*, not wanting to enter (you couldn't anyway), but wanting to emphasise his moment at the boundary between ordinary reality and media reality: 'I actually felt privileged just to turn the knob and try to get in [to the Rover's] ... No, no, it was just brilliant to be photographed outside it' (quoted in Couldry 2000a: 111).

Nor is it just a matter of affirming ritual boundaries in the present at the pilgrimage site; action taken during the visit will allow you retrospectively to confirm your encounter with that boundary when you get home (remember Morinis' insistence that the study of pilgrimage must include the experience of returning home). Hence I found many examples of people phoning, or posting cards, from the *Coronation Street* set, so as to have retrospective evidence that they had entered a media location (Couldry 2000a: 77).

Speaking for the world

In addition – although this is a point more relevant to media sites with a news connotation – there may be another, more subtle, way of affirming the media site's status. This involves claiming, or acting out, the *representative* significance of the site, and therefore of anything you say there. It is after all a mark of ritual action that it has a 'higher' level of significance: media pilgrimage sites do so because somehow they participate in the media's representational power. For example, these comments from American women who visited US mourning sites in the days after Diana's death:

> I came for the boys, I want to show them that we loved their mother and that they have our prayers …
>
> (quoted in Haney and Davis 1999: 235)

> I just wanted to show my respect for the Princess and to show my gratitude for all that she has done for us …
>
> (quoted in Haney and Davis 1999: 235)

> I'm here to show the royal family that even if they did treat her shabby, *the world* loved her.
>
> (quoted in Haney and Davis 1999: 235, my emphasis)

No doubt media discourses have influenced the form of such statements (cf. Chapter 4), but that does not undermine my wider point, that a whole landscape of discourse (of which the media are part) naturalises the idea that media sites are places where you can go and speak in a representative fashion, because they stand in for 'the centre', that is, the place where 'the world' can be imagined as coming together to speak. We will in Chapter 7 apply this idea to talk shows. This 'representative' feature of pilgrimage and other media sites is transferable. Many sites can stand in for that 'centre', precisely because it is not a real place but a constructed one, hence, the countless satellite sites for laying flowers, leaving messages of remembrance, and so on in the days after Diana's death (Walter 1999). What we have here is a strictly materialist version of Durkheim's principle of 'the contagion of the sacred' (1995: 224). The quality attached to the superior term in a categorical difference spreads easily from one object and site to another. So here the quality of standing in for the media 'centre' and/or society's 'centre' is transferable to a whole range of objects, precisely because substitutability is *part of* the myth of the mediated centre. The 'centre', as a mythical 'centre', can be divided as many times as you like.

Note again that, in foregrounding ritualisation, we are nowhere claiming that anything religious is at work. Instead, the argument is about the patterning of actions in space, where central narratives of various sorts are at stake. Media pilgrimage points are compelling because they are the far points of a system of production, distribution and consumption which both separates us from, and draws us towards, its points of power. They represent not the postmodern dissolution of space and place, but 'the compulsion of proximity' (Boden and Molotch 1994). All contemporary systems of power, because of their stretched-out nature, need the myth that *somewhere* is a place where a token of that power can be accessed; this incidentally is the dimension that generalised accounts of flows in the 'information society' tend to miss. Far from being trivial, media pilgrimage points are the real places where the myth of the mediated centre comes to ground, their overdetermination being no more paradoxical than the overdetermination of media power itself.

MEDIA 'PILGRIMAGE' ON THE WORLD WIDE WEB

There is an important question which we must now confront: is the complex, and apparently dispersed, space of the Internet leading towards the dispersal of society's concentrations of symbolic power? If so, then, following the logic of my argument, the force of the media's ritual categories and media rituals themselves should in the longer term wither away, undermining the concept of media pilgrimage among many others. But is this what we see happening? In one way, the Web has transformed the space of fandom (Baym 1999; Pullen 2000) by providing an infinite and at least partly unregulated space in which those across the world with quite specific interests can exchange information, ideas, and images with others unreachable before the Internet. Has this transformation of the discursive space of fandom affected the ritual space in which fans intervene and in terms of which their fandom is partly structured? I will consider this question only in relation to issues of pilgrimage, although of course it is wider than that.

Not surprisingly, the Web has encouraged the proliferation of stories about 'pilgrimages' by fans to sites of all kinds. A Google search (for 'pilgrimage+fans') yielded 18,000 or so references: from my limited trawl, the majority relate to sport and music, not television.[15] In principle, however, the Web should greatly increase the opportunities at least for the exchange of media pilgrimage stories. First, there are Websites which record stories of visits to media sites. These may, or may not, play with the metaphor of pilgrimage, or other quasi-religious language.[16] Here, for example, is part of a report of a 'Pilgrim's Progress' to *X-Files* sites in Vancouver by 'Rev Ma/Sister Nancy (no clever sig)':

> Suddenly I was off to the Holy Land where they film *The X-Files* to stay with ten people who, at the time, I had never met, knowing only that they were *X-F* fans and *shared a soft spot for our Saint* [i.e. Scully]. So with that introduction, I present to you (as promised) a record of *our pilgrimage to the Holy City*.[17]

There follow details of the group's attempt to track down *X-Files* sites, playing with the idea that they are staying in the room where Scully 'lived'. Second, the Web may be a useful medium in which to plan media pilgrimages, as in a site calling for people to take part in 'The *Blair Witch* Camping Trip', which provides basic details of the planned trip and the email address of the organisers.[18]

Most interestingly, the format of Websites, coupled with the increasing ability of people to send not just text but image files, is leading to *virtual pilgrimage sites* where information and relics of people's pilgrimages to actual media sites can be posted for others to consult. It did not take me long to discover a number of sites of this type associated with various pilgrimage targets: the singer KD Lang, the set of *Coronation Street*, the Australian television version of the 1970s UK gameshow *It's a Knockout*, and the UK television series *The Sandbaggers* (Granada TV 1978–80).[19]

The last site provides an example of 'parcelling out' online (see Plate 5.2), with an image of a scene from the programme juxtaposed with photographs of some Australian fans at the same site (which they call 'Burnside's Bridge', after a programme character). They had tracked down the site along the Thames in London. Others

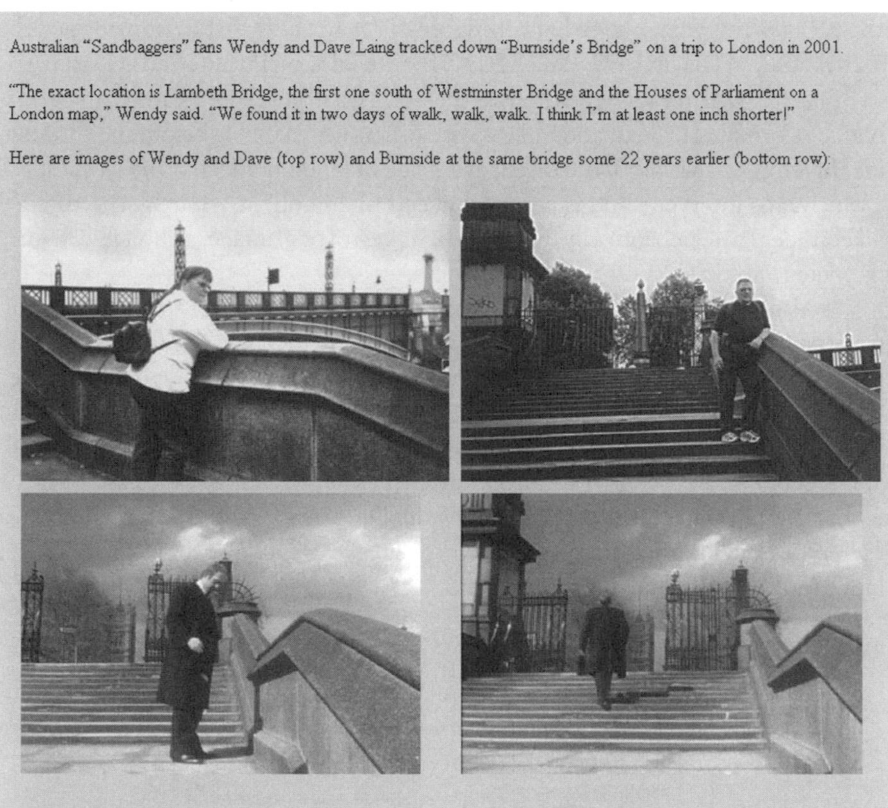

Australian "Sandbaggers" fans Wendy and Dave Laing tracked down "Burnside's Bridge" on a trip to London in 2001.

"The exact location is Lambeth Bridge, the first one south of Westminster Bridge and the Houses of Parliament on a London map," Wendy said. "We found it in two days of walk, walk, walk. I think I'm at least one inch shorter!"

Here are images of Wendy and Dave (top row) and Burnside at the same bridge some 22 years earlier (bottom row):

Wendy added, "The trees seen at the back beyond the gate, on the other side of the road that crosses the bridge (Horseferry Road—Lambeth Bridge—Lambeth Road) are in Victoria Tower Gardens, which run along the banks of the Thames but which were closed to the public when we walked past on Millbank Road (which merges into the Embankment)."

If you make a pilgrimage to Burnside's Bridge and would like to have a photo of your visit featured on the Ops Room, just send it to Roy@opsroom.org. Please also send e-mail if you know of any other "Sandbaggers" locations worth a visit!

Plate 5.2 Pages from *The Sandbaggers* pilgrimage Website

are encouraged to add to the virtual pilgrimage site: 'If you make a pilgrimage to Burnside's Bridge and would like to have a photo of your visit featured on the Ops room, just send it into [address]. Please also send your email if you know of any other 'Sandbaggers' locations worth a visit!'

The Web then is a space well-suited for leaving traces of past media pilgrimages and inciting further ones. It is interesting that these sites, while they may call themselves loosely 'pilgrimage sites', perhaps to attract searchers like myself, seem not to claim that the Website substitutes for the media location. On the contrary, the replication of images of actual pilgrimage sites on the Web reinforces precisely their original significance. The Web, to recall Durkheim once more, is a space where the 'contagion' of the media-related 'sacred' is likely to spread, not die.

CONCLUSION: REVERSE PILGRIMAGES

In this chapter, I have used the term 'media pilgrimages' as precisely as possible, for such a slippery term, to map how certain places have special, ritual significance, and are therefore worthy of pilgrimage. This is connected with the wider myth of the mediated centre. I have concentrated on media pilgrimages relevant to the practice of media *consumers*. It might be interesting to review the same questions from the point of view of media producers' practice, as John Caldwell's (forthcoming, 2003) fascinating recent work suggests: Caldwell writes about ritualised practice at the conventions where writers pitch stories to television and film producers. In either case, the myth of the mediated centre is always a construction; its imaginary spatial form conflicts potentially with the very different form that the media's spatial operations actually take.

I want to end this chapter with a reminder of that potential conflict. We should think not only about media pilgrimages, but their opposite: moments when, instead of us journeying to places in the media, the power gradients that structure the media landscape suddenly pass close to us. For example, when you are involved in a news event and the media are there, putting a camera in your face, paparazzi camped in your front garden. This is a *reverse pilgrimage*: instead of a journey which dramatises the media's ritual hierarchies in a special distant place, those hierarchies are now being enacted *on you*. You are pressed to speak 'to the world', whether you want to or not; you are marked out, most likely, as an 'ordinary person', whether you accept that categorisation or not.

These situations are common in the sense that there are countless examples every day, although, because of the media's regular overaccessing of certain sources, most of us have not experienced it. We know very little about how people deal with such experiences, although there is a growing awareness that they can be traumatic. In any complete analysis of the media process – as a social and ethical form – these encounters should receive more attention.

Sometimes an intended pilgrimage mutates into its reverse, as in this fragment from Mike Davis' wonderful book *City of Quartz* (1990) where he describes a conversation in the Mojave Desert outside Los Angeles with two migrant workers from El Salvador:

> I asked them what they thought about Los Angeles ... One of my new Llano compañeros said that LA already was everywhere. They had watched it every night in San Salvador, in endless dubbed reruns of *I Love Lucy* and *Starsky and Hutch*, a city where everyone was young and rich and drove new cars and saw themselves on television. After ten thousand daydreams like this, he had deserted the Salvadorean Army and hitchhiked two thousand five hundred miles to Tijuana. A year later he was standing at the corner of Alvarado and Seventh Streets ... along with all the rest of yearning, hardworking Central America. No one like him was rich or drove a new car ... More importantly no one like him was on television; they were all invisible.
>
> His friend laughed. 'If you were on TV you would just get deported anyway ...' He argued it was better to stay out in the open weather whenever possible, preferably here in the desert, away from the center.
>
> (Davis 1990: 12–14)

What is so moving, and exceptional, about this passage is the connections it brings out between two worlds that absolutely should *not* be connected, or at least not if they are to retain their hold over us: the ritual space of the media and the coexisting (but, as we shall see in Chapter 6, connected) space of *surveillance*, operated by the state and other agencies. The workers imagined a journey to Los Angeles, taking them to a 'higher' place, somewhere where people 'saw themselves on television'. But it was the grid of surveillance space that they encountered in the real places occupying that supposed ritual centre. 'Being there' meant being tracked on a bank of security screens. Sensing the danger, and perhaps the reversal, they took the best course and left.

This story, dramatised though it is, is not a false dramatisation. It points exactly to the connection – normally obscured – between media rituals and a part of the media system with very different connotations, where mediation works closely with government. It is, not surprisingly, an unusual story, since, if such stories were commonplace, they might corrode our belief in the media's symbolic authority. Sometimes, however, the interfaces between media ritual and other forms of power cannot be avoided, and then must be controlled, as we see in the next chapter.

Chapter 6

Live 'reality' and the future of surveillance

> Nothing has changed, except, you are there ...
>
> (US TV guide describing reality footage, quoted in Nichols 1994: 54)

The most fundamental claim which the media can make is the claim to present 'reality', not any reality but the 'social reality' which we share as members of a society. Since the media's ritual status is based on that underlying claim, 'reality' (and the related term 'liveness', whose significance depends, as we shall see, on the access to 'reality' that it guarantees) are important ritual categories, which deserve a chapter to themselves.

Claims to present 'reality' are multiplying in contemporary societies, but in two ways whose connectedness is not generally discussed: first, the countless new forms of 'reality TV' which have received attention in media studies; and second, the claims to present 'reality' associated with the real-time information processing by government and other systems. This connection, as noted at the end of Chapter 5, risks contaminating the media's ritual status (which requires media to seem to be 'above' power), and is therefore rarely stated explicitly, although, as we shall see, in programmes such as *Crimewatch UK*, the separation between the two has to be carefully managed. It is against this background that I recall Jane Feuer's (1983) argument that 'liveness' is an ideology, an argument that can easily be extended to the claim to present 'reality'. Its full significance, however, only emerges when we examine the media's authority in a wider sociological context, which addresses contemporary forms of governmentality and the media's entanglement with the mediation process otherwise known as 'surveillance'.[1]

LIVENESS AS A RITUAL CATEGORY

It has always mattered that television is 'live' in some sense. I want to argue that 'liveness', however obvious its meaning might appear at different historical moments, is a socially constructed term, tied not just to television's but to the media's claim to present social 'reality'. This is why in an age of 'reality TV' but relatively little live-performance footage, 'liveness' goes on mattering, even if its reference points have changed.[2]

In television's early days, when all programmes were performances broadcast live, television was entirely a 'live' medium. As the proportion of live performance declined, the term 'live' switched its reference. The issue is how exactly this reference point changed. Jerome Bourdon (2000) argues that the reference point of 'liveness' shifted to those parts of television which broadcast *real* events as they happen, excluding fictional programmes. While the term is often used this way (to suggest a direct representation of reality), this is not the only way that connection to reality works. A contradiction in Bourdon's discussion brings this out. He imagines a family watching a programme: what would defeat their belief that what they were watching was live? The only decisive factor, he argues, would be if they found out that a child had in fact taped the programme weeks ago and was showing it to them as if it were being broadcast for the first time now (2000: 535–6). If so, the decisive criterion of liveness is not the factuality of what is transmitted, but *the fact of live transmission itself* (cf. Ellis, J 2000: 31).

Bourdon is, however, right to suggest that factuality has something to do with the wider significance of 'liveness', but the connection is more indirect than he supposes. Live transmission (of *anything*, whether a real event or a fictional narrative) guarantees that someone in the transmitting media institution *could* interrupt it at any time and make an immediate connection to real events. What is special, then, about live transmission is the *potential* connection it guarantees with real events, rather than an actual portrayal of real events themselves. Or at least, I would argue, this is how liveness is now generally constructed. Joshua Meyrowitz expressed the point succinctly some years ago:

> There is a big difference between listening to a cassette tape while driving in a car and listening to a radio station, in that the cassette player cuts you off from the outside world, while the radio station ties you into it. Even with a local radio station, you are 'in range' of any news about national and world events.
>
> (Meyrowitz 1985: 90)[3]

The connection with the media's ritual status is clear: liveness – that is, live transmission –[4] guarantees a potential connection to our shared social realities as they are happening. Because of this connection, 'liveness' can properly be called a ritual category which contributes to the ritual space of the media.

Once we express the issue in these broader terms, it is clear that liveness can apply to a range of media, not just television. Paradigmatically it is television that is live, simply because until recently television has provided the greatest amount of live information. But not only are other media themselves transmitted 'live' in their own right – radio obviously, but also the press (as in the idea of the 'exclusive' report, or the just-printed edition on breaking news) – but those other media contribute to our sense that 'the media' connects us to our shared and current reality (the ritual meaning of 'liveness').

Indeed, the range of media which can contribute to the media's liveness, or claim 'liveness' for themselves, goes on expanding. So considerable claims were made for the epochal significance of the *Big Brother* Website during its first UK series in 2000:

> Yesterday ... the internet ... offered a shared viewing experience of an unusually powerful kind. In offices – or at least hi-tech, media-friendly offices – employees crouched around computer screens to watch the live web transmission from the [*Big Brother*] house [to watch Nick Bateman's expulsion] ... People in homes and offices unable to receive broadcasts on the internet kept up with developments in the house through email and the mobile phone ... As a significant moment of television, the [discovery of Nick's deception] is most remarkable for being the first of the medium's highspots not actually to have occurred ['live'] on TV.
>
> (*The Guardian* (G2 section), 18 August 2000: 2)

It is less clear whether most actual viewers considered the *Big Brother*'s Website so important (Hill 2002). Liveness in any case continues expanding into new media spaces, for instance text messaging, as in this piece on the marketing strategies of UK mobile phone companies during the build-up to the second UK *Big Brother* series and other game-based reality TV series (*Survivor, Castaway*):

> Ultimately the [enhanced] SMS services may all boil down to the quality of the content and characters, not forgetting the giddy excitement that can be generated from a message telling *Big Brother* obsessives of two housemates being in bed together – 'live on the internet now'.
>
> (*The Guardian* (Online section), 24 May 2001: 5)

Clearly, it is the sense of 'liveness' that advertisers seek to capitalise upon when they suggest that it is 'exciting' to get standardised promotional material on your private phone (a strange idea!), but this 'liveness' would be meaningless if *many* media did not contribute to our sense of 'live' connection (in the broad sense of the term). It is not therefore a question of one technology superseding another as the main carrier of 'liveness'; and there is no reason why television cannot retain its own claims to liveness alongside those of other media. Television's 'liveness' continues to mutate into new forms: for example, NBC's striking (although unsuccessful) claim to present 'plausibly live' coverage of the far-away Australian Olympics at later times favourable to its advertising revenue.[5]

This puts into perspective repeated claims that liveness is declining in its overall importance for television. 'Liveness' – as the guarantee of *actual connectibility* to events of central social significance – is not declining, only finding new forms. These forms are surprisingly flexible. In the early 1990s, it was claimed that video timeshifting would kill liveness and with it a crucial element in television's symbolic authority (Cubitt 1991). But liveness – access to current shared realities – can easily accommodate your watching a video recording of a soap or football game broadcast earlier that evening. Indeed it can be argued that liveness in the broad sense is *enhanced* by video, since video extends the time-slot within which we can share the significance of the transmitted-live event. More recently, an interesting argument has been made by John Caldwell (1996: 27–31) that live transmission content has declined as the proportion of multichannel television's output dedicated to reruns of old films or television classics (for example, Sky Gold) increases. Certainly if this archiving function became television's main form, liveness would have lost its ritual force, but this has not happened yet. Indeed, as Bourdon points out, most cable and satellite packages contain at least one live news-only channel (2000: 552). 'Liveness' (and the related notion of 'prime time') is still what cable and satellite television providers market as their distinctive value: think of the Discovery channel's slogans 'Watch with the World' and 'Global Primetime Premiere'.[6] Even in the multichannel environment, the territory of liveness goes on being reclaimed.

Whatever exact form 'liveness' takes, what matters about ideological critiques of liveness, and is missed by non-ideological accounts (however much they tell us about the detailed narrative construction of 'liveness'),[7] is their link from the categories of media discourse to wider relations of power. Brunsdon and Morley's (1978) deconstruction of 'the myth of "the nation, now"' targeted precisely the mythical idea of 'liveness' (in the form of the BBC live current affairs programme *Nationwide*). Liveness is not a natural category but a constructed term. It could not have its broad impact if it rested on simple technological fact. Its significance rests on a whole chain of ideas, which are worth unpacking:

1 that we gain access through liveness to something of broader significance, worth getting access to now, not later;

2 that the 'we' who gain live access is not random, but a representative social group;
3 that the media (not some other social mechanism) is the privileged means for obtaining that access.

'Liveness' is therefore a social construction, an object of belief (Bourdon 2000: 535), but since it is generally treated as 'natural', it is also ideological. 'Liveness' naturalises the idea that, through the media, we achieve a shared attention to the realities that matter for us as a society. This is the idea of the media as social frame,[8] the myth of the mediated centre. It is because of this underlying idea (suggesting society as a common space focused around a shared 'ritual' centre) that watching something 'live' makes the difference it does: otherwise why should we care that others are watching the same image as us, and (more or less) when we are? Critics of liveness were right to sense that something major is at stake in the term.

The most well-known such critic was Jane Feuer in her classic paper 'The Ideology of Liveness' (1983) (cf. Rath 1988). By 'ideology' Feuer meant the ideology of television as an institution, not a political ideology. She was writing against the background of the wider critique of television and film's 'realism' in early film studies (Heath and Skirrow 1977) and in Marxist and Marxist-influenced analysis (Brunsdon and Morley 1978; Dalhgren 1981; Golding 1981; Hall 1977). One problem with that tradition of ideological critique of entertainment was how to link the 'content' of the television or film text to any wider social process that could be called ideological.[9] At the end of her article, Feuer raises, but cannot answer, this question:

> It seems to me that the ideology of 'liveness' must surely act to suppress contradictions. However, I have difficulty theorizing the level at which this occurs ... we remain caught in a hermeneutic circle. Is the spectator positioned by the [television] apparatus, or is the spectator relatively free, and if so, what permits us to analyze texts [as ideological] in the way I have done above, and why is *Good Morning, America* so successful? Or perhaps this manner of articulating the problem is itself the problem?
>
> (Feuer 1983: 20–1)

The way out of this 'hermeneutic circle' – whose apparent closure perhaps discouraged further ideological critiques of the media after the early 1980s –[10] is the concept of ritualisation developed in Chapter 3. The level at which 'liveness suppresses contradictions' (as Feuer puts it) is through its operations as a ritual category; it naturalises a hierarchical notion that media are our privileged connection to a social centre. But this does not require us to believe in a specific ideological content;

it works instead through patterns of thought and action across the wider space of *ritualisation* where the category of liveness is sustained.

Fundamental questions not just of ritualisation, but also of social trust (Silverstone 1994), are in play when we analyse the media's role in our shared 'reality'. This helps to explain why 'liveness' was seen by producers right at the beginning of television history as a category of overriding importance:

> I believe viewers would rather see an actual scene of rush hour at Oxford Circus directly transmitted to them than the latest in film musicals costing £100,000.
>
> (Gerald Cock, producer, quoted in Corner 1999b: 25)

> The primary function of television is to transmit pictures as they are being made ... the basic attraction is not so much the subject matter it presents but the realisation that whatever is happening is happening at the time.
>
> (John Smith, television producer, quoted in Corner 1999b: 25)

Liveness was of course especially notable in the early days of television when its possibility of image transmission was so new. But that only makes it more striking that liveness still matters to us now, when we take the technology of television (and many other forms of instantaneous telecommunication) for granted.

There are broader sociological issues here: 'liveness' is part of a wider coordination of society in time (Scannell 1989).[11] As Jerome Bourdon has recently argued:

> Liveness should be interpreted as a development within media history as a whole. Media technological history at least partly reflects an effort to reduce the gap between events and media users. It is intimately linked to a history of communication as speed ... there has been a mutual adjustment between technique, society and economy. From the top, major institutions have all used news, then radio and television liveness, to create a connection between the masses and events ... At the base, the need to connect oneself, with others, to the world's events, is central to the development of the modern nation.
>
> (Bourdon 2000: 551–2)

But once we make that broader sociological connection, we must not forget the operations of power that are at work within it. It is *not neutral* in terms of power that society is coordinated through one particular medium – the operations of one particular set of institutional practices and resources – rather than another. This cannot be emphasised enough. The point of seeing 'liveness' as not just a sociological but a ritual category is to maintain some distance from the myth of the mediated centre.

Apparently innocent histories of technology and society may obscure this. Why this matters will, I hope, become even clearer by the end of the chapter.

MEDIATED REALITY

If the 'liveness' that media claim to offer is a ritual category (that is, a category which helps to naturalise the media's ritual status as a frame on the social world), then so too is the media's 'reality'. A quotation from the US television anchorman who commentated on the Apollo moon touchdown in 1969 brings out the link:

> [television's] real value is to make people participants in ongoing experiences. Real life is vastly more exciting than synthetic life, and this is real-life drama with audience participation.
>
> (quoted in Marvin 1999: 159)

The overall nature and volume of televised output has changed markedly since then, and not just in the United States; in addition, television now competes with a number of other access points to 'reality', including the World Wide Web. John Ellis (2000) in a lucid analysis has described a shift from an era of television 'scarcity' through television 'availability' to, increasingly, television 'plenty'. Certainly, in the age of channel, and indeed medium, multiplication, television has increasingly relied both on specific claims to present 'live' special events (especially sport) and on generating new forms of exclusivity in entertainment genres such as 'reality television'. There is a link, then, between the changing forms of the media's ritual categories and changes in media institutions and markets.

'Reality–television'

The invention of 'reality–television' (part of its impact is that we no longer see it *as* a paradox) is a fascinating story which has received increasing attention from media scholars.[12] In line with my broader aims, I want here to look quite selectively, not at the whole genre but at what a ritual analysis can contribute to the analysis of that genre's main features. I will be concentrating on programmes which use documentary formats more or less,[13] rather than talk shows, another development involving media's claims to present 'reality' (see Chapter 7).

The claim of television to present 'reality', as with 'liveness', is a thread throughout its history, and is part of a wider 'ideology of naturalism' (Collins 1986); within that consistent history, however, it is clear that different definitions of 'reality' have been fought over at different times. If we take the well-documented case of 1950s and 1960s Britain, a central contest was over the appearance of 'real people' on radio and television, and documentary and news programmes were a key site of conflict. John Corner in a helpful survey of this period quotes Denis Mitchell, a leading documentary maker, on the shift from requiring interviewees to read from a prepared script written on the basis of unrecorded conversations to allowing them to speak *direct* to camera or microphone:

> It was an astonishing success mainly because for the first time ever [people] were listening to real people saying whatever came into their minds …
>
> (quoted in Corner 1991: 50)

How exactly to present 'reality' shifted, as broadcasting changed from a 'social' to a 'sociable' medium (Corner 1991: 57; cf. Scannell 1989). This was, however, no straightforward democratisation, as the increasing appearance of 'ordinary people' was inseparable both from the ideological implications of that category and also the editing to which their testimony was subject (Corner 1996: 167–8). From the 1970s onwards, further developments in video recording and the improved quality of film shot with cheap hand-held cameras changed the technological fundamentals, but did not automatically allow 'ordinary people' to be more widely represented in television's picture of the social world. There was a complex interplay between technological possibilities, the 'cultural' recognition of those possibilities in mainstream television, and subsequent economics, as the 'ordinary person' became in the 1990s a valued television commodity (Corner 1996: 173; see, for the US case, Caldwell 1996). Throughout this period, factual 'reality' developed in parallel with soap operas' (or *telenovelas*') establishment as a fixed part of the television schedule in Britain, the US, Latin America and elsewhere. In fiction, although in a different form, the claim of broadcasting to present social 'reality' also became more insistent, for example by addressing current social issues in soap opera plots (Geraghty 1995). It became commonplace in Britain for fictional narratives to generate news headlines and in *telenovelas* the process went one stage further when real public figures appeared in fictional narratives (see Hamburger 2000, for a case from 1990s Brazil).

Contemporary 'reality TV' therefore emerges from a wider history of how media claim to connect us with a shared social reality. Recent 'reality television' has taken a variety of forms. Perhaps the most useful definition has been provided by Richard Kilborn (1994: 423). Reality TV, he argues, involves (abbreviating his description slightly):

1 recording 'on the wing' of events in lives of individuals or groups; or
2 the attempt to simulate real-life events through dramatised reconstruction; or
3 the incorporation of (1) and (2) in edited form in a packaged programme.

This definition captures well the formal flexibility of 'reality TV':[14] from the mid-1990s explosion of 'docusoaps' in Britain (such series as BBC's *Hotel* and *Driving School*) to programmes based on reconstructions of action by the emergency services (in the UK, BBC's *Emergency 999*, and, in the US, CBS's *Rescue 911* and Fox's *Cops*), to package programmes which run together clips from surveillance footage provided by the emergency services or camcorder footage shot by viewers (in the UK, ITV's *Police, Camera, Action* and *You Have Been Framed*). Other writers, however, have argued for a narrower definition. For example, Jon Dovey (2000: 71) argues that the term should be focused on programmes where the claim to represent 'reality' is at its clearest, as in footage or reconstructions sourced from the emergency services, with no obvious element of fictionality: I will come back later to one example of this narrower definition, *Crimewatch UK*. But to narrow the definition is not necessarily helpful; it obscures the flexibility inherent to 'reality TV' seen as a *ritual* category (cf. above on 'liveness'). The claim to offer special access to 'reality' is quite compatible with many formats, including elements of fictional packaging (the 'docusoap') or humorous commentary (ITV's *Candid Camera*). None of these moves far from the basic claim that television is a *privileged* access point to unmediated reality, even as (to a greater or lesser extent) it can be seen mediating that reality.

To recognise this inherent flexibility is important if (extending Kilborn's definition just a little) we are to take account of this genre's most recent development in the UK, US and Europe: the television game-show (or 'game-doc') which, while at one level explicitly a game between contestants, at another level claims to show us the 'reality' of the participants as people playing a game. The best known example, shown in different formats across the world, is *Big Brother*, but there are many others (including *Survivor* and *Castaway*). The 'game-doc', notwithstanding its clear artificiality, is just as capable of making claims to present 'reality' as the 'docusoap' (which combines documentary claims with an entertainment format of, say, six weekly half-hour shows) or programmes which package surveillance footage. All come within a broad definition of 'reality TV', being broadcasting that claims to present 'reality' but falls between the recognised and clearly separate zones of pure news/documentary and pure fiction.[15] Indeed it is this in-between status of 'reality TV' that is most interesting for a ritual analysis. It is the ambiguity of 'reality TV' programmes with regard to their factual or fictional status that reproduces most effectively television's ritualised claims to present 'reality' (see below).

What underlies the multiplication, indeed the fragmentation, of broadcasting's reality claim in the 1980s and 1990s is difficult to say. Certain factors were clearly important. There were economic imperatives at work: in an era of increasing financial pressures upon, and competition between, programme schedulers, reality TV offered cheap and (more or less) reliable ways of gaining significant audiences (Kilborn 1994; Dovey 2000). As financial pressures on programme makers increased in the mid- to late 1990s, the costs of maintaining a convincing 'reality' component also increased, particularly against the background of press campaigns about some fakery in documentaries and talk shows (Dover 2001; Dovey 2000: chapter 1; Winston 2000). In Britain, at least, an older historical strand of public service-centred 'access television' dating back to the 1960s took on a new revived form in the *Video Diary* and *Video Nation* series (Humm 1998; Kilborn 1998). Can we go further? One possibility, as Garry Whannel has argued,[16] is that in the 1990s television had to adapt, at least in those countries where it was introduced early, for the first time to a population the vast majority of whom had grown up with television and therefore had a high degree of interpretative sophistication. This would account, in part, for the increasing reflexivity in programmes, such as the docusoap, about the fact/fiction boundary, but would not explain the persistence of television's claim to present reality, even against the apparent decline of formal documentary and news outputs. Similarly Umberto Eco's much-cited argument for a shift in the 1980s from 'palaeo-TV' which 'talked about the external world' to 'neo-TV' which 'talks about itself' (Eco 1992: 247), while capturing a broad shift in television's tone and rhetoric of address (its increasingly informal sociability), cannot account for the paradox that television's 'reality' claim *intensified* in the 1990s, although in more varied and more relaxed formats and with a greater emphasis on 'ordinary people's' place in its discourse. Crucial, perhaps, was not the increased competition within the television sector to which Eco points, but the increased competition from other media which television faced in the past decade. Television increasingly must argue for its social centrality against competing claims from film, music production and the Internet. Fortunately, my argument does not depend on resolving this question.

It is time now to clarify what I mean when I say that the 'reality' to which the media claims to give us access involves a *ritual* categorisation.

The ritual dimension of reality TV

In developing my argument about the ritual dimensions of the genre of reality TV, I want to focus on three themes: first, and most obviously, on the claim to reality itself, and then, more briefly, on issues of democratisation and interactivity.

Unmediated reality

The claim to reality, like liveness, is a construction: the very idea of 'reality television', let alone 'unmediated television', is a direct contradiction. And yet it is this contradiction that has always been at the root of television's claim to present the real; 'reality TV' just presents this paradox in starker form. Although the technological possibilities of the camcorder predated by some time its wide usage in broadcasting both in the UK and the US (Caldwell 1996), once it did become more widespread, television producers believed that the hand-held camcorder, since it was flexible enough for non-media people to use, might 'refresh' the medium (UK producer Jeremy Gibson, quoted in Dovey 1993: 168). Certainly camcorder footage (juddery, moving in a confined space) has in some respects become a sign of 'direct' access to 'the real' within television and elsewhere,[17] although not perhaps '*the* privileged form of "TV truth-telling"' (*contra* Dovey 2000: 55). There are many other such truth-signs: for example, those moments in a talk show (see Chapter 7) when 'real' emotions seem to emerge, or the helicopter zoom shot in US breaking news footage focusing in on the details of a street scene. Indeed the camcorder's significance is complicated by its prevalence as a medium for domestic use (Dovey 2000: 65). Does this 'reframe' television's camcorder usage, implying that the tools of truth-telling are now in your hands or mine, not just those of reporters or programme-makers? To argue that would be to ignore precisely the *ritual* form which television supplies for camcorder footage (cf. Caldwell 1996: 283). My camcorder footage of a private event *might* be shown on television but it would remain in status just private footage, unless packaged (for example) as special 'insights' into family life, that is, unless brought within the rhetorical discourse of television more generally. Television's claim to 'reality' is not just a feature of this or that video clip, but a much broader construction.

Indeed it can be argued that the foregrounding of television's representational mechanism, in the form of the shaking, hand-held camcorder, serves not to problematise or weaken television's wider 'reality' claim, but to naturalise it further, familiarising us with television's everyday operations in the 'real world'. We *could* argue the opposite – that reality TV makes the media process more transparent – but do television's presentations of the real matter less now than those of individuals, or other media? As yet, there is no evidence that people are spending their time and money watching or distributing their own camcorder footage in preference to televisions' camcorder-based offerings! If so, television's underlying 'metadiscourse' (in Steve Neale's useful phrase) is unlikely to have changed either.[18]

Nor should we believe the classic postmodern argument that the more television images are produced, the less the claim to 'the real' matters (Baudrillard 1983). Kevin Robins (1995a: 139–40) develops this argument by claiming that in the era of 'karaoke television', participation in the media process seems to matter more than the contents of television's representational space; if so, we might see 'reality TV' as a response to people's desire for connection with others, what Michel Maffesoli (1996a: 12) has called 'the aesthetic of the "we"'. While this captures, perhaps, one reason why television's 'reality' rhetoric insists so much on interactivity (see below), it flies in the face of the intensification of television's claims to be our access point to reality (cf. Dovey 2000: 90).

Sometimes the 'reality' claim depends on liveness itself: for example, the category of news story common in the US of 'breaking news', when live footage of a developing event is shown open-endedly with minimal commentary and editing (for example, live footage of O.J. Simpson's station wagon chased by police cars along a Los Angeles freeway). Here, as Bondebjerg notes (1996: 37), television's live presence seemed to justify its claim to present the 'real' life behind the celebrity facade; it was inconceivable, surely, that this celebrity was acting at this moment. In such cases of *live* 'reality', the framing provided by the television station may be limited to a logo and a short caption, but it is quite enough to assert the ritual status of the television frame. Indeed this is arguably television's ritual frame in its purest form; 'frame' and nothing more.[19]

Having it both ways?

Television's 'reality' claim, however, does not require purity; it can subsist in the most messy and ambiguous of forms, as in recent game-docs. What exactly is at stake in programmes such as *Big Brother* (Channel 4), entering its third year in the UK as I write? The only starting point for analysing the significance of what happens in the *Big Brother* house is that television cameras are present. Hence the importance of television's presentation *underplaying* that fact, and insisting that, in all their details, those events are not directed for media presentation. As Ruth Wrigley, producer of the first series of *Big Brother* in the UK ('BBUK1'), put it: 'I wanted it to look live and exciting ... this was not meant to be a polished drama. *We were filming it for real*, and it was a virtue of the programme that viewers understood that' (quoted in Ritchie 2000: 11, my emphasis). Filming it 'for real', paradoxically, meant ensuring that audiences did *not* believe that what they watched was just ten people performing for the camera. The psychological discourse of the programme (with regular comments from its 'resident' psychologists) had a role here, since it reproduced the idea (hardly uncontestable in itself!) that submitting ten people to national surveillance for two months would reveal their human 'reality'. As Wrigley put it, 'nobody can keep up an act all the time in front of the cameras – the world was going to see them [the participants] as they really were' (quoted in Ritchie 2000: 26). As the programme's official book put it without irony, BBUK1 'should not just show what went on in the house, but should explore human relationships with the help of top psychologists' (Ritchie 2000: 9).

The ambiguity of *Big Brother* – as both artificial entertainment and human 'reality' – is found elsewhere in game-doc discourse. So in a projected BBC variation on the *Survivor* format to be called *Serious Jungle*, children will be placed in the Borneo jungle for two weeks for our entertainment, but the explicit aim once again is to reveal more of human 'reality':

> Because it is focused on children, the viewers will see very clear and honest reactions to their experiences ...
>
> (Marshall Corwin, producer, quoted in *The Observer*, 31 March 2002: 15)

> For the first time, these children will be trying relationships that are no longer about what music they like or what trainers they wear. They will change so much during these few weeks that going home to their old friends could be quite difficult for them.
>
> (Alex Paterson, trip organiser, quoted in *The Observer*, 31 March 2002: 15)

It is found even in studio-based shows such as *Popstars* (ITV), whose producer Nigel Lythgow claimed that 'it's not just an entertainment show, it's a real life drama'.[20] The 'ordinariness' of these shows' contestants has a double significance in ritual terms: first, their 'ordinariness' confirms the 'reality' of what is shown (once their early performance strategies have, we assume, been stripped away by the continuous presence of the camera) and, second, that 'ordinariness' is the status from which the contestants compete to escape into another ritually distinct category, celebrity (Couldry 2002). The apparent contradiction between these two senses of 'ordinariness' – 'ordinary' as 'real' and 'ordinary' as 'merely ordinary' – is only apparent, because both contribute to the wider sense that the media (whether as the frame through which we see 'social reality', or as the space into which we want to go to escape our 'ordinary reality') is special, higher than the 'ordinary world'. Indeed the first claim adds spice to the all too familiar second. This ambiguity – between fiction and reality, pure entertainment and social learning – is precisely the type of ambiguity that Roland Barthes called the 'turnstile effect' (1972) and argued was characteristic of myth more generally.

A complication here is evidence for increasing scepticism, at some level, with television's reality claims. Annette Hill's current audience research suggests (Hill 2002) that, as the output of 1990s UK docusoaps grew, so too did scepticism about their presentations of reality. Clearly the idea that audiences are unaware of the constructedness of these programmes (cf. for talk shows, Gamson 1998: 87, 90; Grindstaff 1997: 187) is as outdated as the loose claims about audience voyeurism or credulity in early discussion of reality TV.[21] But such sophistication is a long way from a *general* loss of belief in television's *underlying* status as our privileged access point to social 'reality'. We would not expect audiences to be unambiguous on such questions, but should remember that the claim to 'reality', like the claim to 'liveness', is, because constructed, inherently transferable. Declining belief in the reality-claims of one television genre is compatible with increasing belief in the reality-claims of another – indeed that was how docusoaps themselves came to prominence and the more ambiguously truthful game-doc represents already an implied response to that emerging scepticism.

Democratisation?

My emphasis on the ritual dimension of reality TV is not designed to rule out the possibility that television is becoming, for example in Britain, more democratic as a medium. Certainly, cutting across television's continued insistence on its privileged access to the real is an increasing emphasis in contemporary television on presenting the apparently unedited individual voice. This is seen (at one end of the spectrum) in the BBC's *Video Diaries* (Kilborn 1998; Dovey 2000: 121–2) where individuals tell their story partly, at least, on their own terms, to (at the other end) the game-doc such as *Big Brother* where contestants, by living before the cameras, are interpreted as 'revealing' more and more private 'realities' about themselves, as the game develops. Within a neo-Durkheimian framework, this is precisely how we might be tempted to interpret these programmes.

If we are to move beyond the prima facie claim of 'democratisation', however, we need to think, first, about the material constraints that lie behind the appearance of these 'ordinary people'; even in the most favourable case (the *Video Diaries*), the ratio of applicants to those appearing on television was *fifty* to one (Keighron 1993: 25), which raises unanswerable questions about the criteria on which selection was based. We also need to think about whether the inequalities underlying the ritual space of the media are reproduced, or challenged, in such programmes and the discourse that surrounds them. Take these two comments quoted by Dovey: 'I need to see myself on television to know that I really exist' (2000: 126); or 'a tattooed biker summed it up when she said that she wanted to show that people like her were "just like everyone else"' (2000: 131). The first quotation is from an account by the producers of a *Video Diary*, and the second is from a newspaper article observing the production of a *Video Nation* programme. The status of television as a space where people can make representative claims (see also Chapter 5) is here *affirmed*, not undermined, although the fact these comments were selected by those working in the media, and then highlighted by a media researcher, may itself be significant! What appears like a simple opening up of the practical boundaries around television's enclosed space may involve a reinforcement of the *symbolic* boundaries which give those practical restrictions meaning. If so, we have an analogy to Bourdieu's analysis of the rite of passage as a 'rite of institution' (see Chapter 3): more than the individual's moment of transition and revelation, what matters are the boundaries which make the rite significant in the first place, that is, in reality TV, the categorical difference between 'media people' and 'ordinary people'. It is this underlying boundary that these programmes reinforce.

Interactivity

Potentially, however, the Web's interactive dimension makes a fundamental difference to the democratic potential of reality TV. 'Interactivity', like all the other terms we have discussed, is not something natural, but constructed.

We are all familiar with countless examples of 'interactivity' in computer-mediated interaction, from interactive exhibits in museums to the constrained interactivity of most service providers' automated phone lines. In relation to society's central media, however, the stakes around the term are much higher. 'Interactivity' here means showing, in performance, the otherwise merely assumed connection between medium and representative social group. The World Wide Web provides many tokens of 'interactivity': the Website hit counter, the one-step connection between information source and 'chatroom'. The online 'chatroom', whatever is said there, is a form whereby the 'liveness', and implicitly the 'reality', of a broadcast can be confirmed by linking it to 'real people's' talk, as the programme happens. A good example from music radio is the chatroom BBC Radio 1 introduced for the Webcast of some live DJ sessions in 1999: as DJ Dave Pearce said, 'it seems like the most instant way to interact with the audience'.[22] We touched earlier on another link between 'interactivity' and media's 'reality' claims in the case of the Website dedicated to *Big Brother*, which enabled you to view through particular cameras around the house (assuming you could download the images at a reasonable speed). Other forms are developing, such as interactive Web-based soap operas (for example, www.onlinecaroline.com, which appeared in April 2000) or the fictional Webcam site (*Big Brother*-style) attached to a BBC drama about a dot-com start-up, *Attachments*.[23]

One underlying sociological question, however, is why interactivity is thought to matter so much. Interactivity here represents a further development of the media's ritual categories of 'reality' and liveness', whether in the form of 'live chat', or 'live interaction' with an interface that stands in for the media system itself. Clearly any bigger claims for such interactivity's representative significance are highly rhetorical, but it is just such rhetorical claims of social connection that need *ritual* enforcement. Reality TV and its 'interactive' offshoots may only give 'sensations of togetherness' (Nichols 1994: 56), but that is hardly trivial in today's vast social spaces. This is one area where, I would argue, we can expect the media's ritual space to go on generating new forms, categories, and boundaries for some time to come.

MEDIA RITUALS AND THE EVERYDAY REALITY OF SURVEILLANCE

I want, however, to pursue a different line to the future. So far in this book I have analysed the ritual forms and practices which help make the media's authority seem natural. I have not discussed specifically how that authority connects with wider forms of power. Indeed one impact of the ritualisation of the media's operations is precisely to make such connections difficult to see. However, the genre of reality

TV, and particularly the sub-genre which deals with state activities, for example the emergency services, raises those questions unavoidably; it is here that the myth of the mediated centre gets quite directly entangled with power structures beyond the media.

A few writers have suggested a general connection between the media's authority to represent the world and society's strategies of control, particularly control exercised through images (surveillance).[24] But these have not been developed in media studies in any detail, excepting John Fiske's important point that the lack of democratic access to the means of making images is true equally of everyday media and of everyday surveillance (1996: 217–18). So it is to work within the sociology of crime that we must turn for insight into the direct *practical* link between police work and media professionals' work in generating information about, and definitions of, 'crime'. Police, of course, use media technologies themselves: for example, the video in the interview room (Ericson and Haggerty 1997: 140), and surveillance camera evidence. Norris and Armstrong make the connection powerfully in their book on the 'maximum surveillance society':

> Television is a visual medium. CCTV is a visual medium. They were made for each other. Add one other ingredient, crime, and you have the perfect marriage. A marriage that can blur the distinction between entertainment and news, between society and spectacle and between voyeurism and current affairs.
>
> (Norris and Armstrong 1999: 69)

This marriage is not a temporary blip in media history. The connection between mediation (as studied by media studies) and more general systems of information control goes back to the foundations of modern societies. Both are part of what Giddens called the control of society's 'authoritative resources' (1984: 262). Indeed mediation in this double sense is a necessary precondition of the large-scale modern state: 'modern societies have been "electronic societies" longer than we ordinarily imagine and 'information societies' since their inception' (Giddens 1985: 178). If we consider the types of authority on which both police and media rely, both are forms of symbolic authority, that is, particular, privileged ways of categorising the world,[25] although the media's authority is of a broader, more all-encompassing sort. Little wonder, then, that media at times pool their symbolic resources with those of the police (Wilson 2000: chapter 1). These connections emerge particularly in reality TV that deals with crime.

A number of countries have programmes which help the police track down crime through televised appeals: for example, in Germany ZDF's *Aktenzeichen XY … ungelost*, in France TFI's *Témoin N° 1*, and in the UK BBC's *Crimewatch UK*.[26] I will concentrate on the British programme, which has run continuously with large audiences since 1984. In *Crimewatch UK*, the myth of the centre has, necessarily, a double reference, to the authority of both media and state; the interesting question is how the relationship between the two types of authority is managed.

Sometimes the overlap between the two seems close, as in this quotation (note also the emphasis on 'liveness' as the frame within which audience and police can interact):

> Good evening, and welcome to the programme where once a month instead of just hearing about crimes you can perhaps actually do something about them. As always we're live, and the detectives here from all around the country are waiting for your call.
>
> (*Crimewatch UK*, 10 November 1987, quoted in Schlesinger *et al.* 1992: 46)

But *Crimewatch UK* has always drawn on the media's own symbolic authority in a specific way, through its meticulous reconstructions of real crimes. Television's claim to represent reality is embodied in those who make these reconstructions, as reflected in these comments from a book written by the programme's first two presenters:

> [A]ll those who take part in a *Crimewatch* reconstruction remark on the responsibility they feel when filming.
>
> (Ross and Cook 1987: 59)

> It wasn't a pleasant experience but I'd go through it again. I was so proud that as a result of our filming that day, those men were caught. I really felt I had a part in that.
>
> (Remy Lister, actress, quoted in Ross and Cook 1987: 61)

So far, however, the media's representational authority, and all the ritual weight it carries, would appear to be at the service of a quite independent state authority.

At other times wider claims are made for the programme's authority, as in this passage about how crimes are selected for reconstruction:

> Any crime that has hit the headlines is followed up for, though the motive may not be entirely virtuous, we believe it is in the programme's interests to be *seen at the centre of the crime detection business.*
>
> (Ross and Cook 1987: 29, my emphasis)

The logic is, on the face of it, strange: why should following crimes which have media attention elsewhere help *the programme* 'be seen at the centre' of crime detection? But, as a reinforcement of 'the media's' ritual role as central social access point, this practice makes perfect sense. The programme's aim is to affirm *the media* (represented by *Crimewatch UK*) as being at the centre of society's crime detection. Sometimes the authority claimed for the programme is virtually a form of surveillance itself, but operating through the enhanced medium of national terrestrial television:

> *Crimewatch* has a big advantage over [local] cable TV. The audience is so huge we can reach a third of the population at one go and, what is more, our viewers are spread across the whole of the United Kingdom. For detectives that is even more important than it may sound, for police forces are still organised on a local basis. In an age when a crook can zip from one end of the country to another in a matter of hours, the police are fairly rigidly confined to their own patches. *Crimewatch* cuts across all that.
>
> (Ross and Cook 1987: 110).

The friendly relationship which people have with TV presenters, they suggest, enables the programme's police officers to gather information which, as 'ordinary' police officers, they could not (1987: 115). The symbolic authority of television is seen as enhancing the power of the police, two operations of 'the centre' working in harness.

Managing the relations between state and media authority became even more complex when the programme and the police started to rely increasingly on surveillance images. We are here right at the boundary between two very different forms of media-based authority: the media's ritual authority to represent the world for us, and state and corporate authority to collect images for law enforcement. Put another way, and drawing on the work of the leading authority on surveillance, David Lyon, we are at the boundary between the organisational process of 'social orchestration' and the 'cultural commitment', indeed desire, fulfilled by television, for 'omniperception' (Lyon 2001: 30, 124–5). It might seem strange to describe the media's ritual power as a desire for 'omniperception', but only because this 'illegitimately' redescribes the media's workings from the perspective of government.

Is there, then, a risk that in the long run the media's ritual authority will be eroded, or at least contaminated, through this proximity to state power? Certainly the contact zone between these two forms of representational authority needs to be carefully managed. The problem is not one of automatic contamination, as with the taboos on contact between the 'sacred' and 'profane' in Durkheim's theory of religion. Both media authority and state authority are part of society's 'centre' and so there is no automatic problem in their power overlapping by being exercised on the same people. They need not therefore be kept absolutely separate, even if their original mixing in *Crimewatch UK* at first seemed daring (Schlesinger and Tumber 1994: 254–6). The problem of contamination arises at the level of means, not ends. Both programme and police increasingly rely on surveillance footage. But if the media's claim to present 'reality' (including through its re-presentation of surveillance footage) were to merge entirely with the surveillant eye of the state or its agents, then the 'social reality' to which the media provides access could no longer be 'naturally' consensual; it would have become in principle contestable, for example through the legal process, and directly linked to the authority of the state. Television's authority cannot however appear directly contestable in this way, if it is to retain a *ritual* (that is, fully naturalised) force.

One way round this risk is to keep these two competing interests in the surveillance process (state's and media's) as separate as possible: in *Crimewatch UK* programmes I analysed, for example, from the mid-1990s (1996, 1997) this separation broadly held, with the programme being generally divided into two distinct parts, television crime reconstructions (occasionally supplemented by brief surveillance footage) and other sequences where clips of surveillance footage were played for identification purposes, sometimes with a uniformed police officer commenting. A recent programme (6 March 2002), however, presented something very different, along with a markedly higher reliance on surveillance footage throughout the programme. Here, the narrative authorities of television reconstruction and contemporaneous surveillance footage were not kept separate, but interwoven in tight narrative sequences, often enhanced by the voice (with or without silhouetted face) *of the actual victim*, reflecting on the moment recorded by the surveillance footage; the practice is not unique to *Crimewatch*, it is also found used by *Emergency 999*.[27] Reconstruction and surveillance footage here become an intertextual unity, with the first reflecting back on the second: the victim's voice against the criminal's image.[28] The treatment of one particular clip from the March 2002 programme illustrates what I mean. It was introduced by a familiar *Crimewatch* comment about the value of CCTV cameras ('If you needed *proof* of how effective CCTV cameras *can* be, have a look at these clips' – my emphasis).[29] We then saw CCTV footage of a man accosting a woman (her face disguised) in a queue at a bank. Over the footage, we hear the voice of the victim, an elderly lady, speaking nervously about the incident. Her testimony ended with these words: 'He's taken away something that I had. I'm not the same person any more.' On the screen, the *Crimewatch* logo is superimposed with the phone number of the studio, and underneath the woman's voice is a version of the *Crimewatch* theme tune playing softly, to provide continuity with the next surveillance clip.

Here the authority of the media gaze is protected from being contaminated by the surveillant gaze, not through separation of their two streams of representation but by separating the *objects* at or for whom the two gazes are directed. There is an implied separation between the media (representing reality for 'us') and the state (scanning social space for 'others'). The voice of the victim puts beyond doubt where our identification should be directed: *away* from the object of surveillance. What we rarely, if ever, get on *Crimewatch UK* is a sense that we, as reflexive subjects, might be represented on the surveillance screen. Adapting the TV guide quoted at the head of this chapter, 'nothing has changed and you are *not* there'.

The media's presentation of the social world and the state's surveillance of that same space retain their necessary separation only through the additional assumption that those under surveillance are not 'us', and are unlikely to be 'us'. It is not accidental that the surveillance process is rarely shown on television from the perspective of *its* 'victims', who may, and probably[30] are, innocent.[31] It helps, of course, that *Crimewatch UK* usually avoids 'political' crimes that might be socially contested (for example, the taking of cannabis!), but it is the underlying shift on which we must focus: the stability of the media's ritual authority has begun to depend on assumptions which are not consensual, let alone 'natural', and which divide up the social world into incompatible zones of victims and criminals.

How then does the general practice of 'reality TV' contribute to the naturalisation of surveillance in everyday life? That this is one role of *Crimewatch UK* is clear: the programme is obviously not the place to look to for debate about surveillance's implications for the future of public, and indeed private, space. When the victim's voice is played over surveillance footage of the very moment of attack, the argument for CCTV could hardly be personalised further, but this form of rhetoric is not innocent; it is part of a wider *individualisation* of society's crime discourse whose corollary may be the decline of more broadly social discourses about crime and its management (Garland 2001: 200–1).

It is striking also that the link between surveillance and mediation (in the conventional media studies sense) is increasingly being reinforced in the opposite direction for the purposes of entertainment. *Big Brother* is only the latest in a line of reality TV programmes, going back to MTV's *Real World* (Andrejevic, forthcoming, 2003), which have accustomed us to the idea that it is meaningful and acceptable for cameras on occasion to monitor our *private*, not public, behaviour for an ultimate public audience. If we juxtapose the reality claims of *Big Brother* with the socialised process of surveillance which it and other similar programmes represent, the logic is disturbing: that the most reliable, and perhaps even socially significant, 'reality' is that 'revealed' under surveillance, provided those seen are not yet, or no longer, aware of the camera's presence. If, as Maurice Bloch (1989) argued, the ritualisation of power is a means to make us forget its operations, then we should watch carefully the developing ritual forms associated with the media's (and the state's) claims to present to us the social world.

Chapter 7

Mediated self-disclosure

Before and after the Internet

> It's as if in order to speak to those close to them, it's necessary [for them] to pass through TV.
>
> (French talk-show producer, quoted in Mehl 1996: 57)

> A bright agent could do worse than checking out the following five top blogs . . .
>
> (*The Guardian* (Online section), 23 August 2001: 4)

The recent growth in the media's, and particularly television's, role as a site for self-disclosure is striking, and has attracted considerable attention.[1] It is hardly surprising that some have seen here a throwback to 'the medieval confessional box' (Hartley 1992: 3). But, as one of the more subtle commentators on this phenomenon has argued, television's confessional 'ritual' is quite different from earlier forms (White 1992a). The relationship between the meanings of self-disclosure and technological form is a subtle one, and goes on changing with the expanded possibilities for self-disclosure on the Internet. In this chapter, I want to explore not so much the details of what individuals disclose through the media, but rather what a ritual analysis adds to our understanding of these forms of self-disclosure. A ritual analysis can cut across and help us rethink from a broader sociological perspective, otherwise indecisive debates about the meaning of self-disclosure in our supposedly 'confessional culture'.

In general terms, it might not seem surprising that more and more people are revealing private aspects of themselves through the media. After all, recent decades have seen a great increase in the mediation of everyday life, making us all familiar with acting for, and with, distant others through mediation (Livingstone and Lunt

1994: 5; Slevin 2000: 159; Thompson 1995: 100–9, 175): why should not the implied boundaries around private space be altered, not only to import new information from the public sphere (cf. Meyrowitz 1985), but also to let out once private information into the public arena? There is a broader sociological dimension to this: as our everyday experience becomes more and more separated, or 'sequestrated', from that of others, so the media are an increasingly important site where experience can be shared (Giddens 1991: 156): why then should private experience not be 'looped through' zones of public disclosure? We return to this argument later, but first let me emphasise a basic point: that the price of this expansion of the boundaries of private experience, if indeed that is what is occurring, is to submit that experience to the power dimensions of the mediation process. The symbolic landscape in which people's mediated confessions occur is neither simple nor even.

We will look at a broad range of mediated self-disclosure: although I will concentrate on television talk shows where guests are required directly or indirectly to reveal something important about their private lives, I will also touch on cases apparently more under the control of those making the disclosures (such as the *Video Diaries* and *Video Nation* series in the UK in the 1990s), and the increasing disclosure of self through text and images on the Internet (even this is to select drastically: much recent 'reality TV' discussed in Chapter 6 can be read from this angle). My approach, as before, will concentrate on questions of form rather than content. Too close a focus on the contents of individual disclosures risks missing the most puzzling aspect of this whole landscape: its links to the ritually reinforced notion that the media provide a 'central' space where it makes sense to disclose publicly aspects of one's life that one might not otherwise disclose *to anyone*.

A formal analysis cuts across another important dimension of self-disclosure: the general spread of the languages of confession and therapy (White 1992a; Mehl 1996), and its implications for family and social relations. But the advantage of this structural approach is to show what is wrong with two other approaches that collapse prematurely the power relations involved in mediated self-disclosure: first, an unqualified celebration of such self-disclosure as the irruption of popular voices into a previously closed public domain (Shattuc 1994, on early 1990s US talk shows), a position that is often close to a functionalist reading of the public spaces created by these shows; and second, an outright dismissal of mediated self-disclosure as a collapse into narcissism of earlier spaces of public representation; Robins (1995a: 139–43) comes close to this in his discussion of 'karaoke TV'. Mediated self-disclosure is a great deal more ambiguous than that, as some excellent recent studies of talk-show production (Dovey 2000; Gamson 1998; Grindstaff 1997) demonstrate. The underlying reason for this ambiguity is that, like any media ritual, self-disclosure takes place within the uneven power relations of the media's ritual space.

DOING STRANGE THINGS ON TELEVISION

When I first saw an episode of the *Jerry Springer Show*, with couples rowing violently before a studio audience, I was physically shaken; I sweated and had goosebumps. A naive reaction, perhaps, linked to the fact that personally I don't like arguments! But Aristotle's diagnosis of tragedy in terms of 'pity and terror' also came to mind.

This might open up an obvious link to ritual analysis, since Aristotle's theory of catharsis has founded countless analyses of ancient Greek tragedy as a ritual process. As Roger Silverstone (1999: 101) has argued, we can interpret the talk show text as a symbolic reversal (cf. Babcock 1978) through which community is reaffirmed by the display and eventual closing off of its opposite, conflict. But there are two paradoxes in that approach. First, as just mentioned, there is not necessarily much ritual intensity for viewers of such shows (watching for the hundredth time); at best, such shows would represent routine, liminoid forms, which carry intensity because of their *rhetorical* claims to restore community. In any case, this reading of the talk-show text takes no account of the process undergone by the performers: where is the evidence that *to them* the process is one of symbolic reversal, let alone community reaffirmation or (Shattuc 1994: 169; 1999: 223) 'carnivalesque'? There is, of course, another, very different ritual interpretation to be considered, whose implications are not affirmative: the ritual of degradation and excommunication (Carey 1998). In any case, we need to start not from textual analysis but from the social process that self-disclosure on such programmes constitutes.

The social process of self-disclosure

What is at stake in these shows from the perspective of the performers, both those who disclose themselves and those who engineer the disclosure? This is surely very different from what is at stake in watching such programmes, although talk show performers may be largely drawn from regular viewers of the genre.[2] If so, it can hardly be that the performers are unaware of the constraints under which they will perform in the talk-show format. Any distance between viewers and performers is not a simple matter of knowledge; indeed it may only be to *some* viewers that talk shows seem strange, in which case the genre divides its potential audience as much as it unites it.

Something more fundamental is at stake in these programmes, I suggest, which relates to the very basis of media ritual. Before we examine this in specifically ritual terms, let us recall a point made by Joshua Meyrowitz in his still highly insightful analysis of television's consequences for social interaction. We will not grasp the workings of television within the social process, he argues, if we look on the level of this or that person's behaviour in particular locations; instead it is 'the overall *pattern* of situated behaviours' (Meyrowitz 1985: 42) – what particular people do here and what they do *not* do there – that we need to understand. If so, then a clue to the significance of talk shows may be the way participation in them is patterned: what is the relation between those likely to perform on the *Jerry Springer Show* and those not, and how is this relation linked to wider relations of power, and particularly media power?

This requires a more subtle analysis of the social process constituted by talk shows. Two recent analyses of talk shows have advanced our understanding greatly. First, Joshua Gamson's (1998) book on the performance of non-mainstream sexual identities on US talk shows makes clear that, whatever the artificiality and indeed cruelty of such shows and their attendant ethical problems, part of their significance *for performers* derives from the opportunity they represent, against the odds, to be seen before a public audience, to emerge from invisibility:

> It is *because* of the cynical use of 'real people', people who feel themselves to be disrespected and in need of television affirmation, that talk shows have offered the most diverse visibility for gay and lesbian and bisexual and transgender people available [in public life].
>
> (Gamson 1998: 215, original emphasis)

This is not to say that these television performances simply extend a democratic public space, since there is just as much scope through talk shows for the expansion of bigotry as of mutual understanding (Gamson 1998: 14, 221). The point rather is that the programmes make sense for many performers, as a means of dealing with their normal invisibility: they are 'struggles of visibility' (Thompson 1995: 247), even if they are also 'visibility traps' (Gamson 1998: 212). 'Visibility' here means being seen before the social gaze, before a representative sample of the social body.

Laura Grindstaff in an article on the production of daytime talk shows develops this point even more forcibly. The viewer/performer gap already noted is not, she argues, accidental since it is based in the social differentials that make these shows' performers distinctive. Although she does not offer a detailed analysis of their social backgrounds, Grindstaff convincingly argues that the attractiveness of appearing in a talk show is connected with certain people's usual exclusion from media representation. The fact that certain people appear on talk shows:

> is less a comment on how trashy they are and more a comment on the exclusivity of television and the limited access of ordinary people to media representation.
>
> (Grindstaff 1997: 193).

'Ordinariness', of course, is not here a natural term (cf. Chapter 2), but directly linked to the social power that television constitutes, and how people are positioned in relation to that power: 'appearing on national television is not part of the daily routine for ordinary people. This is in part what makes them ordinary' (Grindstaff 1997: 177). Which is why you wouldn't expect a *celebrity* to appear on the show and reveal themselves; the power and draw of the programme is linked directly to wider questions of symbolic inequality (Grindstaff 1997: 195–6).

Strategies of excess?

I want to emphasise here that I am not discounting the importance of other readings of the contemporary talk show (or indeed self-disclosure on the Web) which foreground the *uses* to which these spaces are put to challenge important forms of cultural and social exclusion (for example, linked to differences in sexuality). It is certainly arguable that, in particular circumstances of oppression, the fact of getting your story on television outweighs *any* power dimensions of the medium through which you must speak. I take seriously therefore the argument (Shattuc 1999) that, by permitting sexual stories that many regarded as 'bad taste', the 1990s US talk show was a space of therapeutic significance for many participants and often also a space of highly knowing performance that was well aware of the limits of the form.

These issues, in themselves, raise questions of power. Within the context of particular cultural and social conflicts (recalling de Certeau's (1984) fundamental distinction between 'strategies' and 'tactics'), these actions could be seen as strategic interventions, even if, relative to the talk show form, they were merely 'tactical'. My priority, however, in this book are the questions of power condensed within the ritual *forms* of mediated self-disclosure themselves, rather than these broader cultural negotiations.[3]

SELF-DISCLOSURE ZONES: A RITUAL ANALYSIS

Part of the overall meaning of performing on talk shows (notwithstanding the obvious range of detailed reasons people give, which are linked to what precisely they reveal of themselves) is as a crossing over into a rarely entered space of public attention. As Priest (1996: 81) puts it, to appear on a talk show is 'to "step in" to a valued place'. Priest's insight is not new but draws on the argument long ago of Lazarsfeld and Merton (1969) that appearing on television confers status, the status Neal Gabler (2000: 187) calls 'the sanctification of the television camera'. We begin to see here the ritual basis of self-disclosure on television. The talk show is *assumed* to be a valued place, because it is a media place:[4] to enter it is to cross a *category* boundary from 'ordinary world' to 'media world', marked by the phrase 'to step into'. These assumptions are only a naturalised version of the real inequalities in society's distribution of its symbolic resources. But it is precisely such wider resonances that characterise media rituals: media rituals, such as the talk-show form, are formal means of making media power seem natural.

The talk show, then, involves a ritual boundary: it is a 'rite of institution' (Bourdieu 1991) which *confirms* that boundary's significance and legitimacy, regardless of whether it effects any permanent transformation of the performer. The 'ordinary person' may, or may not, succeed in getting recategorised as a 'media person' by appearing on a talk show: generally not. But this does not alter the ritual status of the process, which is based on the unequal status of the 'ordinary person' and the media institution. We cannot understand talk shows unless we see that people perform on them under pressures that are connected to the meaning the media/ordinary boundary has to them, which relates, in turn, to their own variable symbolic capital.

Let's now make this point more specific by showing how in a number of ways the media/ordinary boundary is negotiated and reaffirmed in talk shows. It is necessary here to cut across the obvious variety within the talk show genre: from the studio discussion format focused on the meeting between 'ordinary people' describing and debating their experiences with relevant 'experts' (in the UK, BBC's *Kilroy* and ITV's *The Time The Place*), to shows involving more direct personal conflict between friends and family, but with a strong therapeutic element (in the US, *Oprah* and *Joan Rivers*, and, in the UK, *Trisha*), to shows whose main focus is the staged confrontation between guests (*The Jerry Springer Show*).

These programmes, of course, vary in their detailed format and, even within shows with an explicit therapeutic content, there are variations between types of therapeutic discourse (Brunvatne and Tolson 2001). None of these differences, however, affect the underlying ritual form in which I am interested: the fact that it *makes sense* to enter television space, before a studio and domestic audience, to reveal aspects of one's life that until then were largely, if not entirely, private. The principles that emerge are crucial for understanding why and how the media in general can function as a site for important self-disclosures.

The ritual of confession

First, there is a range of evidence that the media/ordinary boundary is present, and reworked in various ways, where people disclose themselves in the media. If those who appear in the shows and also watch them are 'ordinary people who watch television' (interviewee, quoted in Livingstone and Lunt 1994: 119), they have a very different status from those who host or produce the shows. We should not underestimate the fierceness with which this division may be underlined in talk-show production. Take this striking comment from a producer:

> I'm always amazed – *amazed* – that these little people from their trailer parks don't totally freak out [i.e. go silent] on camera more often.
>
> (quoted in Grindstaff 1997: 179, original emphasis)

Gamson also reports how television producers may be well aware of the class differential between themselves and the performers (or studio audience):

> It's like you go [as a talk-show guest] from never leaving town – like Houston was the biggest city they ever went to, and some people had never been there – and it's like you're [as a talk-show producer] offering them this vision of grandeur, and [your aim] is to exploit them.
>
> (quoted in Gamson 1998: 83)

In a similar spirit, one producer of a UK television phone-in show casually referred, in conversation with me, to those who spoke on the show as 'pond life'.

A similar sense of boundary emerges, less brutally, in another producer's recollection of the gratitude expressed to him by audience members just for the fact of them *being there* in the studio:

> A lot of people in the studio audience would say, 'Thank you so much. Thank you, this is the first time that like we're going to be seen on TV.'
>
> (quoted in Gamson 1998: 62)

Those who go on shows recognise it as an experience that is 'out of the ordinary' (Syvertsen 2001: 322). More than that, it may be seen by them as an act of *social* significance:

> I felt like I had contributed something to society.
>
> (guest on *Donahue*, quoted in Priest 1996: 74)

> In my down times, and when I think I'm useless . . . I think 'But wait, I've touched these people [i.e. people out in the social world].'
>
> (guest on *Donahue*, quoted in Priest 1996: 74)

The media/ordinary boundary is present also, in a displaced form, in standard notions of how people should perform on such shows. It is a cliché of media discourse noted by a number of writers that, to appear as significant *agents* in the media world, 'ordinary people' have to do 'extraordinary things';[5] they have to be 'over the top'.[6] This is hardly surprising, since the terms 'ordinary' and 'extraordinary' are just another way of expressing the media/ordinary hierarchy. The boundary is just translated into prescriptive terms: if you're 'ordinary', then 'of course' you can't expect to get on the media by 'just' being ordinary, or as another producer quoted by Gamson put it: 'if you behave the way I'm asking, you're more likely to be on TV' (Gamson 1998: 87).

It is hardly surprising, then, that in talk shows, just as in the less intensely performative zone of reality TV, the ritual category of the 'media person' is preserved. This does not require anything as crude, or definitive, as talk show guests becoming, or regarding themselves as, celebrities. It comes out more subtly in performers' sense that they and their story have somehow been validated or certified (cf. Priest 1995: 163; 1996: 74); they 'matter' now because they have been on television. Although the format of talk shows (programmes with a cast that changes each week, and, indeed, before and after the advertising break) militates against any stable form of celebrity for performers, the ritualised boundary that *underlies* celebrity is clearly reinforced. We can reverse Dovey's comment that on reality television 'everyday life has become the stage upon which the new rituals of celebrity are performed' (2000: 104), since the talk show 'stage' is the media's version (more or less artificial) of 'everyday life'. Instead of 'postmodern' television deconstructing the authenticity of the traditional media celebrity (Tolson 1991), the forms of celebrity have become not less, but more, pervasive.

Self-disclosure on talk shows is not, in any case, a *simple* transition from 'ordinary' to 'media' person, because it results from a real, antecedent situation of conflict. Just as important, therefore, as the effect of the media/ordinary boundary on the person disclosing is the effect of the ritual on what is said, its transformation from something merely personal into something special, something representative. It is here that the talk show's status as media ritual shapes the meaning of the act of disclosure, its very *possibility* as a meaningful act for a private person to perform.

The connection, specifically, between ritual and self-disclosure was expressed powerfully, although outside any broader theory of ritual, by Michel Foucault in his analysis of confession in Volume 1 of *The History of Sexuality*:

> The confession is a ritual of discourse in which the speaking subject is also the subject of the statement; it is also *a ritual that unfolds within a power relationship*; for one does not confess without the presence (or virtual presence) of a partner who is not simply the interlocutor but *the authority who requires the confession*, prescribes it and appreciates it, and intervenes in order to judge, punish, forgive, console and reconcile; a ritual in which the truth is corroborated by the obstacles and resistances it has had to surmount in order to be formulated; and finally a ritual in which the expression alone independently of its external consequences, produces intrinsic modifications in the person who articulates it: it exonerates, redeems, and purifies him …
>
> (Foucault 1981a: 61–2, my emphasis)

Mimi White was the first to apply Foucault's insights to television confessionals (1992a: 7–8), but she rightly pointed out that the television form brings very different consequences from a confession before a priest, doctor or psychoanalyst. First, the talk-show audience is multiple: it encompasses those on stage, including the host, the studio audience and the assumed domestic audience. Second, the structures within which confession is acceptable and permitted are different and closely linked with the economic and formal imperatives of the televisual medium. This is undoubtedly true.

Even so, Foucault's analysis goes to the heart of the ritual power of mediated confessions in three respects. First, the confession gains meaning and strength ('is corroborated' in Foucault's words) from the resistance it encounters, that is, from the difficulties that attend it (including the stress of appearing before a large audience, which is assumed also to be a significant audience). Second, as in all ritual, its performance (the act of speaking on television) has a direct transformative effect on the speaker. Third, both these effects are based in a power relationship, that is, they happen because of the significant power *differential* condensed in 'the authority who requires [the] confession'.

Who exactly is this 'authority' in the television talk show? It cannot be the talk-show host as such; she or he generally has celebrity status, but only rarely (Oprah Winfrey is the obvious exception) a broader cultural or personal authority. Nor can it be the studio audience, which is a general group, without any formal expertise. The 'authority who requires the confession' is rather the authority of *television itself*, as the *assumed* representative of the social centre and our access point to social reality. To recall the *Donahue* guest quoted by Priest (1996: 74): 'I felt like I had contributed something *to society* [by speaking on the show].' Talk-show host and studio audience stand in for this assumed ritual authority.

This *representative* dimension of the disclosure space that talk shows provide can be traced in other comments by guests, and in a way that reflects the ritual status of their disclosures. Particularly interesting work has been done here on French talk and reality shows, first by Patrick Ehrenberg, and then in greater empirical depth by Dominique Mehl. Here is a woman speaking on television who had gone on the French programme *Bas Les Masques* (Beneath the Masks) to condemn her estranged mother:

> I've broken a taboo, which is the taboo of silence. She's [the mother] not going to see it. She's strong. But so what? I've spoken. It's over.
>
> (quoted in Mehl 1996: 38)

A few months later Mehl interviewed this same woman and she reflected on that moment of public disclosure:

> I didn't think that I was acting in public. It was an announcement done for me. And that produced a liberating effect. When I saw the programme, I saw myself, me, adult, speaking calmly about mother. I wasn't a girl of three years any more.
>
> (quoted in Mehl 1996: 38)

Note how the act of self-disclosure carried a meaning which was not articulated at the time by the performer: 'it was an announcement done for me'. This is the fundamental aspect of ritual (carrying meanings 'not entirely encoded by the performers') that Rappaport (1999: 24) identified. The effect, especially when confirmed by viewing from the outside (through the frame of the domestic viewer) is transformative, as Foucault insists the ritual of confession is: it 'produces intrinsic modifications in the person who articulates it' (1981a). They are *intrinsic* modifications, because they are based not on the exact details of what is said, but in the power relationship that is the context in which anything is sayable. Whether one speaks before God's representative (the priest) or science's representative (the doctor) or society's representative (television), it is one's belief in the power differential naturalised in the confession form that makes the act of confession possible.

Mehl takes the issue one stage further to an important, although speculative, conclusion: that mediated self-disclosures represent not so much the flouting of boundaries around private life through reckless self-disclosures, but a more subtle transformation: the regular embedding of mediated public performance into individual practices of self-definition. Hence, the (probably self-promoting) statement of the television producer quoted in part at the head of this chapter:

> It's as if, in order to speak to those close to them, it's necessary [for them] to pass through TV. One could say that, in order that these people are reintroduced into the social circuit, they must pass through television … which is their home [*qui est chez eux*].
>
> (quoted in Mehl 1996: 57)

Mehl expresses the point even more boldly in the conclusion to her book:

> The emergence of the intimate onto the public stage doesn't kill off the intimate but reformulates it and changes its boundaries. The mutual flow between exhibition and secrecy doesn't suppress the zones of shadow and silence; it remodels them … intimacy can hardly make sense of itself without publicity … 'Exteriority' is consitutive of interiority/intimacy [*'L'extimité' est constitutive de l'intimité*].
>
> (Mehl 1996: 158, 163)

Whether or not you go this far, depends, in part, on whether you believe that these effects are universal, or limited to particular groups of people. Does the televised confession mean more to those for whom crossing the media/ordinary boundary is more significant? That requires further research, but what is clear is that this boundary's ritual status is intrinsic to the act of mediated self-disclosure.

Producing ritual

The performers are, of course, only one element in the social process of talk shows. There are also the producers. Both Gamson and Grindstaff have analysed the constraints on producing moments of self-disclosure, day in day out, to a regular schedule and a tight budget from unpredictable human 'raw material'. The arbitrariness and artificiality of much of the result is, they both acknowledge, inevitable to some degree (Gamson 1998: 15–17; Grindstaff 1997: 189; cf. Dovey 2000: 11). The producers must produce 'reality': live performance which (given the obvious constructedness of aspects of the performance setting) must not just be 'real', but '*really* real'. The 'really real', as Gamson discusses, is the moment when something 'genuinely' uncontrolled happens in the highly controlled setting of the studio: for example, a fight (Gamson 1998: 91). Indeed the very purpose to which the talk shows' structure is directed is often to increase the likelihood of such *unconstructed* moments, what Grindstaff, borrowing from the parlance of pornographic production, calls the 'money shot': the 'moment of raw emotion' that 'proves' that the whole performance really is real (Grindstaff 1997: 168).[7]

It is the money shot, as something unplannable, that is the token of the 'reality' the talk shows claim to represent. Not all talk shows have a money shot as dramatic as *The Jerry Springer Show*, but they all focus on moments of confrontation. What form of 'reality' is favoured? Above all, the outbreak of extreme *emotion*, although it could, in theory, be other things (a sudden thought connection, a suddenly improvised joke). The automatic link between 'reality' and 'emotion' is clear from the talk of one producer quoted by Grindstaff, discussing a moment of extreme rage (a daughter flying at her hated mother) captured on television:

> It was – this one scene is just like the best television *moment* you'll ever see. It was so powerful and real ... It was just a wild card because there was so much emotion there. It was a wild card and we got lucky.
>
> (quoted in Grindstaff 1997: 183–4, original emphasis)

The same language of inflated emotion is reproduced in routine directions to guests and audience also. Emotion, it is implied, is important and it has a representative power:

> Don't hold back on those emotions because this is your big chance to show millions of people you really care about this issue. If you're going to laugh, laugh big.
>
> (advice to guest, quoted in Grindstaff 1997: 180–1)

> Remember you represent all those viewers out there who can't ask questions for themselves. You represent America.
>
> (instructions to audience, quoted in Grindstaff 1997: 180–1)

Note here how the ritual nature of the studio situation *as* a representative space is portrayed as something that is the responsibility of the audience to sustain; what is more, it is associated automatically with heightened displays of emotion.

Here the myth of the mediated centre has turned into stage directions, whose 'naturalness' is deceptive, as are all ritual instructions. Inside the space where that myth is reproduced (the studio), the distinction between 'real' and 'constructed' is inevitably blurred. Every act there is both constructed (from the perspective of everyday action) and real in its ritual intent: in the precisely calibrated acts of talk-show performance we have a contemporary form of 'ritual mastery' (Bourdieu), the attuned acts of the ritualised body. An unknown factor here, however, is the degree to which performers' internalisation of these directions makes their emotion false: are talk shows evidence of the spread of the simulations Mestrovic calls 'postemotions' (1997)? But it remains unclear how we could tell a real emotion from a 'postemotion', so the point is, as yet, unanswerable.

The basis of the talk-show ritual, however, remains an *assumption* that such sites of self-disclosure carry a representative significance. This (not some looser, more comforting notion of community) is the 'consensus' such shows reinforce, and they do so whether or not we see the shows' emotional displays as 'real' or simulated. Thus Gamson's interviewees at various points use the metaphor of 'out' or 'out there' (1998: 74, 79, 104), a banal but hardly trivial expression of the representative public status of what is performed within the talk show 'frame'. Without some degree of 'trust' (here in the media's representative status), no exposure of self-identity can take place (Giddens 1991: 41). The representative and expressive aspects of ritual are both important, and in no way undermine the show's ritual status; on the contrary, they go together. Ritualisation requires, first, a sense that a wider consensus is engaged about transcendent forces (in this case, the imaginary transcendence of 'society', reinforced by that other comforting transcendental reference point, 'human nature'), and second, an allowance for individual acts of appropriation (Bell 1992: 169, 220). Ritual forms are reproduced precisely through the frames within which extreme individual expression makes sense, at least to the performers.

MONITORING SELF-DISCLOSURE

In the case of talk-show disclosures, there are at least three, and possibly four, quite distinct processes superimposed upon one another:

1 the individual acts of self-disclosure or performance;
2 the process of production that contains them (I have concentrated on these first two themes);
3 the process of watching the programme (which I have not analysed because (cf. Chapter 2) it is not a media ritual in itself).

A fourth level comes when we analyse the broader phenomenon of the talk show and the other reality television forms that crowd our broadcast schedules. If, as we argued in Chapter 6, 'reality TV' shows, taken as a genre, are a process of socialised surveillance, what should we conclude about the talk show and other mediated forms of self-disclosure? In spite of the difference in ritualised formality between the talk show's emotional studio audience and the 'reality TV' series shot on location, there are important similarities. Both sub-genres show us that surveillance is the price of entering the most widely available spaces of self-disclosure: as Handelman puts it, 'the spectacle becomes the representation of social order under surveillance' (1998: xxxix). There is no systematic information gathering and retrieval (we assume!) behind the talk show, but we have here nonetheless the raw material from which the stereotypical categories of a broader *surveillance culture* might be forged. The price of appearing on television to speak in your own name is to be categorised in terms over which you have very limited control, categories (for example, the misfit, the eccentric, the waster) that are entangled with the more general categories of media rituals ('ordinary person' versus 'media person').

While this basic point affects everyone, different groups of people have different spaces of self-disclosure available to them, depending on their cultural and symbolic capital, and those spaces come with different constraints. The written autobiography (a form available to very few) allows very different strategies of self-monitoring and defensive adjustment from appearing on a prime-time television show, edited usually to foreground those moments when you have lost your self-control; moreover the opportunities for reflexive self-adjustment in, for example, *The Jerry Springer Show*, are very different from that in the celebrity chat show.

Worse, appearing on television or other central media exposes you to monitoring far beyond the original act of disclosure. The press, in particular, tend to monitor quite closely 'ordinary people' as they pass backwards and forwards across the media/ordinary boundary; not surprisingly, because it is the boundary on which the media's own authority, in part, depends. Here is an example from the UK tabloid *The Sun* concerning one of the contestants of the second UK series of *Big Brother* (just one of the overlaps between reality TV and talk shows as zones of self-disclosure). This story appeared a few weeks after the television series had finished. Under the front page headline 'PAUL AND HELEN BONK', *The Sun* wrote that:

> *Big Brother* star Paul has revealed last night he HAS bedded blonde housemate Helen ... Paul Clarke, 25, revealed intimate details of his relationship with Helen Adams, 23, to 400 revellers at a nightclub ... Paul's boasts came just THREE DAYS after he vowed never to divulge details of his sex life with Welsh hairdresser Helen ...
>
> (*The Sun*, 25 August 2001: 1, 7)

On the face of it, why should a newspaper highlight the duplicity of one of its potential informants? Doesn't this in the long run serve to undermine similar revelations in its own pages? But there is no paradox from a ritual perspective. Tracking people's uncertain dealings with a ritual boundary only reinforces the wider significance of that boundary. There is a similar boundary play in talk shows themselves, which now may place concealed cameras in 'off-stage' areas, so that the performers can be tracked as they negotiate their entries, exits, and re-entries into and from the official television arena.

Talk shows, of course, represent just one part of the wider field of mediated self-disclosure. Sometimes non-media people use the broader ritual space of television to frame new forms of action. We discussed in Chapter 6 the *Video Diary* as one version of this. An example in which media institutions had no hand, it would seem, is the distressing case of a British woman who had been stalked by a man for many months, and in despair decided to confront him face-to-face *on television* (*The Guardian* (G2 section), 19 July 2001: 8–9). This might seem like a simple attempt to generate legal evidence, but it was not, since the stalker was *already* the subject of a court order which he had broken; in any case, the filming of the meeting was prearranged and, it seems, consented to by both parties. The meeting was distressing for the woman concerned, but the piece that told the victim's story in the *Guardian* ended with a defiant statement: 'I'm not a victim, I like to think of myself as a survivor.' What is intriguing about this case is the woman's idea that a *television* camera would make a positive difference to her situation. Why? If it was that cameras were thought essential as security, why not have police filming? Why perform this meeting in public in any case? Was the act of doing so intended as a way of confirming the reality of the meeting? We see here, if only in fragmentary form, how the assumed 'representative' nature of mediated situations can shape individual actions, and well outside the standard television genres. As argued throughout the book, the ritual space of the media extends much further than the actions we might formally call 'media rituals'.

SELF-DISCLOSURE ON THE INTERNET

I want finally to examine how the Internet offers new directions, as well as complexities, for the ritual analysis of mediated self-disclosure.

It has been clear for a long time that the Web offers unprecedented opportunities for self-disclosure (or at least *apparent* self-disclosure), from the early literature on MUDs (Multi-User Domains) and bulletin boards (Turkle 1996), to the more recent work on personal Websites (Chandler 1997; Chandler and Roberts-Young 1998), to the new and little studied phenomenon of Webcam sites and Web diaries.[8] I want to explore how far the notion of ritual boundary can help us understand what is at stake for those who make these forms of self-disclosure. First, however, let me make some more general points.

Some forms of Web-based self-disclosure (Webcams) involve a significant degree of skill and resources, and those without them need to make compromises. They may place their site in a general 'umbrella' site for Webcam sites (such as http://www.camcentral.com and http://webcamworld.com) along with hundreds of other Webcam sites. Some Webcam-site authors use the standard site format which the organisers supply, although most people try within that framework to develop their own more personalised material. A second restriction, which may or may not be significant for particular individuals, is that your site is likely to be presented by the general Website organisers alongside pornographic material, simply because this is one of the most obvious ways in which the organisers of general Webcam sites can make money. My point is not specifically an ethical one, but more about the risk of miscategorisation which any individual site producer has to negotiate in order to get seen. Webcam site producers have only limited control over the interpretative context in which people will encounter their site.

The second general point is that, to a greater degree than on television, it is often difficult to decide whether or not there is a ritual dimension to Internet acts of self-disclosure. Some language used by site authors suggests that a personal Website, diary, or 'Cam' is an act of disclosure 'to the world' (conceiving the Web in effect as a stretched-out version of the media's mythical centre). Other language describes the act of self-disclosure quite differently, as a semi-private act of information circulation directed at existing friends and family, or, at most, at new friends recently encountered through the Web. The Internet as a 'many-to-many medium' is always potentially ambiguous as to whether you are communicating with 'the world' or some private zone, or something in between, which makes the ritual dimension of self-disclosure on the Internet equally uncertain. Closer analysis is needed of particular cases.

Miller and Slater (2000: 16) have noted the ambiguity between the many personal Internets (involved in individual uses) and '*the* Internet', the reified, naturalised, space of social coordination which much Internet discourse constructs. It is the latter that is more likely to generate ritual forms, although it will be some time, I suspect, before these forms become stable. Performance, including identity performance, is ambiguous on the Internet (Lindlof and Shatzer 1998: 178), but in any case the idea of Internet *ritual* is particularly difficult, if one follows Bourdieu in emphasising the importance of the ritual *body*. As Lindlof and Shatzer put it (1998: 173): 'in virtual space, most behavior is inscribed as visible discourse only'. A shift may occur when a larger proportion of transmitted material is non-text, for example live audio and video streaming. For now, however, uncertainty about the long-term ritual significance of the Internet is unavoidable.

To illustrate the ambiguity, take on the one hand this promotional description of the pleasures of the 'weblog' or 'blogging': writing a personal diary or story for your Website (once again there are general sites, which collect together these diaries for a price). One such diary, Mike Anderiesz writes, hints:

> at a time when ordinary people will have the means to command mainstream media attention directly from their keyboards. Whether new writers, artists, and celebrities will be discovered this way remains to be seen, but a bright agent could do worse than checking out the following top five blogs ...
>
> (*The Guardian* (Online section), 23 August 2001: 4)

Here the public status of 'blogging' sites is emphasised, but the crucial question is begged: how can you secure public attention for one among millions of personal sites? Already, it is worth noting, there are forms of 'celebrification' in this area, for example the 'Bloggies' awards for the best piece of writing (http://www.bloggies.com).[9]

On the other hand, in their study of personal Webpages, Chandler and Roberts-Young discovered some striking cases where the Webpage author conceived of the site as private:

> The main reason for *my secrecy* [about my site] was that people who are not familiar with the internet do not understand why my homepage is up, they do not know about it, and to me it would be quite embarrassing for people in school to read the pages and ins and outs of my life! ... I tend to see the internet as something that people only understand if they actually use it, and personal homepages like mine may seem strange to them, you know, why would I put a page up on the Internet about my life? – *they don't realise who it is for.*
>
> (quoted in Chandler and Roberts-Young 1998: 12, my emphasis)

This last example is in fact at odds with Chandler's supposition in an earlier article that Webpages are a form of 'asynchronous *mass* communication' (Chandler 1997:

2, 3). Given the enormous difficulty, even if you wanted to, of getting your personal homepage noticeable by a general browser, there is little scope as yet for 'asynchronous *mass* communication', except perhaps through commercially managed umbrella sites which collect together large numbers of private sites in a generic package, in which case, how 'personal' would your message ever be? There is therefore a real ambiguity about the personal/public nature of the World Wide Web as a site for self-disclosure and its relation, therefore, with the ritual space of the media, as it existed before the Web. This, arguably, is as it should be, given that the Internet is not one single thing or space, but 'numerous new technologies used by diverse people, in diverse real-world locations' (Miller and Slater 2000: 1).

Less ambiguous, however, is some of the rhetoric surrounding the Web and its possibilities for self-disclosure. We have already seen one optimistic writer discussing the democratic potential of 'blogging'. Take this advertisement for the new Panasonic e.Cam displayed on the London Underground[10] where the association, already noted in the television talk show, between the 'reality' of self-disclosure and emotional display is unambiguous:

> *Months* to get to know her
> *Weeks* to fall in love
> *Seconds* to show the world
> Showing your feelings is easy with an e.Cam.

On the face of it, the individual Webcam site *could* start a wider *de*naturalisation of the myth of the mediated centre: we would begin at last to realise Mark Poster's description of a 'second media age' in which '"reality" becomes multiple' (Poster 1995: 85). But this is to draw on another deep, if recent, myth of the Internet's prophets, most notably Nicholas Negroponte's slogan 'prime time becomes my time'. Such visions, as I argue in the next chapter, are certainly *not* to be derided. But, as we saw in Chapter 6, even the concept of 'interactivity' on which they depend has begun to be appropriated to support the media's traditional claims to represent a *centralised* social reality (as in *Big Brother*).

In any case, and against the trend of this speculation, some personal Websites list basic personal information about their author's likes and dislikes, but only as the *form* for pursuing a very different purpose. One female Webcam site-author, whom I interviewed via email as part of ongoing research on Webcam sites, put it this way:

> I simply set it up to offer something different on my personal home page . . . There are millions of personal home pages [without Webcams], it's hard to get yours seen . . . My website isn't aimed at anyone in particular. Due to my interest in the computer industry and the Internet, then it is expected that you have a home

> page and an email address. My site simply helps me do that! ... I don't really know what impression I want to give people, *I'm not making the pages for them, they're for me* ... I don't cover anything personal on my website ... and I don't feed people my address/contact details etc. Obviously as I don't want people turning up on my doorstep!
>
> (email interview, 7 January 2002, my emphasis)

We have here perhaps the 'degree zero' of media ritualisation. The author denies that there is a personal message communicated by her site, except enough conventional personal content to enable her to pass on a public message about her Web skills. Even this limited personal presence on the World Wide Web is hedged around with defences: not only the exclusion of details which would expose the author to unwanted 'pilgrimages', but, as the author explained, a front page to the site covered with links to pornographic sites. When I asked why, the reason given was purely defensive:

> If I don't have those links, I tend to get a lot of emails asking why I don't get naked on my cam. So I simply link to these sites to help get rid of the people that are simply looking for porn, and not a webcam.
>
> (email interview, 7 January 2002)

It is clear, at least, that, if a 'democratic' space of self-disclosure opens up on the World Wide Web, it will have to work *against* many other powerful forces: the sheer difficulty of obtaining more than random exposure for one's site in a universe of millions of sites,[11] the costs of maintaining individually distinctive sites (especially if production standards go on being raised by those with access to the more expensive skills and equipment), and the difficulties of staking out in an already heavily commercialised cyberspace somewhere where private individuals can give an account of themselves without constantly being mistaken for pornography or other for-profit sites.

The long-term impacts of such developments are uncertain. We may be at the start of a gradual transformation and de-legitimation of the media's ritual categories – including the dismantling of the category of the 'ordinary person' – or we may be at the start of a period where those ritual categories simply operate under heavier disguise. It would be foolish to predict which is more likely.

CONCLUSION

The tentativeness of these last comments is justified by a wider uncertainty which this book can hardly hope to change. This is the uncertainty about how the relationship between media and ritual will develop in the Internet era: towards the gradual dispersal of the media's ritual space in the vast, fractal space of the Web, or towards the further intensification of that ritual space's coordinating power, at least in the Web's central zones (the zones which the typical user will come to know)?

In the course of this chapter, I have discussed how different people may be positioned differently by media rituals that, as *rituals*, must draw on boundaries and categories with a general social reference. But I have said little about the ways in which different sites of self-disclosure seem appropriate and representative to different performers. For many viewers, *The Jerry Springer Show* is simply *not* a space where they could imagine disclosing aspects of their private life. Does this suggest that the apparent unity of the media's ritual space, even without considering the Internet, is fracturing into 'public sphericules' (Gitlin 1998) in ways that would undermine, once and for all, a Durkheimian view of the media's integrative social 'function'? This fracturing of the television audience into sub-communities of taste is of course a much wider phenomenon than the talk show. It is especially paradoxical on talk shows, because a sense of a 'representative' space is built into the form. Given, however, that the notion of the media's social function implied here is always only a construction, there is no reason why this construction cannot be played out in different (but parallel) forms, and as such engaged with by groups occupying a range of positions in social space.

Having raised, however, the question of the potential fracturing of the myth of the mediated centre, the issue arises: can we think beyond that myth, and beyond media rituals, at least in their current form? I want in the concluding chapter to explore how we might open up new ways of imagining the future of media rituals; imagining, against the grain, a new way of orienting ourselves, as private individuals and as citizens, to the ritual authority of the media, in whatever form it survives.

Chapter 8

Beyond media rituals?

> [We must look] within public events, making their interior workings problematic, and focusing our attention there. It is this angle of perception towards horizons of the possible that turns representation on its head and into an issue.
>
> (Handelman 1998: xiii)

Ritual may be universal, even if media rituals are not. For Rappaport (1999), rituals are universal because they are actions whose form points to a world beyond human action, the divine. For Durkheim (1995), rituals do not refer to the transcendental in a metaphysical sense, but to the transcendental which is human beings' way of imagining the absolute nature of the bond they share as members of a social group; if so, ritual is as universal as the existence of social groups. While particular rituals will lapse, and while ritual practice itself may be disrupted at times when social experience is profoundly disturbed, the *urge* to create ritual forms is, according to Durkheim (1995: 215), universal. For Bloch (1989), ritual is as universal as practices of domination, and the will to mystify domination. In this book I have not sought to choose definitively between these positions, although, in Chapters 2 and 3, I argued for a way of working with Durkheim's legacy that takes account of questions of power and ideology. Instead my aim has been to bring us to the point where we can answer a different question: are *media* rituals (and the wider space of ritualisation on which they draw) universal?

The answer is no, and not for the obvious reason that our current forms of mediation (radio, television, the Internet, and so on) are historically recent. Media rituals, at least in their *current* forms, are not universal, because they are social forms which legitimate a fact about the current organisation of mediation, in most parts of the world at least, that is contingent, not necessary: namely, the intense concentration of society's symbolic resources in centralised institutions that we call 'the media'. This concentration is not necessary, and we can imagine beyond it; and so we can imagine beyond the current forms of media ritual too. In this concluding chapter, I want to do just that.

DIFFERENT HORIZONS

To think beyond the current forms of media ritual, and the forms of social organisation in which they seem natural and which they in turn help naturalise, we must make two important preliminary moves. First, we must clear our heads of any romanticism in our thinking about mediation; second, we must reject any romanticism in our thinking about 'society'. I will take each in turn, which means making explicit arguments which have so far been largely implicit.

An enormous step forward in clarifying our thinking about mediation has been made by John Durham Peters in his book *Speaking Into the Air* (Peters 1999). Through careful historical argument and an extremely broad range of philosophical and cultural reference, he has demolished, once and for all, the romantic notion that communication must *either* be based on face-to-face dialogue *or* doomed as defective; from which it follows that mediation (communication that is mediated, and therefore cannot in principle be based on face-to-face dialogue) is not, for that reason alone, flawed. Although much of Peters' argument is philosophical, it has major consequences for a sociology of mediation, because it demonstrates the unhelpfulness of philosophers' *ex ante* claims that communication is necessarily or ideally face-to-face. That is not to say that all the potential issues raised by contemporary forms of communication and mediation are magically solved, in some local replay of Fukuyama's (1992) notorious 'end of history', but to say that such issues are always *sociological*, not philosophical;[1] or rather they are always sociological first, before they become philosophical (we shall see that contemporary forms of mediation, as forms of social organisation, may raise philosophical issues for the longer term).

Only with this principle in place can we see through clearly to the actual issues raised by communication and media, which are about power, access and participation (cf. Peters 1999: 65; Peters and Rothenbuhler 1989: 23–4). These questions, though their urgency takes contemporary forms, have considerable historical depth, dating back at least to the Enlightenment (Garnham 2000: chapter 8) and having antecedents in the concentration of symbolic power in much earlier societies, for example the medieval Catholic church in Western Europe (Curran 1982). To see clearly what is at stake in media's current social organisation, we need to reject not only the romanticism which sees media's consequences for society as automatically negative, but also the romanticism which sees those consequences as intrinsically positive or at least as assessable in isolation from questions of power.[2]

Let me turn now to the second form of thinking to be rejected, a romanticism in our thinking about 'society'; this has been our target more directly throughout, since it is closely entangled with classic arguments about ritual, and the media's ritual dimensions. Returning to the quotation from Norbert Elias at the start of this book, we must be ready to see the 'contradiction and ... disproportions' in social forms and social structure (Elias 1994: 520). That means outlawing any *assumptions* that society is a functioning unity, let alone that mediation works to maintain such a unity. If 'in a world of paradox, easy communication is necessarily false' (Peters 1999: 133), no less false are easy assumptions that society functions like an organism with a real centre and periphery (Shils 1975) which therefore requires for its healthy operation a *centralised* system of symbolic production and distribution ('the media') to represent what goes on at its 'centre' to those on its 'periphery'. We have come across such functionalist assumptions in many places, explicitly in Dayan and Katz's theory of media events and implicitly (with or without acknowledgement of their classic Durkheimian premises) in positive readings of 'talk shows' or 'reality TV'. The challenge to such functionalist arguments is in every case quite simple: where is the evidence? What reason is there not to take the opposite starting point, that, in societies that segregate their members' life-worlds in many other basic respects, centralised media work as much to entrench conflict and exclusion as to restore unity and shared values.[3]

With such romantic notions of mediation and of society out of the way, the way forward would seem clear. But it is obscured by another factor: that all debates on mediation, until recently, were marked by the question of the 'legitimacy' of *mass* media (along with 'mass' culture, and so on). This has obscured more urgent issues. But once we see, following John Durham Peters, that the massification of media or cultural production is not automatically and totally flawed, we can examine the *actual* constraints affecting *current* forms of mass communication, and the social (and perhaps philosophical) consequences which flow from them. As Peters puts it: 'communication becomes a political problem of access and opportunity, not a psychological or semantic one of purifying the media' (1999: 65). If we want to think effectively about what social process contemporary media systems constitute, we must be clear on what is at stake; we must define, as Alberto Melucci (1996: 4) put it, 'the field of conflict'.

The field of conflict is contemporary societies' unequal distribution of symbolic resources and symbolic power, of which media institutions are both paradigmatic examples and chief beneficiaries. The enormous pull of functionalist assumptions about society and mediation's role within society (and the legitimacy those assumptions give to processes of centralisation) has made the issue of symbolic power difficult to see; this is why we need alternative ways of imagining the mediation process.

Can we imagine a social world in which mediation is characterised by a different, more even, distribution of symbolic power? Yes, provided our assumptions do not rule it out arbitrarily in advance.

What might this alternative horizon be? There is one utopian possibility which we must immediately reject. In large complex societies and global formations, a totally decentred pattern of media production and distribution is impossible, and not so much because it runs against all principles of political economy, but more simply because in that chaotic world individual agents would always work to make selections and to make its complexity manageable and liveable (cf. Neuman 1991: 163); so effective 'centres' of *some* sort would emerge, and it is no use pretending otherwise. In any case, there is nothing in principle wrong with certain centres of communication emerging for certain purposes and under certain limited conditions. Communication cannot be all face-to-face dialogue or interactive co-production. There is an unavoidable role for 'scatter' or 'dissemination' (as John Durham Peters calls it): that is, messages broadcast across space from particular centres without being aimed at anyone in particular.

The alternative vision of the media process we should work towards, then, is not a chaotic 'Tower of Babel', but a world with *many* 'centres' that produce and distribute media messages, each of them only a relative centre, in whose formation and operations a very wide range of people can participate, and which holds no entrenched monopoly that would prevent further 'centres' forming. Instead of the absurd nightmare of everyone broadcasting simultaneously, our alternative image of mediation could be a non-hierarchical space in which people have some degree of choice over *whether* to broadcast *or* to receive messages and images, at least for a significant number of purposes and contexts.

It hardly needs emphasising that current media systems, whether market-based or publicly funded, do not constitute such a non-hierarchical space, or anything like it. Indeed, all basic economic principles (economies of scale, economies of scope), operating by themselves, work against the possibility of such a space. If we are serious, then, in imagining such a space, we need to develop critical reflection in the teeth of economic constraints. In these final pages, rather than closing off possibilities, I want to discuss a range of ways in which we might begin to imagine beyond the current horizon of an overwhelmingly centralised media process, in which most people do not participate. I mean a world where 'media' comprise a 'scatter' from many sources, a succession of sources, with a very different balance for individuals between possibilities of production and possibilities of consumption. Within this new horizon, current forms of media rituals (surrounding celebrity, the media's special access to 'reality', 'liveness', and so on) should seem less necessary, even redundant.

But isn't it naive, you might object, given the massive centralisation of so many other aspects of contemporary societies (the state, the economy), even to *imagine* this less centralised media world? That charge, however, can be reversed: if this alternative image of the mediation process (quite possible in principle) must for ever be ruled out of court because of its 'lack of fit' with current structures of media power, that only demonstrates how complicit in those power structures our standard, centralised concept of mediation is. The point here is not to claim unrealistically that 'everything is possible', but as Alain Badiou put it in a recent discussion of utopian thinking (2001: 115; quoted in Giroux, forthcoming, 2003) to show 'how the space of the possible is larger than the one we are assigned – that something else is possible'.

None of this is to undermine the fundamental social importance of communication, and our need for connection with distant others through media – to see both, in other words, as social facts, in Durkheim's sense.[4] The point is to develop an alternative image of what *forms of* mediation sustain best the conditions of social life and democratic politics. There are a number of places where we can turn for further inspiration.

Remembering Durkheim's century-old thought experiment, we could return to the arid centre of the Australian subcontinent, and the work of Eric Michaels (1985; 1994) which, unlike Durkheim's, was based on actually observing the social (and media) practices of aboriginal societies in their accelerated transition from entirely oral cultures to cultures with (limited) access to broadcasting resources. The point is not, of course, to copy the 'informational economy' (Michaels 1985) of aboriginal societies with their intense restrictions on speech and image production; Michaels rejects any romanticism of the supposedly 'archaic' for its own sake. Instead, he insists that this distinctive informational economy is as much part of modernity as our more centralised one; it is therefore equally relevant to our attempts to imagine a different social form of mediation. The aboriginal informational economy sees mediation as a local process of communication that requires the existence of many centres (Michaels 1994: 100), a process whose ethical, social and political implications are always open, in principle, to local deliberation. As Helen Molnar puts it:

> Aborigines see their local areas as the centre from which information emanates … [Aborigines'] information/communications model is completely the reverse of the European model which sees the urban cities as the centre and the remote communities as the periphery.
>
> (quoted in Ginsburg 1995: 280)

This, on the face of it, is the opposite of scatter but, when taken together with Peters' very different notion, it can help us produce a better depth-image of the mediation process, as we might wish to develop it.

Recent discussions of new media 'networks' also can be read as combining the image of scatter (assumed to be from one centre) with the multiplication of centres:

the result is an image of a more or less *decentred network*. Although it was this image that inspired many Internet pioneers, its incompatibility with the dominant commercial forces now shaping the Internet's development is increasingly obvious (cf. Castells 2001). But this lends all the more interest to the recent attempt by the leader of the Zapatistas, Subcomandante Marcos, to sustain in his writings the network image as a political notion, without claiming that it is somehow inherent in the Internet's technological base. Marcos' broad vision of 'a new relation between power and citizens' imagines a network to be built over time that:

> will attempt to create channels so that words may flow to all paths that resist … this network is not an organising structure … nor does it have a central command or hierarchies. We are the network, all of us who speak and listen.
>
> (Marcos 2001: 125)[6]

We have here not a crude rejection of mainstream media spaces, but a vision of the mediation process as a social form that can, and should, *extend beyond* them (cf. Marcos 2001: 174–6).

There are, in fact, many sites of media production and consumption where the centralisation of symbolic resources has been challenged, both before and after the arrival of the Internet: in the area of production called variously 'radical media' (Downing 2000), 'alternative media' (Atton 2001) and 'citizens' media' (Rodriguez 2001), which for so long has been treated as marginal to the agenda of media and communications studies, but whose concerns with media's implications for democratic participation now look increasingly central; and in the area of fan production that Henry Jenkins and others have explored (Bacon-Smith 1992; Hills 2002; Jenkins 1992). New, dispersed possibilities of production and distribution challenge the naturalised hierarchies between media people and non-media people, suggesting a different, less unequal vision of the mediated public sphere (Bolin 2000). What, perhaps, has been lacking until now is a broader alternative vision that would *connect* all these specific visions into an effective challenge to the dominant centralised conception of media. There are dangers, of course, in this alternative vision (for example, that the specialised worlds of fan communities reduce the possibilities for dialogue on a larger scale); and also major uncertainties (how decentralised a medium will the Internet be for most users once it reaches a stable commercial format?). Nonetheless it is clear that the Internet (or aspects of the Internet) will be fundamental to any shift in our dominant metaphors for understanding media.

The possibility that right now we are in the middle of a fundamental shift in how we think about communication technology and its places in our imaginative lives should surely encourage us to pursue, not close down, new metaphors.[7] Establishing a new vision will, however, take time. In the short term, it is perhaps more important to be clear on why we need such alternatives in the first place. Quite simply, my argument is that only by imagining mediation as something other than the 'necessary' expression of a social 'centre' can we address the *depth* of the current crisis of public communication (Blumler and Gurevitch 1995). This is to make explicit the contemporary political context that so far has been only implicit in this book's (to some, 'archaic') concern with media rituals.

FROM PRIVATE TO PUBLIC WORLDS

The promise of the neo-Durkheimian approach to media, as represented most clearly by Dayan and Katz, was that it would enable us to see how 'social integration of the highest order is ... achieved via mass communication' and in so doing confirm that in 'the full potential of electronic media technology' lies the answer to Durkheim's fundamental questions about social order in modernity (1992: 15, viii). The claim is an important one, since Durkheim's questions are no less urgent now than when the neo-Durkheimian approach was first developed, indeed they are probably more urgent.

We saw, however, that media rituals are at least as much about confirming categories and divisions as they are about establishing social unity. The media's ritual categories are socially divisive, not because they are understood directly in those terms (if they were, they would be less effective), but because they entrench a *naturalised* division of the world into two, which in turn helps legitimate society's unequal distribution of its symbolic resources. Media rituals, and the boundaries they encourage us to draw, are therefore necessarily entangled in the broader notion of politics at stake in the distribution of symbolic power; this is a crucial dimension of the current crisis of representative democracy. I am relying here on a broader notion of 'politics' that encompasses people's sense of connection with society's 'centres', people's sense of having an active stake in deliberations about the future of social spaces that remain profoundly unequal, people's sense of their own symbolic resources and worth (cf. Benhabib 1995).

There are two sides to this. On the one hand, there are people's connections to a shared space of action and deliberation. Nina Eliasoph (1998: 113–23) has analysed some working class and middle class communities in the USA, where at least in her analysis (and it is a controversial one) the only 'rituals' and 'traditions' are consumption rituals, and there is only the most perfunctory sense of a social bond; worse, the connections of that social bond to any possible shared politics are systematically disavowed in all but the most private settings. Henry Giroux (2001: 4) has argued something similar in his wide-ranging work on cultural and political practice in contemporary America and, following the analysis of Zygmunt Bauman (1999), suggested that the very 'bridges between private and public life are [being] dismantled'. One important issue is whether the 'reality' with which the media presents us enhances, or reduces, the distance between our everyday concerns and the public world.[8] Paul Virilio has expressed these doubts as strikingly as anyone:

> The proliferation of the global city's *discrete virtuality* results in the increasing unreality of the legitimate state's territorial foundation. This privileges **contemporaneity** unfairly over **citizenship** and so causes the metropolitan virtuality of the **live broadcast** to dominate the geopolitical reality of the **town.**
>
> (1999: 74, original emphasis)

Whatever our conclusions – and there are issues to debate, perhaps, in Virilio's romanticisation of 'the town' – we must at least ask whether the forms of contemporary media analysed here in ritual terms (media events, reality TV, talk shows, and so on) are building overall a sense of connection with a wider social world, or reinforcing people's sense of disconnection. The current problems of democracy are as much about *symbolic* capital and symbolic resources, as about 'social capital' (in Robert Putnam's (2000) important recent argument).

Rather than taking at face value neo-Durkheimian claims for modern media, we should be asking for evidence based on everyday thought, talk and action. What if contemporary media isolate us as much as they sustain connection, create false proximity as much as real connection (Silverstone 2002)? There is a whole new subject of media ethics (the ethics of the social process of mediation, rather than journalistic ethics in a narrow sense) to be opened up here.

Transposing Durkheim's (1984: 24) question about the long-term sustainability of the division of labour to the current social division[9] between media producers and media consumers, what if the latter division also fails to sustain the type of social connections that we need? If participating in the representations of one's shared world is (Rodriguez 2001: 20) one important way of 'enacting ... citizenship', then how positive for citizenship are practices that naturalise the absence of the majority of a population from that process?

Does this mean we should abandon any notion of media rituals altogether? No, but we should suspend that notion's automatic connection to belief in a social 'centre', and a centralised media system that is our route to that 'centre'. We need, in other words, to imagine an alternative horizon within which media can still bridge our personal and public worlds, but differently from in the past; if so, we should expect media rituals to take future forms that as yet we cannot imagine.

MAKING THE STRANGE FAMILIAR

Rituals make things happen. They are ways of organising practice (Asad 1993: 78), and it is a common, but misleading, thought that rituals can only confirm, or re-present, a social order that is already in place. Even so, by acting upon, and not merely alongside, the social world, rituals may entrench very different organisational principles from those suggested by their surfaces. So in *Big Brother* and elsewhere, media rituals which seem to affirm the shared significance of an individual's transition to celebrity in fact entrench further the working division between 'media people' and 'ordinary people' (cf. Couldry 2002). Heavily ritualised processes such as media events, which seem to affirm the shared significance of media institutions' picture of the world, in fact insist upon the hierarchy of that picture over any possible other.

It might seem, then, that this book's critical approach to media rituals – looking within them, as Handelman says, and 'making their interior workings problematic' – merely confirms the pessimistic readings of media's contribution to political space. It might seem that 'media rituals' can only ever enact abstractions, confirming through their tired formalities the voiding of public space that the philosopher Søren Kierkegaard long ago diagnosed:

> Only when the sense of association in society is no longer strong enough to give life to concrete realities is the Press able to create that abstraction 'the public', consisting of unreal individuals who never are and never can be united in an action situation or organisation – and yet are held together as a whole.
>
> (Kierkegaard 1962: 66)

But, where Kierkegaard and countless other writers have seen the media's relation to the social as an unending one-way street, leading to ever more public disconnection, it is better to see this as only one historical trajectory – the trajectory, in Foucault's chilling phrase, of 'the rarefaction of speaking subjects' (1981b: 61). There are other possible trajectories.

The need to communicate, and the need for connection, as both Durkheim and Carey saw clearly, are universal, however varied the forms they take. People, in their desire to be heard, will go on pressing for new connections to be made, and for old abstractions and formalities to be dismantled. Media studies has been slow to address the underlying question about representation: not representation in this or that text, but representation in the overall social process of making representations (the process of mediation). Just as political philosophy can no longer ignore the 'politics of presence' (Phillips 1995), so media studies must face up to the long-term consequences of an entrenched politics of absence – most people's absence from the process of representing whatever worlds we share.

In analysing current media rituals, we have been dealing with the mystified outcome of that politics of absence: a mystification of the inequalities currently (but not inevitably) surrounding one of the fundamental resources at stake in social life – the resource of representing our lives, both apart and together. If those mystifications are, because they are the most general, also the most difficult to disentangle, the benefits of disentangling them are correspondingly high. In making contemporary media's ritualised categories and boundaries seem strange, we are paving the way, I hope, for other, less unequal, spaces of media representation to become familiar.

Notes

Chapter 1: Media rituals: the short and the long route

1 Arguably, there were several such 'inventors': see Flichy (1995: chapter 8).
2 In Briggs (1961: 549), quoted in Flichy (1995: 141).
3 The importance of this shift is gradually becoming accepted in media studies. See Couldry (2000a: chapter 1), Elliott (1982), Ginsburg (1994; 1995), Martin-Barbero (1993), Michaels (1994), Rothenbuhler (1993), Saenz (1994), Silverstone (forthcoming).
4 For example, Douglas (1984: 63–4), Humphrey and Laidlaw (1994: 88–9), Lewis (1980: 25), Myerhoff (1977: 199), Rappaport (1999: 24), Smith (1987: 109–10). Cf. also Carey (1989: 21), Rothenbuhler (1998: 57) in media theory.
5 See Ginsburg (1998), Hobart (2000), Spitulnik (1993).
6 For more detail, see Couldry (2000a: chapters 1, 3), drawing on Durkheim (1995).
7 Of course, you *can* analyse the relationship between media and religion in the contemporary world within a broadly Durkheimian framework (Clark and Hoover 1997), but it is not part of this book's remit to pursue that interesting line of enquiry. See also Frow (1998) and Hills (2002: 125–9) for an interesting hybrid case: the 'neo-religiosity' of fan practices.
8 For discussion, see Couldry (2000a: 22–3).
9 Note that Silverstone (1994) largely goes beyond this earlier neo-Durkheimian position.
10 This division is to some degree an oversimplification: see Stedman Jones (2001: 212–14) for a helpful discussion on how the emotive and the cognitive are intertwined in Durkheim's explanation of the generative force of the social gathering (cf. Giddens 1972: 110).
11 It should be clear, I hope, that I am not assuming any crude binary opposition between the 'cognitive' and the 'emotive'; each impacts upon the other in more and less subtle ways.

12 See Dayan and Katz (1992: viii), Maffesoli (1996a: 149, note 14; 1996b: 55–67). Others adopt a Durkheimian model of media ritual without clarifying their position on Durkheim's rather different argument in *The Division of Labour in Society*, for example Bar-Haim (1997), Marvin (1999: 129–30; 159), Mestrovic (1997), which is not to suggest that those positions are necessarily wrong, only that they are seemingly at odds with Durkheim's own position.

13 For example, Bloch (1989: chapter 1), Lukes (1975), MacCannell (1992: chapter 11), Ortner (1978), Pickering (1984), Sahlins (1976: 117), and in media studies Carey (1989: 53–4).

14 Cf. Lukes (1975).

15 Cf. Bloch (1989: 135), Carey (1989: 65), Thomas (1991: 206).

16 Cf. Bourdieu (1977: 203, note 49).

17 The term 'ideology' has a long and controversial history. I adopt John Thompson's useful definition of 'ideology' as 'the ways in which meaning serves to establish and sustain relations of domination' (1990: 56), but with two qualifications: first, I use 'meaning' in a broad sense to include patterns of organisation embedded in action (but not necessarily articulated as 'meaning' by the actors); second, the relation of domination with which I am concerned is that constituted by the concentration of symbolic power in media institutions (or 'media power', as I define it above), which is to use the term 'symbolic power' in a sense different from Thompson's (see, further, Chapter 3).

18 On the importance of 'banality' in the analysis of power, see Billig (1995).

19 See Asad (1993: 78–9), Bell (1992; 1997), Handelman (1998: x) and, above all, Bourdieu (1977; 1990; 1991). Cf. in media studies Saenz (1994: 584).

20 See Asad (1993: 53), Bell (1997: 81–2), Bloch (1989), Bourdieu (1991), Elliott (1982: 145).

21 See Couldry (2000a: chapter 1).

22 The term 'ritual space' is used by White (1997: 61); cf. MacAloon (1984) on the 'space' of contemporary spectacle. Neither of these usages, however, fits exactly with mine.

23 For the metaphor of 'black box', see also Actor Network Theory (Callon 1991).

24 Baudrillard argues that such value judgements are now meaningless: this is only plausible if you accept Baudrillard's totalising account of social life, which I don't.

25 As Bourdieu (2000: 27) argued, even Heidegger's historicist attack on modern science's status is developed from a standpoint that is profoundly ahistorical.

26 For recent positions, see Boltanski (1999), Derrida and Stiegler (1996), Luhmann (1999).

27 See, for example, Carey (1989: 110).

28 Durkheim (1995: 421), discussed in Stedman Jones (2001: 214).

Chapter 2: Ritual and liminality

1 See Douglas (1970: chapter 1; 1975: 57; 1984: 69) and Thompson (1994).

2 See Lembo (2000: 101, 124–5, 156–7), Nordenstreng (1972: 341), Rubin (1984). So, too, Mellencamp (1990) analyses media disaster coverage as comforting 'rituals', implying that it

is their routineness that makes them effective, although in other ways her analysis might fit well into mine.

3 Bell (1997: 245), Crain (1992), Hughes-Freeland (1998), Rudie (1998).

4 Lewis (1980: 10), Rappaport (1999: 38), Rothenbuhler (1998: 9).

5 Herzfeld (1992: 68), Marvin (1999: 131); cf. Silverstone (1981: 66–7).

6 For a discussion of how the naturalness of media authority may in certain situations be deconstructed, see Couldry (2000a: part 3).

7 For a rare opposing view from a sociologist of religion, see Ruel (1998).

8 In anthropology, Douglas (1984: 63–4), Lewis (1980: 30–1), Myerhoff (1977: 199), Smith (1987: 109–10); and in media theory Dayan and Katz (1992: 178–83), Elliott (1982: 147), Silverstone (1981: 75–7).

9 In this book I will not develop the theme of celebrity in any detail. However, I am sceptical about the idea that media persons fulfil a social 'function' or are even necessarily important social reference points, however much we are told that they are. Needless to say, this goes against the grain of much celebrity research and media comment.

10 For an attempt to extend Turner's work that I feel falls prey to this danger, see Deegan (1989).

11 Cf. more recently the bold – surely too bold – argument by the Colombian media and cultural theorist Jesus Martin-Barbero (1997) that television has *reunited* the 'sacred' and the 'profane'.

12 Compare the much more cautious argument by Don Handelman that the rise of new forms of mediated public event is connected to the problems of living in an era of 'failed centricity' (1998: 266).

Chapter 3: Ritual space: unravelling the myth of the centre

1 In addition, as pointed out in Chapter 2, ritual need not always involve formal symbolic content, since patterns and categories (that are expressible in explicit symbolic form: an image, a statement) may also be condensed in bodily actions. This does not alter the fact that ritual action belongs to the general domain, not of economic or political power, but of symbolic power.

2 Crucially, Thompson (1995: 269, note 8) rules out an important possibility, that certain major concentrations of symbolic power are necessarily misrecognised, precisely because they are so pervasive.

3 See Couldry (2000a: chapter 3) for analysis of how this misrecognition works in detail.

4 This is one place where, quite directly, Bourdieu strives to merge a Marxist and a Durkheimian perspective. For an interesting, but ultimately unconvincing, argument that this merger is impossible, see Garnham (1994).

5 Callon and Latour (1981: 287).

6 For a brilliant demolition of this myth in relation to early notions of 'cyberspace', see Robins (1995b).

Chapter 4: Rethinking media events

1 For an important earlier precedent, see Silverstone (1981).
2 Cf. Raboy and Dagenais (1992: 13): 'One can almost say that it is in times of crisis that the media reveal themselves, their workings and their motivations.'
3 Quoted in Wallerstein (1991: 137).
4 For example, Cardiff and Scannell (1987: 160–1).
5 It is easy to forget that the 1953 coronation occurred when the habit of television watching was itself only just being established.
6 Cf. Meyrowitz (1985) on the more general shift in forms of public performance through television.
7 MacAloon is careful to distinguish between the neoliminal, the spectacular, and the ritual. His argument, in sum, is that while the Olympics as a whole may not be a ritual, they are spectacles with quasi-liminal features, within whose framework many localised rituals can take place.
8 For example, Puijk (1999), Rothenbuhler (1988: 64), and for discussion see Roche (2000: 163–7).
9 We might also argue this for political authorities, but this would go beyond the scope of this book.
10 As Chris Harris (1999: 101) puts it, reflecting on the problems faced by Durkheimian accounts of the gatherings in London to mourn Princess Diana: 'Whereas for Durkheim the assembly engenders the effervescence, in the Diana case the media-generated effervescence created the assembly.' This point was insufficiently recognised in debates about the supposed significance of these events.
11 This point was ignored in much writing about reactions to Diana's death; contrast Nava (1999) with the sensible caution of Walter (1999).
12 Cf. Davies (1999).
13 Visiting New York almost a year later, I found the authority of that coverage continued to be reproduced in videos and booklets for sale on Manhattan streets, recycling television and press images of the attack.

Chapter 5: Media 'pilgrimages' and everyday media boundaries

1 Cf. Couldry (2000a: 72).
2 I owe this useful phrase to Vicki Mayer.
3 Maffesoli's social theory (1996a; 1996b) is an expansion of this.
4 For specific examples, see Bowman (1991), Eade (1991), McKevitt (1991).

5 For a subtle examination of this point and the commodification of fandom generally, see Hills (2002).

6 So, too, Dayan and Katz's neo-Durkheimian interpretation of media events, while on the face of it paying great attention to space (the organisation of media ritual around a ceremonial centre), in fact works through collapsing the complexity of lived space into a set of relations to a mythical 'centre'.

7 Scannell and Cardiff (1991: 311–14).

8 I discussed this passage in a different context in Couldry (2000b).

9 When I returned in 2001, the 'graveyard' had been replaced by an area for serving tea.

10 Cf. Couldry (2000a: 45).

11 'Weatherfield' is the programme's fictional region and 'the Rovers' is the programme's fictional pub.

12 Lévi-Strauss (1981: 672–5), quoted in Smith (1987: 111).

13 See, for example, Harrington and Bielby (1995), Jenkins (1992), Jensen (1991).

14 Thanks to Matt Hills for originally sending me this article.

15 Date of search via www.google.com, 24 February 2002.

16 Again there is a larger question, which I do not have the space to deal with, of the significance of quasi-religious language in contemporary mediated cultures. How, for example, are we to interpret the following language from the December 2000 Napster newsletter (http://www.newsletter.napster.com/archive/dec2000.php, consulted 24 February 2002): 'Screensavers: Like seeing that Napster Kitty on your desktop? Want another way to preach the gospel of Napster? Let the Napster Kitty be your screensaver by downloading one of our cool designs here – just one more way to spread the word'?

17 Thanks to Andrea Feddersen for discovering this material at: http://www.scifi.about.com/gi/dynamic/offsite.htm?site=http%3A%2F%2Fwww.obsse,com%2Foct97,htm%23pilgrim (downloaded 20 February 2002, my emphasis).

18 http://www.angelfire.com/ca3/blairwitch/plan.html consulted 24 February 2002. Thanks again to Andrea Feddersen for telling me about this site.

19 Respectively: http://www.geocities.com/Hollywood/Hills/6880/pilgrima.htm, http://www.nwnet.co.uk/the_street/coro2pge.htm, http://www.geocities.com/Colosseum/Bleachers/2492/pilgrim.htm, http://www.opsroom.org/burnsides-bridge.html, all consulted on 24 February 2002.

Chapter 6: Live 'reality' and the future of surveillance

1 Image surveillance is only one part, and arguably a diminishing part, of surveillance in the 'maximum surveillance society' (Norris and Armstrong 1999; cf. Lyon 2001). I concentrate here on image surveillance, not database surveillance, since only the former can take a ritualised form, although it is the latter's lack of visual traces that makes it so disturbing (see also Agre and Rotenberg 1998).

2 Cf. Bourdon (2000).

3 To be fair, Bourdon (2000: 552) makes the same point, although without seeing its implications for his definiton of liveness.

4 As conventionally organised; there could of course be a rule that transmission was never interrupted.

5 Thanks to Garry Whannel for making this connection (in discussion at MeCCSA conference, January 2002, University of Westminster).

6 I owe this point to an excellent recent paper by John McMurria (McMurria 2002).

7 Ellis, J (2000: 31–6), Dayan and Katz (1992), Scannell (1996: chapter 4).

8 See Couldry (2000a: 42–4), Silverstone (1981; 1988).

9 Cf. Hay (1992: 365–6) and for further discussion (Couldry 2000a: chapter 1).

10 But see Heath (1990), White (1992b).

11 And also space (see McCarthy 2001: 15, on the 'scale-shifting' implied by live broadcasting).

12 Corner (1995: chapter 1), Dovey (2000), Hill (2000; 2002), Kilborn (1994; 1998).

13 I say 'more or less' to allow for the important argument that recent 'reality TV' constitutes an historic break from the journalistic responsibilities of the documentary tradition and the beginning of a 'post-documentary' era (Corner 2002).

14 For studies of this formal flexibility or hybridity, see Bondebjerg (1996), Corner (1995), Kilborn (1994), Schlesinger and Tumber (1994: chapter 9).

15 The 'docudrama' (Paget 1998) falls clearly within the pure fiction zone, since it is a scripted, fully directed version of a real historical event.

16 Comment made in discussion at MeCCSA conference, January 2002, University of Westminster.

17 For example in film, *The Blair Witch Project* being the best-known play upon this.

18 See Neale (1976: 121). Indeed there is a link between my argument here and Neale's 1970s argument, about (then) New Hollywood Cinema, such as Robert Altman's work, that its foregrounding of the cinematic mechanism only served to naturalise still further the wider claim of Hollywood to present 'reality'. Thanks to Nigel Morris for suggesting this connection.

19 Hence I disagree with Bourdon's view (2000: 538) that live coverage, stripped down to a camera just looking, is no longer 'live', merely absurd.

20 Nigel Lythgoe, quoted in *The Guardian*, 10 January 2001: 7.

21 For such early arguments, see Nichols (1994), Rath (1985). For criticism, see Dovey (2000: 91, 99), Hill (2000).

22 Quoted in *The Guardian* (Online section), 17 June 1999: 2.

23 See respectively *The Guardian* (Online section), 13 April 2000: 11 and *The Guardian* (Media section), 28 August 2000: 5.

24 See Chaney (1993: 7, 34–7), Stevenson (1995: 139–40). I became aware of Gareth Palmer's interesting and highly relevant work on *Big Brother* and surveillance (see Palmer 2002) too late to take account of it here.

25 See Loader (1997) for an interesting discussion of policing as an exercise of symbolic power.

26 For useful background, see Dovey (2000: chapter 4).
27 Thanks to Annette Hill for this latter point.
28 If the victim appeared in the surveillance footage, she or he was, of course, pixelled out to preserve anonymity.
29 For analysis of this common rhetorical claim, see Norris and Armstrong (1999: 63–7).
30 Unless you assume that more than half of everything caught by all surveillance cameras is criminal activity!
31 A striking exception was the third episode in Darcus Howe's documentary series *White Tribe* (Channel 4, 27 January 2000), shot on a poor housing estate in North-East England, which asked young people about their reactions to the surveillance cameras under which they conduct their public lives.

Chapter 7: Meditated self-disclosure: before and after the Internet

1 Dovey (2000), Ehrenberg (1995), Gamson (1998), Livingstone and Lunt (1994), Mehl (1996), Priest (1995), Shattuc (1994), White (1992a).
2 See Gamson (1998: 87), Grindstaff (1997: 182), but, for a contrasting case, Priest (1995: 194).
3 Interestingly Shattuc writes of the 'prescribed rituals' of *Ricki Lake*, but without further comment (1999: 218).
4 So, too, the media person is assumed to be linked to valuable places, by virtue of his or her connection to television (Hoover 1988b: 197, 203).
5 Couldry (2000a: 46), Grindstaff (1997: 166), Langer (1998: 48).
6 Radio talk-show producer quoted in O'Sullivan (2001: 4).
7 See also now Grindstaff (2002), published unfortunately after this book was completed.
8 For a brief survey, see Snyder (2000).
9 For a useful brief discussion of 'blogging', see Coleman and Gotze (2001: 34–5).
10 Seen August 2001.
11 See Introna and Nissenbaum (2000) on the hidden material constraints of search engines.

Chapter 8: Beyond media rituals?

1 Hence I agree with Peters' preference for Merton's view of mass mediation as potentially positive over Adorno's insistence that it is in principle flawed (Peters 1999: 221–5), even though my reading in Chapter 4 of Merton's warbond drive study differs from Peters'.
2 Cf. Chapter 1, criticising Scannell's recent work.
3 See Jock Young's classic article (Young 1974; cf. Young 1999) on 'the mass media in a segregated society'. For classic arguments against functionalism generally, see Lukes (1975), Mann (1970).

4 For the continued fundamental importance, in this sense, of the link back to Durkheim, see Elliott (1982), Rothenbuhler (1993).
5 Quoted in *Le Monde Diplomatique*, March 2001: 17.
6 For discussion of Marcos' concept of communication, see Rodriguez (2001: 155–8).
7 See Havelock (1963) for a classic account of how the introduction of writing underlay the profound shift in philosophical outlook that peaked with Plato and Aristotle.
8 Raboy (1992), Robins (2001), Virilio (1999).
9 See Baudrillard (1981: 169).

References

Agre, Philip and Rotenberg, Mark (eds.) (1998) *Technology and Privacy: The New Landscape.* Cambridge, MA: MIT Press.

Andrejevic, Mark (forthcoming 2003) 'Little Brother is Watching: The Webcam Subculture and the Digital Enclosure' in N. Couldry and A. McCarthy (eds.) *Media/Space.* London: Routledge.

Asad, Talal (1993) *Genealogies of Religion.* Baltimore: The Johns Hopkins Press.

Atton, Chris (2001) *Alternative Media.* London: Sage.

Babcock, Barbara (ed.) (1978) *The Reversible World.* Ithaca: Cornell University Press.

Bacon-Smith, Camille (1992) *Enterprising Women.* Philadelphia: University of Pennsylvania Press.

Badiou, Alain (2001) *Ethics: An Essay on the Understanding of Evil.* London: Verso.

Bakhtin, Mikhail (1984) *Rabelais and his World.* Bloomington: Indiana University Press.

Bar-Haim, Gabriel (1997) 'The Dispersed Sacred: Anomie and the Crisis of Ritual' in S. Hoover and K. Lundby (eds.) *Rethinking Media, Religion and Culture.* Thousand Oaks: Sage.

Barthes, Roland (1972) *Mythologies.* London: Paladin.

Bateson, Gregory (1973) *Steps Towards an Ecology of Mind.* London: Fontana.

Baudrillard, Jean (1981) 'Requiem for the Media' in *For a Critique of the Political Economy of the Sign.* St Louis: Telos Press.

—— (1983) *Simulations.* New York: Semiotext(e).

—— (1988) *America.* London: Verso.

Bauman, Zygmunt (1999) *In Search of Politics.* Cambridge: Polity.

Baym, Nancy (1999) *Tune in Log Out: Soaps, Fandom and Online Community.* Thousand Oaks: Sage.

Becker, Karin (1995) 'Media and the Ritual Process', *Media, Culture and Society* 17: 629–46.

—— (1998) 'The Diana Debate', *Screen* 39(3): 289–93.

Bell, Catherine (1992) *Ritual Theory, Ritual Practice.* New York: Oxford University Press.

—— (1997) *Ritual: Perspectives and Dimensions.* New York: Oxford University Press.

Benhabib, Seyla (ed.) (1995) *Democracy and Difference.* Princeton: Princeton University Press.

Billig, Michael (1995) *Banal Nationalism.* London: Sage.

—— (1997) 'From Codes to Utterances' in M. Ferguson and P. Golding (eds.) *Cultural Studies in Question.* London: Sage.

Bloch, Maurice (1989) *Ritual History and Power.* London: The Athlone Press.

Blumler, Jay and Gurevitch, Michael (1995) *The Crisis of Public Communication.* London: Routledge.

Boden, Dierdre and Molotch, Gregory (1994) 'The Compulsion of Proximity' in D. Boden and G. Molotch (eds.) *NowHere: Space, Time and Modernity.* Berkeley: University of California Press.

Bolin, Goran (2000) 'Film Swapping in the Public Sphere: Youth Audiences and Alternative Cultural Publicities', *Javnost* 7(2): 57–74.

Boltanski, Luc (1999) *Distant Suffering.* Cambridge: Cambridge University Press.

Bondjeberg, Ib (1996) 'Public Discourse/Private Fascination', *Media, Culture and Society* 18: 27–45.

Boorstin, Daniel (1961) *The Image: Whatever Happened to the American Dream.* London: Weidenfeld and Nicolson.

Bourdieu, Pierre (1977) *Outline of a Theory of Practice.* Cambridge: Cambridge University Press.

—— (1990) *The Logic of Practice.* Cambridge: Polity.

—— (1991) *Language and Symbolic Power.* Cambridge: Polity.

—— (1996) *The State Nobility.* Cambridge: Polity.

—— (1998) *On Television and Journalism.* London: Pluto.

—— (2000) *Pascalian Meditations.* Stanford: Stanford University Press.

Bourdon, Jerome (2000) 'Live television is still alive', *Media, Culture and Society* 22(5): 531–56.

Bowman, Glenn (1991) 'Christian Ideology and the Image of a Holy Land' in J. Eade and M. Sallnow (eds.) (1991) *Contesting the Sacred.* London: Routledge.

Braudel, Fernand (1972) 'History and the Social Sciences' in P. Burke (ed.) *Economy and Society in Early Modern Europe.* London: Routledge and Kegan Paul.

Briggs, Asa (1961) *The BBC : A History. Volume 1.* Oxford: Oxford University Press.

Brunsdon, Charlotte and Morley, David (1978) *Everyday Television: 'Nationwide'* London: BFI.

Brunvatne, Raina and Tolson, Andrew (2001) '"It Makes it OK to Cry": Two Types of "Therapy Talk" in Television Talk Shows' in A. Tolson (ed.) *Television Talk Shows.* Mahwah, NJ: Lawrence Erlbaum.

Caldwell, John (1996) *Televisuality: Style, Crisis and Authority in American Television.* New Brunswick: Rutgers University Press.

—— (forthcoming 2003) 'Geography Lessons of the Film/Television Production Culture' in N. Couldry and A. McCarthy (eds.) *Media/Space.* London: Routledge.

Callon, Michel (1991) 'Techno-economic Networks and Irreversibility' in J. Law (ed.) *A Sociology of Monsters*. London: Routledge.

Callon, Michel and Latour, Bruno (1981) 'Unscrewing the Big Leviathan' in K. Knorr-Cetina and A. Cicourel (eds.) *Advances in Social Theory and Methodology*. London: Routledge and Kegan Paul.

Cardiff, David and Scannell, Paddy (1987) 'Broadcasting and National Unity' in J. Curran *et al.* (eds.) *Impacts and Influences*. London: Methuen.

Carey, James (1989) *Communication as Culture*. Boston: Unwin Hyman.

—— (1998) 'Political Ritual on Television' in T. Liebes and J. Curran (eds.) *Media Ritual and Identity*. London: Routledge.

Carpentier, Alejo (1990) [1949] *The Kingdom of this World*. London: André Deutsch.

Castells, Manuel (1996) *The Rise of the Network Society*. Oxford: Blackwell.

—— (2001) *The Internet Galaxy*. Oxford: Oxford University Press.

Certeau, Michel de (1984) *The Practice of Everyday Life*. Berkeley: University of California Press.

Chandler, Daniel (1997) 'Writing Oneself in Cyberspace' [WWW document] http://www.aber.ac.uk/~dgc/homepgid.html, visited 3 July 2001.

Chandler, Daniel and Roberts-Young, Dilwyn (1998) 'The Construction of Identity in Personal Homepages of Adolescents' [WWW document] http://www.aber.ac.uk/media/documents/short/strasbourg.html, visited 3 July 2001.

Chaney, David (1983) 'A Symbolic Mirror of Ourselves: Civic Ritual in Mass Society', *Media, Culture and Society* 5(2): 119–36.

—— (1986) 'The Symbolic Form of Ritual in Mass Communications' in P. Golding *et al.* (eds.) *Communicating Politics*. New York: Holmes and Meier.

—— (1993) *Fictions of Collective Life*. London: Routledge.

Clark, Lynn Schofield and Hoover, Stewart (1997) 'At the Intersection of Media, Culture and Religion' in S. Hoover and K. Lundby (eds.) *Rethinking Media Religion and Culture*. Thousand Oaks: Sage.

Coleman, Stephen and Gotze, John (2001) 'Bowling Together: Online Public Engagement in Policy Deliberation'. London: The Hansard Society. [Also at http://www.hansard-society.org.uk, visited 14 March 2002]

Collins, Richard (1986) 'Seeing is Believing: The Ideology of Naturalism' in J. Corner (ed.) *Documentary and Mass Media*. London: Arnold.

Corner, John (1991) 'Documentary Voices' in J. Corner (ed.) *Popular Television in Britain*. London: BFI.

—— (1995) *Television Form and Public Address*. London: Arnold.

—— (1996) 'Mediating the Ordinary: The "Access" Idea and Television Form' in J. Corner and S. Harvey (eds.) *Television Times: A Reader*. London: Arnold.

—— (1999a) Review of T. Liebes and J. Curran (eds.) (1998) *Media Ritual and Identity*, in *European Journal of Cultural Studies* 2(3): 416–19.

—— (1999b) *Critical Ideas in Television Studies*. Oxford: Oxford University Press.

—— (2002) 'Performing the Real: Documentary Diversions', *Television and New Media* 3(3): 255–70.

Couldry, Nick (1999) 'Remembering Diana: The Geography of Celebrity and the Politics of Lack', *New Formations* 36: 77–91.

—— (2000a) *The Place of Media Power.* London: Routledge.

—— (2000b) 'Media Organisations and Non-Media People' in J. Curran (ed.) *Media Organisations in Society.* London: Arnold.

—— (2002) 'Playing for Celebrity: *Big Brother* as Ritual Event', *Television and New Media,* 3(3): 283–94.

—— (forthcoming) 'Beyond the Televised Endgame' in N. Chitty, R. Rush and M. Semati (eds.) *Studies in Terrorism.* Penang: Southbound Press [in association with *Journal of International Communication*].

Crain, Mary (1992) 'Pilgrims, "Yuppies" and Media Men: The Transformation of an Andalucian Pilgrimage' in J. Boissevain (ed.) *Revitalising European Rituals.* London: Routledge.

Cubitt, Sean (1991) *Timeshift.* London: Routledge.

Curran, James (1982) 'Communications, Power and Social Order' in M. Gurevitch *et al.* (eds.) *Culture, Society and the Media.* London: Routledge.

—— (1998) 'Crisis of Public Communication: A Reappraisal' in T. Liebes and J. Curran (eds.) *Media Ritual and Identity.* London: Routledge.

Dahlgren, Peter (1981) 'Television News and the Suppression of Reflexivity' in E. Katz and T. Szecsko (eds.) *Mass Media and Social Change.* London: Sage.

Davies, Christine (1999) 'Jokes on the Death of Diana' in T. Walter (ed.) *The Mourning for Diana.* Oxford: Berg.

Davis, Mike (1990) *City of Quartz.* London: Verso.

Dayan, Daniel and Katz, Elihu (1992) *Media Events: The Live Broadcasting of History.* Cambridge, MA: Harvard University Press.

Debord, Guy (1983) *Society of the Spectacle.* Detroit: Black and Red.

Deegan, Mary Jo (1989) *American Ritual Dramas.* New York: Greenwood Press.

Deleuze, Gilles and Guattari, Felix (1988) *A Thousand Plateaus.* London: The Athlone Press.

Derrida, Jacques and Stiegler, Bernard (1996) *Echographies: Entretiens sur la Télévision.* Paris: Galilée/INA.

Devereaux, Eoin (1996) 'Good Causes, God's Poor and Telethon Television', *Media, Culture and Society* 18(1): 47–68.

Douglas, Mary (1970) *Natural Symbols.* London: The Cresset Press.

—— (1975) *Implicit Meanings.* London: Routledge and Kegan Paul.

—— (1984) [1966] *Purity and Danger.* London: Routledge.

Dover, Caroline (2001) 'British Documentary Television Production: Tradition, Change and "Crisis" Within a Practitioner Community', unpublished doctoral thesis, University of London.

Dovey, Jon (1993) 'Old Dogs and New Tricks: Access Television in the UK' in T. Dowmunt (ed.) *Channels of Resistance*. London: BFI.

—— (2000) *Freakshow*. London: Pluto.

Downing, John (2000) *Radical Media*. (2e) Thousand Oaks: Sage.

Durkheim, Emile (1984) [1893] *The Division of Labour in Society* (tr. W. Halls). (2e) Basingstoke: Macmillan.

—— (1995) [1912] *The Elementary Forms of Religious Life* (tr. K. Fields). Glencoe: Free Press.

Eade, John (1991) 'Order and Power at Lourdes' in J. Eade and M. Sallnow (eds.) (1991) *Contesting the Sacred*. London: Routledge.

Eade, John and Sallnow, Michael (eds.) (1991) *Contesting the Sacred*. London: Routledge.

Eco, Umberto (1992) 'A Guide to the Neo-Television of the 1980s' in Z. Baranski and R. Lumley (eds.) *Culture and Conflict in Postwar Italy*. London: Macmillan.

Ehrenberg, Alain (1995) *L'Individu Incertain*. Paris: Hachette.

Elias, Norbert (1994) *The Civilising Process*. Oxford: Blackwell.

Eliasoph, Nina (1998) *Avoiding Politics*. Cambridge: Cambridge University Press.

Elliott, Philip (1982) 'Press Performance as Political Ritual' in H. Christian (ed.) *The Sociology of Journalism and the Press*. University of Keele.

Ellis, Bret Easton (2000) *Glamorama*. New York: Vintage.

Ellis, John (2000) *Seeing Things*. London: Tauris.

Ericson, Richard and Haggerty, Kevin (1997) *Policing the Risk Society*. Toronto: Toronto University Press.

Ettema, James (1990) 'Press Rites and Race Relations: A Study of Mass-Mediated Ritual', *Critical Studies in Mass Communication* 7(4): 309–33.

Feuer, Jane (1983) 'The Concept of Live Television' in E. Kaplan (ed.) *Regarding Television*. Los Angeles: American Film Institute.

Fiske, John (1996) *Media Matters*. Minneapolis: University of Minnesota Press.

Flichy, Patrice (1995) *Dynamics of Modern Communication*. London: Sage.

Foucault, Michel (1981a) *The History of Sexuality, Volume I*. Harmondsworth: Penguin.

—— (1981b) 'The Order of Discourse' in R. Young (ed.) *Untying the Text*. London: Routledge.

Frow, John (1998) 'Is Elvis a God?', *International Journal of Cultural Studies* 1(2): 197–210.

Fukuyama, Francis (1992) *The End of History and the Last Man*. Harmondsworth: Penguin.

Gabler, Neal (2000) *Life: The Movie*. New York: Vintage.

Gamson, Joshua (1994) *Claims to Fame: Celebrity in Contemporary America*. Berkeley: University of California Press.

—— (1998) *Freaks Talk Back*. Chicago: University of Chicago Press.

Garland, David (2001) *The Culture of Control*. Oxford: Oxford University Press.

Garnham, Nicholas (1994) 'Bourdieu, the Cultural Arbitrary and Television' in C. Calhoun, E. Lipuma and M. Postone (eds.) *Bourdieu: Critical Perspectives*. Cambridge: Polity.

—— (2000) *Emancipation, the Media and Modernity*. Oxford: Oxford University Press.

Geertz, Clifford (1973) *The Interpretation of Cultures*. Chicago: Chicago University Press.

Gennep, Arnold van (1977) [1908] *The Rites of Passage*. London: Routledge Kegan Paul.

Geraghty, Christine (1995) 'Social Issues and Realist Soaps' in R. Allen (ed.) *To Be Continued*. London: Routledge.

Giddens, Anthony (1972) *Capitalism and Modern Social Theory*. Cambridge: Cambridge University Press.

—— (1984) *The Constitution of Society*. Cambridge: Polity.

—— (1985) *The Nation-State and Violence*. Cambridge: Polity.

—— (1990) *The Consequences of Modernity*. Cambridge: Polity.

—— (1991) *Modernity and Self-Identity*. Cambridge: Polity.

Ginsburg, Faye (1994) 'Culture/media: A Mild Polemic', *Anthropology Today* 10(2): 5–15.

—— (1995) 'Mediating Culture' in L. Devereaux and R. Hillman (eds.) *Fields of Vision*. Berkeley: University of California Press.

—— (1998) 'Shooting Back: From Ethnographic Film to Indigenous Production/Ethnography of Media' in T. Miller and R. Stam (eds.) *Companion to Film Theory*. Oxford: Blackwell.

Giroux, Henry (2001) *Public Spaces, Private Lives*. Boulder: Rowman and Littlefield.

—— (forthcoming 2003) *The Abandoned Generation: Democracy Beyond the Culture of Fear*. New York: Palgrave.

Gitlin, Todd (1998) 'Public Sphere or Public Sphericules' in T. Liebes and J. Curran (eds.) *Media Ritual and Identity*. London: Routledge.

—— (2001) *Media Unlimited*. New York: Metropolitan Books.

Gluckman, Max (1971) *Politics, Law and Ritual in Tribal Society*. Oxford: Basil Blackwell.

Godelier, Maurice (1986) *The Mental and the Material*. London: Verso.

Goethals, Gregor (1997) 'Escape from Time: Ritual Dimensions of Popular Culture' in S. Hoover and K. Lundby (eds.) *Rethinking Media Religion and Culture*. Thousand Oaks: Sage.

Goffman, Erving (1975) *Frame Analysis*. Harmondsworth: Penguin.

Golding, Peter (1981) 'The Missing Dimensions' in E. Katz and T. Szecsko (eds.) *Mass Media and Social Change*. London: Sage.

Goody, Jack (1977) 'Against Ritual' in S. Moore and B. Myerhoff (eds.) *Secular Ritual*. Assen/Amsterdam: Van Gorcum.

Grindstaff, Laura (1997) 'Producing Trash, Class and the Money Shot' in J. Lull and S. Hinerman (eds.) *Media Scandals*. Cambridge: Polity.

—— (2002) *The Money Shot*. Chicago: Chicago University Press.

Haggerty, Kevin and Ericson, Richard (2000) 'The Surveillant Assemblage', *British Journal of Sociology* 51(4): 605–22.

Hall, Stuart (1977) 'Culture, Media and "the Ideological Effect"' in J. Curran, M. Gurevitch and J. Woollacott (eds.) *Mass Communications and Society*. London: Edward Arnold.

Hallin, Daniel (1994) *We Keep America on Top of the World*. London: Routledge.

Hamburger, Esther (2000) 'Politics and Intimacy: The Agrarian Reform in a Brazilian Telenovela', *Television and New Media* 1(2): 159–79.

Hamelink, Cees (1999) *The Ethics of Cyberspace*. London: Sage.

Handelman, Don (1998) *Models and Mirrors: Towards an Anthropology of Public Events.* (2e with new preface) Oxford: Berg.

Haney, C. Allen and Davis, D. (1999) 'America Responds to Diana's Death' in T. Walter (ed.) *The Mourning for Diana.* Oxford: Berg.

Hardt, Michael and Negri, Antonio (2000) *Empire.* Cambridge, MA: Harvard University Press.

Harrington, C. Lee and Bielby, Denise (1995) *Soap Fans.* Philadelphia: Temple University Press.

Harris, Chris (1999) 'Secular Religion and the Public Response to Diana's Death' in T. Walter (ed.) *The Mourning for Diana.* Oxford: Berg.

Hartley, John (1992) *The Politics of Pictures.* London: Routledge.

—— (1999) *Uses of Television.* London: Routledge.

Hay, James (1992) 'Afterword' in R. Allen (ed.) *Channels of Discourse, Reassembled.* London: Routledge.

Havelock, Eric (1963) *Preface to Plato.* Cambridge, MA: Harvard University Press.

Heath, Stephen (1990) 'Representing Television' in P. Mellencamp (ed.) *Logics of Television.* Bloomington: Indiana University Press.

Heath, Stephen and Skirrow, Gillian (1977) 'Television: A World in Action', *Screen* 18(2): 7–60.

Heelas, Paul, Lash, Scott and Morris, Paul (eds.) (1994) *Detraditionalization.* Oxford: Blackwell.

Heidegger, Martin (1962) *Being and Time.* Oxford: Blackwell.

Herzfeld, Michael (1992) *The Social Production of Indifference.* Chicago: University of Chicago Press.

Hill, Annette (2000) 'Fearful and Safe: Audience Response to British Reality Programming' *Television and New Media* 1(2): 193–213.

—— (2002) '*Big Brother*: The Real Audience', *Television and New Media* 3(3): 323–40.

Hills, Matthew (2002) *Fan Cultures.* London: Routledge.

Hobart, Mark (2000) *After Culture.* Yogyakarta: Duta Wacana University Press.

Hoover, Stewart (1988) 'Television, Myth and Ritual: the Role of Substantive Meaning and Spatiality' in J. Carey (ed.) *Media Myths and Narratives.* Newbury Park: Sage.

—— (1988b) *Mass Media Religion.* Thousand Oaks: Sage.

Hughes-Freeland, Patricia (1998) 'From Temples to Television: the Balinese Case' in P. Hughes-Freeland and M. Crain (eds.) *Recasting Ritual.* London: Routledge.

Humm, Peter (1998) 'Real TV: Camcorders, Access and Authenticity' in C. Geraghty and D. Lusted (eds.) *The Television Studies Reader.* London: Arnold.

Humphrey, Caroline and Laidlaw, James (1994) *The Archetypal Actions of Ritual.* Oxford: The Clarendon Press.

Huyssen, Andreas (1995) *Twilight Memories.* New York and London: Routledge.

Introna, Lucas and Nissenbaum, Helen (2000) 'Shaping the Web: Why the Politics of Search Engines Matters', *Information Society* 16: 169–85.

Jenkins, Henry (1992) *Textual Poachers.* New York: Routledge.

Jensen, Joli (1991) 'Fandom as Pathology: The Consequences of Categorization' in L. Lewis (ed.) *The Adoring Audience*. London: Routledge.

Jones, Steven (1998) 'Information, Internet and Community' in S. Jones (ed.) *Cybersociety 2.0*. London: Routledge.

Keighron, Peter (1993) 'Video Diaries: What's Up Doc?', *Sight and Sound* 3(10): 24–5.

Kershaw, Ian (1987) *The 'Hitler Myth'* Oxford: The Clarendon Press.

Kierkegaard, Søren (1962) [1846/7] *The Present Age*. New York: Fontana.

Kilborn, Richard (1994) '"How Real Can You Get?" Recent Developments in "Reality" Television', *European Journal of Communication* 9(4): 421–40.

—— (1998) 'Shaping the Real: Democratisation and Commodification in UK Factual Broadcasting', *European Journal of Communication* 13(2): 201–18.

Klein, Naomi (2000) *No Logo*. London: Flamingo.

Laclau, Ernesto (1990) *New Reflections on the Revolution of Our Time*. London: Verso.

Lang, Kurt and Lang, Gladys (1969) [1954] 'The Unique Perspective of Television and its Effects: A Pilot Study' in W. Schramm (ed.) *Mass Communications*. (2e) Urbana: University of Illinois Press.

Larson, William and Park, Heung-Soo (1993) *Global Television and the Politics of the Seoul Olympics*. Boulder: Westview Press.

Lash, Scott (2002) *Critique of Information*. London: Sage.

Lazarsfeld, Paul and Merton, Robert (1969) [1948] 'Mass Communication, Popular Taste and Organised Social Action' in W. Schramm (ed.) *Mass Communications*. (2e) Urbana: University of Illinois Press.

Lefebvre, Henri (1991a) [1958] *Critique of Everyday Life, Volume I*. London: Verso.

—— (1991b) *The Production of Space*. Oxford: Blackwell.

Lembo, Ron (2000) *Thinking Through Television*. Cambridge: Cambridge University Press.

Lévi-Strauss, Claude (1981) *The Naked Man*. London: Jonathan Cape.

Lewis, Gilbert (1980) *Day of Shining Red: An Essay on Understanding Ritual*. Cambridge: Cambridge University Press.

Liebes, Tamar (1998) 'Television's Disaster Marathons' in T. Liebes and J. Curran (eds.) *Media Ritual Identity*. London: Routledge.

Lindlof, Thomas and Shatzer, Milton (1998) 'Media Ethnography in Virtual Space', *Journal of Broadcasting and Electronic Media* 42(2): 170–89.

Little, Paul (1995) 'Ritual, Power and Ethnography at the Rio Earth Summit', *Critique of Anthropology* 15(3): 265–88.

Livingstone, Sonia and Lunt, Peter (1994) *Talk on Television*. London: Routledge.

Loader, Brian (1997) 'Policing and the Social: Questions of Symbolic Power', *British Journal of Sociology* 48(1): 1–18.

Luhmann, Nikolas (1999) *The Reality of the Mass Media*. Cambridge: Polity.

Lukes, Steven (1975) 'Political Ritual and Social Integration', *Sociology* 29: 289–305.

Lundby, Knut (1997) 'The Web of Collective Representations' in S. Hoover and K. Lundby (eds.) *Rethinking Media, Religion and Culture*. Thousand Oaks: Sage.

Lyon, David (2001) *Surveillance Society: Monitoring Everyday Life*. Milton Keynes: Open University Press.

MacAloon, John (1984) 'Olympic Games and the Theory of Spectacle in Modern Societies' in J. MacAloon (ed.) *Rite, Drama, Festival, Spectacle*. Philadelphia: ASHI Press.

MacCannell, Dean (1992) *The Tourist Papers*. London: Routledge.

Maffesoli, Michel (1996a) *The Time of the Tribes*. London: Sage.

—— (1996b) *The Contemplation of the World*. Minneapolis: University of Minnesota Press.

Mann, Michael (1970) 'The Social Cohesion of Liberal Democracy', *American Sociological Review* 35(3): 423–39.

Marcos, Subcomandante (2001) *Our Word is Our Weapon*. London: Serpent's Tail.

Martin, Berenice (1981) *A Sociology of Contemporary Change*. Oxford: Blackwell.

Martin-Barbero, Jesus (1993) *Communication Culture and Hegemony*. London: Sage.

—— (1997) 'Mass Media as a Site of Resacralisation of Contemporary Cultures' in S. Hoover and K. Lundby (eds.) *Rethinking Media Religion and Culture*. Thousand Oaks: Sage.

Marvin, Carolyn (1999) *Blood Sacrifice and the Nation*. Cambridge: Cambridge University Press.

Massey, Doreen (1994) *Space, Place and Gender*. Cambridge: Polity.

Matta, Roberto da (1984) 'Carnival in Multiple Planes' in J. MacAloon (ed.) *Rite, Drama, Festival, Spectacle*. Philadelphia: ASHI Press.

Mattelart, Armand (1994) *The Invention of Communication*. Minneapolis: University of Minnesota Press.

Mattelart, Armand, Delcourt, Xavier and Mattelart, Michelle (1984) *International Image Markets*. London: Comedia.

McCarthy, Anna (2001) *Ambient Television*. Durham, NC: Duke University Press.

McKevitt, Christopher (1991) 'San Giovanni Rotondo and the Shrine of Padre Pio' in J. Eade and M. Sallnow (eds.) *Contesting the Sacred*. London: Routledge.

McMurria, John (2002) 'Discovering the World: Globalisation and Television Documentary', paper presented to the Media in Transition conference, MIT, Boston, May 2002.

Mehl, Dominique (1996) *La Télévision de l'Intimité*. Paris: Seuil.

Mellencamp, Patricia (1990) 'Television Time and Catastrophe, or Beyond the Pleasure Principle in Television' in P. Mellencamp (ed.) *Logics of Television*. Bloomington: Indiana University Press.

Melucci, Alberto (1989) *Nomads of the Present*. London: Hutchinson Radius.

—— (1996) *Challenging Codes*. Cambridge: Cambridge University Press.

Merton, Robert (1946) *Mass Persuasion: The Social Psychology of a Warbond Drive*. New York: Harper and Brothers.

Mestrovic, Stjepan (1997) *Postemotional Society*. London: Sage.

Meyrowitz, Joshua (1985) *No Sense of Place*. New York: Oxford University Press.

Michaels, Eric (1985) 'Constraints on Knowledge in an Economy of Oral Information', *Current Anthropology* 26(4): 505–10.

—— (1994) *Bad Aboriginal Art*. Minneapolis: University of Minnesota Press.

Miller, Daniel and Slater, Don (2000) *The Internet: An Ethnographic Approach*. Berg: London.

Moore, Alexander (1980) 'Walt Disney World: Bounded Ritual Space and the Playful Pilgrimage Center', *Anthropological Quarterly* 53: 207–18.

Moore, Sally and Myerhoff, Barbara (eds.) (1977a) *Secular Ritual*. Assen/Amsterdam: Van Gorcum.

—— (1977b) 'Introduction' in S. Moore and B. Myerhoff (eds.) *Secular Ritual*. Assen/Amsterdam: Van Gorcum.

Morinis, Alan (1992) 'Introduction' in A. Morinis (ed.) *Sacred Journeys*. New York: Greenwood Press.

Myerhoff, Barbara (1977) 'We Don't Wrap Herring in a Printed Page: Fusion, Fictions and Contingency in Secular Ritual' in S. Moore and B. Myerhoff (eds.) *Secular Ritual*. Assen/Amsterdam: Van Gorcum.

Nava, Mica (1999) 'Diana and Race: Romance and the Reconfiguration of the Nation' in A. Kear and D. Steinberg (eds.) *Mourning Diana*. London: Routledge.

Neale, Steve (1976) 'New Hollywood Cinema', *Screen* 17(2): 117–22.

Neuman, W. Russell (1991) *The Future of the Mass Audience*. Cambridge: Cambridge University Press.

Nichols, Bill (1994) *Blurred Boundaries*. Bloomington: Indiana University Press.

Nordenstreng, Karl (1972) 'Policy for News Transmission' in D. MacQuail (ed.) *Sociology of Mass Communication*. Harmondsworth: Penguin.

Norris, Clive and Armstrong, Gary (1999) *The Maximum Surveillance Society*. Oxford: Berg.

Ortner, Sherry (1978) *Sherpas through Their Rituals*. Cambridge: Cambridge University Press.

O'Sullivan, Sara (2001) 'Understanding Talk Radio', paper presented to the fifth conference of the European Sociological Association, Helsinki, September 2001.

Paget, Derek (1998) *No Other Way to Tell It: Dramadoc/Docudrama on Television*. Manchester: Manchester University Press.

Palmer, Gareth (2002) '*Big Brother*: an Experiment in Governance', *Television and New Media* 3(3): 295–310.

Parkin, Frank (1972) *Class Inequality and Political Order*. London: Paladin.

Peters, John Durham (1999) *Speaking Into the Air*. Chicago: Chicago University Press.

Peters, John Durham and Rothenbuhler, Eric (1989) 'The Reality of Construction' in H. Simons (ed.) *Rhetoric in the Human Sciences*. London: Sage.

Phillips, Anne (1995) 'Dealing with Difference: A Politics of Ideas, Or a Politics of Presence?' in S. Benhabib (ed.) *Democracy and Difference*. Princeton: Princeton University Press.

Pickering, W. (1984) *Durkheim's Sociology of Religion*. London: Routledge & Kegan Paul.

Poster, Mark (1995) 'Postmodern Virtualities' in M. Featherstone and R. Burrows (eds.) *Cyberspace/Cyberbodies/Cyberpunk*. London: Sage.

Priest, Patricia Joiner (1995) *Public Intimacies*. Creskill, NJ: The Hampton Press.

—— (1996) '"Gilt by Association": Talk Show Participants' Televisually Enhanced Status and Self-Esteem' in D. Grodin and T. Lindlof (eds.) *Constructing the Self in a Mediated World*. London: Sage.

Puijk, Roel (1999) 'Producing Norwegian Culture for Domestic and Foreign Gazes' in A. Martin Klausen (ed.) *Olympic Games as Performance and Public Event*. New York and Oxford: Berghahn Books.

Pullen, Kirsten (2000) 'I-love-Xena.com: Creating Online Fan Communities' in D. Gauntlett (ed.) *Web.Studies*. London: Arnold.

Putnam, Robert (2000) *Bowling Alone*. New York: Simon and Schuster.

Raboy, Marc (1992) 'Media and the Invisible Crisis of Everyday Life' in M. Raboy and B. Dagenais (eds.) *Media, Crisis and Democracy*. London: Sage.

Raboy, Marc and Dagenais, Bernard (1992) 'Media and the Politics of Crisis' in M. Raboy and B. Dagenais (eds.) *Media, Crisis and Democracy*. London: Sage.

Rappaport, Roy (1999) *Ritual and Religion in the Making of Humanity*. Cambridge: Cambridge University Press.

Rath, Claus-Dieter (1985) 'The Invisible Network' in P. Drummond and R. Paterson (eds.) *Television in Transition*. London: BFI.

—— (1988) 'Live/life' in P. Drummond and R. Paterson (eds.) *Television and Its Audience*. London: BFI.

Reader, Ian (1993) 'Conclusions' in I. Reader and T. Walter (eds.) *Pilgrimage in Popular Culture*. Basingstoke: Macmillan.

Reader, Ian and Walter, Tony (eds.) (1993) *Pilgrimage in Popular Culture*. Basingstoke: Macmillan.

Real, Michael (1975) 'Super Bowl: Mythic Spectacle', *Journal of Communication* 25(1): 31–43.

—— (1989) *Super Media*. Thousand Oaks: Sage.

Ritchie, Jean (2000) *Big Brother: The Official Unseen Story*. London: Channel 4 Books.

Robins, Kevin (1995a) *Into the Image*. London: Routledge.

—— (1995b) 'Cyberspace and the World We Live In' in M. Featherstone and R. Burrows (eds) *Cyberspace/Cyberbodies/Cyberpunk*. London: Sage.

—— (2001) 'Seeing the World from a Safe Distance' (an interview by Mark Terkessidis), *Science as Culture* 10(4): 531–9.

Roche, Maurice (2000) *Mega-Events and Modernity*. London: Sage.

Roderiguez, Clemencia (2001) *Fissures in the Mediascape*. Creskill, NJ: The Hampton Press.

Rojek, Chris (1993) *Ways of Escape*. London: Routledge.

Rose, Nikolas (1996) 'Governing "Advanced" Liberal Democracies' in A. Barry, T. Osborne and N. Rose (eds.) *Foucault and Political Reason*. London: UCL Press.

Ross, Nick and Cook, Sue (1987) *Crimewatch UK*. London: Hodder and Stoughton.

Rothenbuhler, Eric (1988) 'The Living Room Celebration of the Olympic Games', *Journal of Communication* 38(4): 61–81.

—— (1989) 'The Liminal Fight: Mass Strikes as Ritual and Interpretation' in J. Alexander (ed.) *Durkheimian Sociology: Cultural Studies*. Cambridge: Cambridge University Press.

—— (1993) 'Argument for a Durkheimian Theory of the Communicative', *Journal of Communication* 43(3): 148–53.

—— (1998) *Ritual Communication*. Thousand Oaks: Sage.

Rubin, Alan (1984) 'Ritualized and Instrumental Television Viewing', *Journal of Communication* 34(3): 64–77.

Rudie, Ingrid (1998) 'Making Persons in a Global Ritual? Embodied Experience and Free-Floating Symbols in Olympic Sport' in P. Hughes-Freeland and M. Crain (eds.) *Recasting Ritual*. London: Routledge.

Ruel, Malcolm (1998) 'Rescuing Durkheim's "Rites" from the Symbolising Anthropologists' in N. Allen, W. Pickering and W. Watts Miller (eds.) *On Durkheim's Elementary Forms of Religious Life*. London: Routledge.

Sack, Robert (1986) *Human Territoriality*. Cambridge: Cambridge University Press.

Saenz, Michael (1994) 'Television Viewing as a Cultural Practice' in H. Newcomb (ed.) *Television: The Critical View*. New York: Oxford University Pres.

Sahlins, Marshall (1976) *Culture and Practical Reason*. Chicago: Chicago University Press.

Said, Edward (1988) 'Identity, Negation and Violence', *New Left Review* 171: 46–62.

Sakolsky, Ron and Dunifer, Stephen (eds.) *The Airwaves – A Free Radio Handbook*. Edinburgh and San Francisco: AK Press.

Scannell, Paddy (1989) 'Public Broadcasting and Modern Public Life', *Media, Culture and Society* 11(1): 135–66.

—— (1996) *Radio, Television and Modern Life*. Oxford: Blackwell.

Scannell, Paddy and Cardiff, David (1991) *A Social History of British Braodcasting, Volume I: 1922–1939*. Oxford: Blackwell.

Schlesinger, Philip *et al.* (1992) *Women Viewing Violence*. London: BFI.

Schlesinger, Philip and Tumber, Howard (1994) *Reporting Crime: The Media Politics of Criminal Justice*. Oxford: The Clarendon Press.

Scott, John (2001) *Power*. Cambridge: Polity Press.

Shattuc, Jane (1994) *The Talking Cure*. New York: Routledge.

—— (1999) '"Go Ricki": Politics, Perversion and Pleasure in the 1990s' in C. Geraghty and D. Lusted (eds.) *The Television Studies Book*. London: Arnold.

Shils, Edward (1975) *Center and Periphery*. Chicago: University of Chicago Press.

Shils, Edward and Young, Michael (1956) 'The Meaning of the Coronation', *Sociological Review* 1(2): 63–82, reprinted in Shils (1975).

Silverstone, Roger (1981) *The Message of Television*. London: Heinemann Educational Books.

—— (1988) 'Television Myth and Culture' in J. Carey (ed.) *Media Myths and Narratives*. Newbury Park: Sage.

—— (1994) *Television and Everyday Life*. London: Routledge.

—— (1999) *Why Study the Media?* London: Sage.

—— (2002) 'Regulation and the Ethics of Distance' in A. Mahan, R. Mansell and R. Samarajiva (eds.) *Networking Knowledge for Information Societies*. Delft: Delft University Press.

—— (forthcoming) 'Media and Communication' in C. Calhoun, C. Rojek and B. Turner (eds.) *The International Handbook of Sociology*. London: Sage.

Slevin, James (2000) *The Internet and Society*. Cambridge: Polity.

Smith, Jonathan Z. (1987) *To Take Place: Toward Theory in Ritual*. Chicago: Chicago University Press.

Snyder, Donald (2000) 'Webcam Women' in D. Gauntlett (ed.) *Web.Studies*. London: Arnold.

Spitulnik, Debra (1993) 'Anthropology and the Mass Media', *Annual Review of Anthropology* 22: 293–315.

Stedman Jones, Sue (2001) *Durkheim Revisited*. Cambridge: Polity.

Stevenson, Nick (1995) *Understanding Media Cultures*. London: Sage.

Syvertsen, Trine (2001) 'Ordinary People in Extraordinary Circumstaces', *Media, Culture and Society* 23(2): 319–37.

Tambiah, Stanley (1985) *Culture, Thought and Social Action*. Cambridge, MA: Harvard University Press.

Thomas, Nicholas (1991) *Entangled Objects*. Cambridge, MA: Harvard University Press.

Thompson, John (1990) *Ideology and Modern Culture*. Cambridge: Polity.

—— (1994) 'Tradition and Self in a Mediated World' in P. Heelas, S. Lash and P. Morris (eds.) *Detraditionalization*. Oxford: Blackwell.

—— (1995) *The Media and Modernity*. Cambridge: Polity.

Tilly, Charles (1998) *Durable Inequality*. Berkeley: University of California Press.

Tolson, Andrew (1991) 'Television Chat and the Synthetic Personality' in P. Scannell (ed.) *Broadcast Talk*. London: Sage.

Turkle, Sherry (1996) *Life on the Screen*. London: Weidenfeld and Nicolson.

Turner, Victor (1974) *Dramas, Fields and Metaphors*. Cornell: Cornell University Press.

—— (1977a) *The Ritual Process*. Cornell: Cornell University Press.

—— (1977b) 'Variations on a Theme of Liminality' in S. Moore and B. Myerhoff (eds.) *Secular Ritual*. Assen/ Amsterdam: Van Gorcum.

—— (1982) *From Ritual to Theater.* New York: Performing Arts Journal Publications.

Turner, Victor and Turner, Edith (1978) *Image and Pilgrimage in Christian Culture*. Oxford: Blackwell.

Turnock, Robert (2000) *Interpreting Diana*. London: BFI.

Urry, John (1990) *The Tourist Gaze*, London: Sage.

—— (2000) *Sociology Beyond Societies*. London: Sage.

Vermorel, Fred and Vermorel, Julie (1985) *Starlust: The Secret Life of Fans*. London: W.H. Allen.

Virilio, Paul (1999) *Open Sky*. London: Verso.

Wallerstein, Immanuel (1991) *Unthinking Social Science*. Cambridge: Polity.

Walter, Tony (1999) 'The Questions People Asked' in T. Walter (ed.) *The Mourning for Diana*. Oxford: Berg.

Wark, McKenzie (1994) *Virtual Geographies*. Bloomington: Indiana University Press.

White, Mimi (1992a) *Tele-advising*. Chapel Hill: University of North Carolina Press.

—— (1992b) 'Ideological Analysis and Television' in R. Allen (ed.) *Channels of Discourse, Reassembled*. London: Routledge.

White, Robert (1997) 'Religion and Media in the Construction of Culture' in S. Hoover and K. Lundby (eds.) *Rethinking Media Religion and Culture*. Thousand Oaks: Sage.

Wilson, Christopher (2000) *Cop Knowledge*. Chicago: Chicago University Press.

Winston, Brian (2000) *Lies, Damned Lies and Documentary*. London: BFI.

Wuthnow, Robert (1987) 'Ritual and Moral Order' in *Meaning and Moral Order*. Berkeley: University of California Press.

Young, Jock (1974) 'The Mass Media in a Segregated Society' in P. Rock and L. Mackintosh (eds.) *Deviance and Social Control*. London: Tavistock.

—— (1999) *The Exclusive Society*. London: Sage.

Zelizer, Barbie (1993) *Covering the Body: The Kennedy Assassination, the Media and the Shaping of Collective Memory*. Chicago: Chicago University Press.

Zukin, Sharon (1991) *Landscapes of Power: From Detroit to Disney World*. Berkeley: University of California Press.

Index

INDEX